RENAISSANCE MAN & MASON

RENAISSANCE MAN & MASON

A Miscellany of Talks Given Over 20 Years

PIERS ALLFREY VAUGHAN

PREFACE BY

ROBERT G. DAVIS

First Printing: 2016

ISBN 978-0-9815421-8-8

DEDICATION

I dedicate this book to all those men and women, who have helped me to grow spiritually throughout my life, from the many priests and deacons both in mainstream and independent churches who have helped me form my particular understanding of my relationship with God; the organizations – Masonic and otherwise – which have provided me with a safe environment in which to explore my relationship to my fellow men and women on this earth; and to those people close to me who have helped me to better understand myself.

Especially dedicate this book to those Masters, past and present, who have helped me along the Path, who have encouraged, initiated and educated me, and helped me pull the veil aside for myself. I am particularly grateful to those, alive or passed, who have given me an opportunity to hear, first hand, their stories of those we now revere, the ones who went before us into the Great Light. Their names are written in the Great Book, and I will not name them here, for it is not our tradition to do so.

I also acknowledge those friends who have traveled this Path with me, for it is a long and lonely journey to undertake alone. Your support and guidance have been invaluable.

Finally, I dedicate this book in particular to my long-suffering partner and fellow traveler, Jason Sheridan, for his constant encouragement, and his understanding when rooms were blocked with weird wands, wardrobes filled with bizarre regalia, and my experiments threatened to burn the house down!

CONTENTS

FOREWORD

The title of this book is aptly named. The Renaissance began in Italy in the 14th century and lasted through the life of Michelangelo to 1534 – roughly the same time period that the foundational rules which would later become the charges and landmarks of Freemasonry were working their way through the experience of governance in the towns and guild corporations of the Middle Ages. The inspiration of the Renaissance was the growth of knowledge and the rediscovery of classical learning, including the Hebrew Kabbala, which is the only spiritual system of which we have any knowledge that reconciles reason with faith, power with liberty, and science with mystery – ideas which are now woven within the teachings of Freemasonry.

In this seminal book of essays, originally delivered as lectures in various Masonic and related Esoteric Orders, the author gives the reader his inspired interpretations of the essential themes and traditions which are plaited into the allegories and symbols of Masonic Degrees.

Brother Vaughan is well positioned to do so, having been raised in English Freemasonry, belonging to Lodges in England, Belgium, France and Canada. He has presided over Lodges and Royal Arch Chapters in America; and has translated a number of French texts relating to Freemasonry and related Orders. He brings to the student a wealth of knowledge in Masonic history, the ancient mysteries, spirituality, alchemy, Rosicrucian studies and related esoteric disciplines.

He immanently understands the language, symbols and ceremonial forms which have made Freemasonry an Initiatic Art. The Renaissance influence over 16th and 17th century theology, philosophy, science and art stirred the men of the 18th century to embrace the enlightenment ideals of liberty, equality, and fraternity. The Masonic organization evolved as one of the premier societal institutions of the Enlightenment.

These global influences stirred men toward a path of contemplating their own nature, the nature of God, and their relationship to Divinity. Suddenly, men could embrace a world of ideas; they had a framework in which they could work out the challenges in their life and recreate themselves with a better understanding of their spirituality and their higher purpose. The call of liberty profoundly influenced free thought and the advancement of metaphysical ideas. Freemasonry became a venue in which men could meet in private assemblies, and meditate on the great questions of existence.

In this wonderful book, Brother Vaughan takes us on a journey of the structure of the lodge, purpose of initiation, the process of spiritual healing, the mystery schools, the significance of the related disciplines of Alchemy, Rosicruciania and Martinism; as well as the necessity of employing meditation as a vehicle we can all use for elevating ourselves as men of higher thinking through an awakening consciousness.

The author adds several chapters regarding our fraternal origins, along with some of the differences which exist between English Freemasonry and his own jurisdiction of New York. Finally, he presents important ideas that are presented in our York Rite and related orders.

This is a book that can be read with much enjoyment from cover to cover. Its individual chapters can also be perused by the student in augmenting his own knowledge about specific Masonic and esoteric ideas.

We are delighted that Brother Vaughan has chosen to share his labors with the broader Masonic community. This is an important book which covers material not readily available in a normal tyled setting. It offers the reader many insights he can use in his own journey toward "improving himself in Masonry." Perhaps most importantly, it makes us all aware that we are indeed Renaissance Men as well as Brothers of the Royal Art. This is, after all, what distinguishes us from the rest of the community.

Robert G. Davis, 33°, G∴C∴
Guthrie, Oklahoma

PREFACE

I was initiated into Freemasonry in Southwick, England in 1979. While there had been Masons in my family my father was not, but he introduced me to a friend who was. However, in those days it took three explicit request for information over the course of a year before my father's friend acknowledged my interest. It was almost six months before I received a letter inviting me to an interview, and following that another six months before I received a letter informing me I had been accepted. This was not a step to be taken lightly: in England in those days, there was nobody standing on street corners handing out petitions for admission, or proudly displaying '2B1ASK1' fender stickers on their cars. There were no lapel pins proudly proclaiming membership; and no 'One Day Classes'. Persistence was the only way in.

However, this was not my first brush with the esoteric side of life. I came from a family which had numerous experiences with the 'other' way of life. Several relatives frequently saw ghosts, both strangers and family members (I myself was visited by my paternal grandfather at the age of seven, only to find out he had died in hospital that very evening). I witnessed my mother visiting a stately house which had long since passed out of our family's hands due to death duties (Friston Place, Alfriston – my matronymic being 'Allfrey', a modernization of 'Alfreye', a Norman name), and nearly fainting on entering a particular bedroom: we then learned from Lady Birley that it was the very room in which a distant relative had taken their own life. When my great aunt died, her collection of Tarot cards, crystal balls, and other paraphernalia were found. Apparently I inherited this family hobby: while at boarding school, while others' tuck boxes were filled with 'tuck' (i.e. soda pop and candy)[1], mine was filled with strange herbs and potions, books, and my first Tarot deck.

So I joined my local Lodge, and was instantly transported to another manner of existence. I was *'home'*!

---

[1] My apologies to my English friends. Whilst being born and raised in England, I have lived in the United States for the past 25 years, so I tend to use American spelling and terminology nowadays...

Let me immediately add for the benefit of those who would use religion to attack our honorable Order (none of whom will be reading this book, I am certain), that our Fraternity is *not* a religion. Rather, it encourages us, through its requirement that all its members believe in a Supreme Being and the Immortality of the Soul, that its members are solid supporters of their respective faiths. Being raised in England, I was taught in the weekly school Divinity class that, while the Church of England was the established religion of my country, this was a historical coincidence, and therefore I had no right to consider my religious system superior to anyone else's. Indeed, comparative religion framed a major part of religious education in school, notwithstanding the fact that every morning began with morning prayers in the chapel, and bedtime was preceded with prayers in the dormitories. I had attended church from the age of five, singing in the choir and attending Sunday School. At college I sang, played the organ, and later joined a local Anglo-Catholic Church where I also sang, eventually became choir master, conducted the choir and occasional orchestras, wrote music and arranged scores. Finally, on coming to the States, I completed a Master's Degree in Divinity with the Sophia School of Divinity, attached to the Independent Catholic Apostolic Church of Antioch, and now serve as Primate of the Pre-Nicene Church, a gnostic church founded by Richard, Duc de Palatine. So no, Masonry is not a religion: but it teaches us to grow in our own faith and not to claim an arrogant superiority over anyone else's.

In parallel with my Masonic education, I found myself increasingly drawn to other paths towards Truth. As the Rosicrucians teach, there are many paths up the mystical Mount Abiegnus to its summit, where one may finally gaze on God without a veil. I used to use the analogy of visiting a museum, and walking into a room to behold a beautiful statue. Standing at this entrance, perhaps the Western door, one can admire its beauty of form, the artist's intent, the background to this inspiring *objet d'art*. But for all this, one is looking at a two-dimensional view. This is enough for most, and indeed it is all one is given in a picture or portrait, or icon. But now imagine coming into the same gallery from, say, the Southern door. One sees the same statue: there is no doubt of that. But now one sees new features, and those with which one is already familiar can be contemplated from a new angle, new insights derived, and a greater understanding of the artist's intention understood. I am sure the point is clear: one may derive great pleasure out of a masterpiece; but if one can get to see the same opus from a number of different viewpoints, one's overall understanding and appreciation of this work increases considerably.

And so began my journey for 'more light', and not necessarily in Masonry. Over the coming decades I would join many Orders. My only personal rule was inspired by C. S. Lewis's *The Screwtape Letters*: not to jump from one variety of the same Order to another in search of 'novelty'. In other words, while there may be new teachings, or new 'views' in different Orders, there was no point joining twenty-five manifestations of the same Order, since they all descended from the same point of origin, and therefore if one persevered one would understand the same purposes, however they were presented. It is the egocentric nature of human organizations that the reason so many flavors of the same thing exist is normally more due to the vanity of its leaders than the unfolding of greater mysteries! And so I searched, but was cautious in whom I selected as my guides.

Then, in the early 1990s, I was relocated by my job to the United States.

Academically, as well as a Master's in Divinity, I possess a Master's Degree in Experimental Psychology from Oxford University, an M.B.A. in Business Studies from Cranfield University, England, and a teaching diploma in music from Trinity College of Music, London. I guess you could say I tried my best to be a Renaissance Man in the modern world. The bizarre collection of knowledge I had amassed was at least useful in solving The Times cryptic crossword puzzle clues! My profane profession was Project Management and internal consulting for Operations and Technology in the international banking world, focusing on business process reengineering, or making old and outmoded processes better. This led me to live for varying periods in England, France, Germany, Switzerland, and finally the United States. This also gave me an opportunity to belong to Masonic – and other – bodies in England, France, Belgium, Canada and North America. My travels gave me an opportunity to observe, and to learn from, a number of Masonic and esoteric bodies which descended from a variety of different philosophical and cultural backgrounds.

When I arrived in New York, after six months I was offered a permanent position, so transferred my Masonic memberships to this state. I quickly found out that the level of education in those days (the early 1990s) was somewhat lacking. The average talk in Lodge tended to focus more on famous dead Masons, or how to invest your money, that on the stunning lessons afforded by a study of our rituals. And so, with the arrogance of youth, I started to give talks in Lodges.

Now, I was lucky enough to join St. John's Lodge No. 1, Antient York Masons, the oldest Lodge in New York State. Founded by the Premier Grand Lodge of England by warrant in 1757, it eventually found itself under the newly formed Grand Lodge of New York following the Revolutionary War. Its great claim to fame is its ownership of the Washington Inaugural Bible, the bible on which George Washington took his oath of office as first President (we must remember that Washington was a Worshipful Master of a Lodge; and that his Aide de Camp, General Jacob Morton, was Master of St. John's Lodge; Chancellor Livingston, who administered the oath, was Grand Master of Masons in the State of New York; even Samuel Fraunces the President's chef, of Fraunces' Tavern fame, was a newly-minted Mason of Holland Lodge No. 8). Being a member of such a Lodge was both a blessing and a curse (I have since had the honor of serving twice as its Master), and giving lectures on esoteric and spiritual topics when most Masons were used to hearing about how to buy life insurance quickly earned me the nickname of 'Piers the Nut'!

While early talks were quite a battle, over time more and more attended. The younger Masons, who had joined because they thought this is what we did in Freemasonry, now openly discussed philosophy and spirituality; and finally, even the 'back row' Masons started to ask questions.

Fast forward twenty-five years, and I can now look back on a most satisfying career in which I have seen the focus in our beloved Craft shift from quantity to quality, where phrases like: 'guard the West Gate' are no longer seen as contrary to Masonic strategy, and where the focus had returned to 'making good men better', in far more ways than simply meaning digging deeper into their pockets and give yet more to charity. At last they are learning to work upon *themselves*.

I have had the good fortune to be invited to speak across the United States and in three other continents. I am amazed and excited by our Brothers' desire to learn and grow, and their keenness to hear the views of those who come from very different cultural backgrounds to their own. But then, that is the beauty of our universal Fraternity. The strength of Freemasonry lies in the fact that one can travel anywhere in the world, and find an instant circle of friends whose common experience transcends any other parochial differences, and who will always welcome you, like the patriarchs of old, into their tent and call you 'friend'.

Masonry is 'an house of many mansions', containing a wonderful variety of societies, societies which focus on history, esotericism, charity, fun, exegesis, the preservation of lost Orders, the preservation of ritual. I am proud of my thirty-seven years' membership in this global organization, an organization whose lack of religious restrictions means that those who hold any devout religious stance may converse as equals; whose lack of dogma means that we can bring any philosophy, any teaching to the table for intelligent consideration under the strong light of reason; and whose inclusiveness means any man who seeks more in life than the mundane daily routine can expand his understanding of life and mix with others who, to quote the famous phrase, 'might otherwise have remained perpetually at a distance.'

As advice to those who have managed to climb to the top of the pile of Masonic honors and titles, I would caution that you have not 'arrived'; you have merely become an administrator! If you do not still follow the Golden Rule of 'making a daily advance in knowledge', then you have let *hubris* replace the search. The day you have nobody to look up to is the day you fail to grow.

Since this is a collection of talks, rather than a novel or book, you will find various ideas revisited time and again. This is in the nature of speeches. I hope you do not find this repetitive, but rather reinforcing. My determination to introduce Rosicrucian ideas, my delight in encouraging members to study symbolism and to draw their own conclusions from what they see, and above all a desire to fan the flame of desire to learn more and to get more out of Freemasonry drive me to revisit concepts and ideas through my talks.

I have used the pronoun 'he' throughout. This is in no way intended to be a slight towards any female readers: it is simply due to the fact that I assume the major part of my audience will be Masons, and the majority of Masons are, for good or ill, men.

Finally, I would add the *caveat* that, in all my years of giving talks, of which these which follow are hopefully a representative sample, the contents reflect my own personal ideas and interpretations, and are in no way intended either to reflect any official position in Freemasonry or of the intentions of the original authors of the rituals or monitors. This is *my* journey, and if it encourages others to make their own, discover their own interpretation of the symbols, and grow to better understand this thing we call life on their own terms, then my purpose will have been accomplished.

Piers A. Vaughan
St. John's Day, 2016

INTRODUCTION

In the late 1990s and early 2000s I had to sit through innumerable pronouncements by leaders of Freemasonry who said 'there are no secrets in Freemasonry'. Regrettably here are still a few fossils who do it now.

I never did work out whether it was because they had genuinely spent forty or fifty years in the Craft without the slightest idea what it was about; or whether they thought by 'demystifying Masonry' they would attract new members. The former would be a tragedy and a waste of a life; and the latter was a disaster for the Craft, since it effectively scared an entire generation of seekers away.

I can categorically state that there *are* secrets in Freemasonry. They may not be the ones the general public hope for. We are not lizard men. We do not run the planet. We do not control the police (though we may have some voting right on a few golf courses…). We are not descendants of Jesus/Genghis Kahn/Noah/Akhenaten. But within our ritual monitors are hints of profound insights into man, his relationship with his fellow men and God, and even indications on how to communicate with all of these and how to effect change, for those who are willing to put in the time and effort to discern these lessons.

The title of this book takes its inspiration from two sources. Firstly, just about every title I tried had already been taken! Secondly, as I reflect upon my life I realize that, like the Renaissance Man of old, I seem to know a moderate amount about a lot of things. This may not be valued quite so much in an age where specialization is critical to pursue most professional careers. On the other hand, it affords me the luxury to seeing connections between facts which are not immediately obvious, and my wide background has resulted in a library which covers the gamut of subjects, from history to religion, esoteric studies and grimoires to bilingual dictionaries, philosophy to old rituals in varying languages. Do not expect a tidy house if you visit: you will have to negotiate piles of books and papers at every turn!

In this book you will find a collection of talks ranging from the historic through the spiritual to the esoteric. I have deliberately mixed them up because I want the reader to enjoy the sheer variety of approaches to the teachings in Freemasonry. If I collected the tasks under headings I suspect that some would immediately go to that section, and that is not the point. To the esoteric seeker, there is much to be gained by learning about our amazing history; and to the historian, there are hidden treasures in our rituals which will bring insights into your daily life.

In former times the biggest conundrum used to be: what to reveal and what to keep secret? Well, the internet changed all that. With a little help from internet search engines there is almost no ritual which cannot be found (though I can assure you from practical experience that reading a ritual is no substitute for experiencing it, any more than reading a hundred books on how to play the piano will make you a concert pianist!).

Even from those who ignore the internet, publishers such as Kessinger have made available much material, monitors and rituals which were hitherto only available to its members. Even yard sales and online auction sites have made the private collections of fastidious assemblers of first editions and private printings available to any with a PayPal™ account and a keen eye.

So I have not held back from my interpretations of Masonic rituals, since these are freely available everywhere. But I do promise that you will never find a sign or a password, or anything which is not in the public domain, in my musings, other than my own observations.

All the papers contained within this book were given as talks in Lodges, Chapters, etc. Although many of the original papers also appeared as handouts, containing many illustrations, glossaries and bibliographies, the wide range of topics would make a bibliography random at best, and so I have decided not to include one, to avoid confusing the flow of the papers. I hope that any academics who read this book will forgive me. Unlike certain television programs and sensationalist books, I promise that, given my academic background, I do not make a habit of drawing theories and out of thin air.

That said, while I have tried to be as accurate as possible, any inaccuracies in this book are entirely due to me!

THE SEVEN LIBERAL ARTS & SCIENCES

1. Introduction

We are all familiar with the Middle Chamber Lecture in the Second Degree. For many it signifies a test of memory, to demonstrate the prowess of the Senior Deacon and his fitness to take the senior offices of Warden and Master in the Lodge. For others it is the beauty of this moving oratory which inspires. For others still it is the fact that the Lecture is pregnant with allegory. In this talk I would like to focus on one small part of the Lecture – the Seven Liberal Arts and Sciences. Why are they mentioned in a Masonic Ritual? Where do they come from? What are we to make of them today? While this brief talk will only dig a little beneath the surface, I hope that by the end you will know what the Seven Liberal Arts and Sciences are; have an idea of their history and why it is so extraordinary they survived in a Christian culture; how the Age of Enlightenment was founded on their practice and therefore why they were adopted in Freemasonry; and finally look at some of the extraordinary insights and ideas they have afforded prominent Masonic writers.

This paper gives away no secrets of the Fellowcraft Degree: the fact that the Seven Liberal Arts and Sciences are mentioned in the Middle Chamber Lecture is common knowledge and can easily be discovered by the most casual search of the Internet.

2. Recapitulation and other Countries

The Lecture traces the progress of the Entered Apprentice into the Middle Chamber to receive his wages "without scruple or diffidence" as some versions state. In some jurisdictions – as in ours – the Lecture is given in the form of a drama with several people taking roles and physical movement introduced; in other jurisdictions the Fellowcraft stand about the Tracing Board of this degree while a Brother invited by the Master gives the Lecture, indicating the various objects referred to with a pointing stick. In some jurisdictions – the English for example – the Seven Liberal Arts and Sciences are merely named in passing, together with the fact of the Temple taking "seven years and upwards to build". In our jurisdiction of New York rather more is made of them. I will quote from our Ritual book (which is not in code, and therefore reproducible), omitting the examples and analogies which in the case of music, verge on the maudlin:

"The seven steps allude to the seven Liberal Arts and Sciences which are Grammar, Rhetoric, Logic, Arithmetic, Geometry, Astronomy and Music.

"Grammar is the science which teaches us how to express our ideas in correct language.

"It is by Rhetoric that elegance of diction is taught.

"Logic is that science which teaches us how to form clear and distinct ideas, and prevents us being misled by similitude or resemblances.

"Arithmetic is the science of numbers, or that branch of mathematics which considers the properties of numbers in general.

"Geometry treats of the powers and properties of magnitudes in general, where length, breadth and thickness are considered...

"Astronomy is that science which treats of the heavenly bodies, their motion, magnitude, distances, and physical constitutions...

"Music is that art which affects the passions by sound."

One interesting exchange from the Questions of the Third Degree in England, where the Master examines the Candidate in open Lodge on his knowledge of the Fellowcraft Degree, is the following:

"WM: What are the peculiar objects of research in this Degree?

"Can: The hidden mysteries of Nature and Science."

4

Should this suggest to us that, far from being a quaint turn of phrase, the Candidate was expected to be versed in the Seven Liberal Arts and Sciences in order to proceed? We will return to this idea later.

So where did this 'syllabus' originate?

3. Origins of study

Although the term 'liberal arts' is nowadays used to lump together unspecialized and nonscientific courses available to students in universities, it originally referred to a very precise and invariable course of basic study offered at all universities. Its origins may be traced to Ancient Greece.

Around 387 B.C.E. Plato established The Academy, an informal school in which he based education on his principles of philosophy, including scientific testing, critical originality and the rejection of accepted assumptions. At the same time, Isocrates, a Greek orator, founded a school based on literary ideals. His goal was to form an intellectual elite of skilled orators capable of assuming the mantle of power (an objective also close to Plato's Republic, in which children were taught to regard all adults as 'mother' and 'father', and would follow schooling to prepare them for preordained stations in life). Isocrates' method taught students moral virtues, good judgment and prudent decision-making to prepare them for office, and study of the *Iliad* and *Odyssey* were central to his syllabus. However, there were no particular number of liberal arts defined, and the first clear mention of Seven Liberal Arts can be found in the writing of Marcus Terentius, a Roman scholar, in the 1st Century B.C.E., who also wrote treatises on the 'practical' arts of architecture and medicine.

4. Martianus and Codification

It was not until the fifth Century B.C.E. that a Roman writer in Africa – Martianus Capella – put these ideas into a book which became so popular that the Seven Liberal Arts were frozen from that moment forward. His book was entitled "*De nuptiis philiogiae et Mercurii*", or "*The Marriage of Philology and Mercury*".

Martianus was working as a lawyer in Carthage at the time, and wanted to write an encyclopedia of the liberal culture of his time, dedicated to his son Marianius. This was to be based on the ancient "*Satyra*" format, which were romances mixing prose and verse.

In his extraordinary (and, I must say, extraordinarily tedious) book Mercury has grown weary of celibacy, but has been refused by Wisdom, Divination and Soul. Apollo tells him of a charming and wise maiden called Philologia. The gods give their consent to the marriage provided Philologia is made divine. She assents to this. Her mother Reflection, the Muses, the Cardinal Virtues and the Three Graces surround and bedeck her, and she drinks the ambrosia. She is now immortal, and is introduced to the gods. The wedding gifts are listed, including seven maidens who will be Philologia's slaves. These are, as you must have guessed by now, our old friends Grammar, Logic, Rhetoric, Geometry, Arithmetic, Astronomy and Music. In the following seven books, the Liberal Arts each give an exposition of the principles of the science they govern. Interestingly, although Architecture and Medicine are present at the nuptials, they care nothing for earthly things and are condemned to remain silent. The writing, as you can tell from the brief description, is allegorical in nature. As I mentioned before, it is not an easy read. I quote one example from an English translation from Grammar's discourse:

"Disyllabic words have an acute accent on the first syllable when both syllables are short, as in *citus*; or when both are long by position, as in *sollers*; or when the final syllable is long by position, as in *cohors*. If, however, the first syllable is long by nature and the final syllable short, then the first syllable bears the circumflex, as in *luna*; if the final syllable is long by position or by nature, the first syllable bears the acute accent, as is *codex*, *docte*; in a disyllable work the grave accent will never be found on the first syllable."

With seven speeches like this, it must have been a long and tedious wedding banquet indeed!

The impression is, while this book attempts to set down an encyclopedia of the knowledge of the Seven Liberal Arts, the very act of writing it as a romance, and not a textbook suggests to me that this was not a formally adopted course of study in schools of the time. Certainly these subjects were covered, but there is a strong indication that other subjects were taught. Could it be that the Universities of the Middle Ages ended up basing their curriculum on the romantic fancy that they were reproducing the great schools of learning of Plato, Aristotle and Martial, when in fact no school teaching the Seven Liberal Arts as laid out in Capella's book ever existed?

5.   Adoption by Christian Society Against the Odds

Now the miracle occurs.

The 'Marriage' was a comprehensive if turgid book written by a decadent pagan writer at the time of the taking of Rome by Alaric in 410 C.E. This, remember, was when the majority of the Roman Empire was Christian (the Emperor Theodosius had prohibited all pagan cults and closed the Mystery Schools by 392 C.E.). In 429 Northern Africa was sacked by the Vandals. By 450 all remaining pagan temples had been destroyed and no pagan could hold office. And yet, fifty years later, a Christian writer, Flavius Magnus Aurelius Cassiodorus uses the term 'Seven Liberal Arts', and we also find a similar reference in the works of the Spanish scholar St. Isidore of Seville.

By the end of the fifth Century another Christian writer, Fulgentius, had written a work based on it, and in the sixth Century Gregory of Tours tells us it had become, in a way, a school manual! By the middle of the sixth Century Securus Memor Felix, a professor of rhetoric in Rome, received a copy of this pagan book.

So during these ages when priority was given to Christian persecution of anything pagan, particularly religion and education, and the focus was on the eradication of all non-Christian scholarship (fortunately for us, some wise Pachomian monks buried many such books following the decree by St. Athanasius to destroy all gnostic writings, which are now known to us as the Nag Hammadi Library), a book written by a minor pagan writer rose to be the cornerstone of the education system of the Christian world for nearly a thousand years.

Perhaps the ultimate irony was the appearance of the Seven Liberal Arts on the facades of the great cathedrals, for example Chartres Cathedral in Northern France. So we have the operative masons of the time carving the Liberal Arts into the entrances of the holiest buildings in Christendom during this great gothic architectural period. Perhaps a question we might ask ourselves is: were the Masons of old adding this detail merely upon the request of the sponsors; or were they introducing a subversive element of non-Christian education, seeing that they had considerable latitude in building these great structures?

6.   The Structure of the Syllabus: Trivium and Quadrivium

In Medieval schools and universities, the syllabus was divided into the elementary *trivium* (meaning the three roads), consisting of grammar (and the study of literature), logic and rhetoric (including the study of law). This approach is still followed in outline in European Colleges, where the first year is spent following general courses ending with Preliminary examinations, before the student passes on to take the elective courses for the following two or three years, which culminate in the Final examinations. It is this Latin word that gives us the modern English word 'trivial'. Upon completion of these courses the student received his Baccalaureate.

The *quadrivium* (Meaning the four roads) followed successful completion of the *trivium* and included the study of arithmetic, geometry (including geography and natural history), astronomy (and astrology), and music. Each built upon the previous 'road': number (arithmetic), number in space (geometry), number in time (music), and number in space and time (astronomy). On completing these four courses the student received the degree of Master of Arts. A further requirement would often be that the post-Graduate had to teach the *trivium* to the next generation of students, in order to maintain membership of a college in order to study for his Master's degree. A Doctorate would require special research into a particular area of interest and proof of original scholarship.

The Seven Liberal Arts and Sciences flourished through the Middle Ages and into the Renaissance, and suited that period of deep interest in the arts which survived up to the Age of Enlightenment, until being ultimately superseded by the burgeoning interest in science and economics brought about by the technological advances of the Industrial Revolution. The Seven Liberal Arts was the curriculum taught in colonial America during the 17th and 18th Centuries, and I suspect this may be why their description in the American rituals is often far more lavish than the brief allusion in the English rituals.

7.   One example – the art of Rhetoric and the Art of Memory

I want to take a very brief look at one of the Seven Liberal Arts, Rhetoric. To set the scene, let us recall the origins of the so-called *Ars Memoria*, or Art of Memory. The story goes as follows: a banquet was given by Scopas of Thessaly, at which Simonides of Ceos gave an oration. Simonides was later called out of the banquet by a messenger. During his absence the roof of the banqueting hall collapsed killing all the guests. The corpses were so mangled that relatives could not identify their dead, but Simonides remembered the places at which all the guest had sat, restoring the bodies to the next of kin. From this he realized that orderly arrangement is essential for good memory.

The challenge was how to memorize a long and difficult speech in such a way as to deliver it faultlessly.

Cicero developed this theme in his masterpiece "*De oratore*", when he introduces a brief description of mnemonics of places and images (*loci* and *imagines*). Thus, the Art of Memory because one of the five parts of the Liberal Science of rhetoric, so was taught to all students in the universities. The technique is not difficult. One imprints upon the memory a series of *loci* or places, for example, imagining walking about a large building, such as a Temple; perhaps Solomon's Temple? The place, according to Quintillian, another source of this technique, should have many rooms, all different, and be as spacious and varied as possible. Now the things needed to be remembered are placed in these rooms, in order, and associated with objects in those rooms. Perhaps there is a painting on the wall, of an ear of corn by a waterfall, and we associate this with an important biblical battle. Or perhaps we ascend seven steps, and are reminded of the time it took to build the Temple and the Seven Liberal Arts.

The 'Palace' we design is one with many rooms, each furnished with a number of objects. The idea was for the student to place ideas he need to remember in a logical sequence in those rooms, associating each with an object to make it easy to remember, and the sequence of rooms and objects would retain the sequence of ideas. This idea was keenly followed by Masons – one has only to look at a traditional Tracing Board to see this in action.

So now we can see that the entire Middle Chamber Lecture is one long exercise in the traditional Art of Memory!

8.   Foundation of the Age of Enlightenment and Introduction to Freemasonry

It is interesting to note that even in the oldest manuscripts known to refer to Masonry – the Regius and Cooke Manuscripts, dating back to 1390 and 1410 respectively, the Seven Liberal Arts and Sciences are not only referred to but listed in detail. This is not surprising, since as we have seen, this was the normal curriculum of universities of the time and therefore the knowledge common to all educated men. Let us read a passage on the Seven Liberal Arts from the Regius manuscript (in modern translation):

> "Many years after, the good clerk Euclid
> Taught the craft of geometry full wonder wide,
> So he did that other time also,
> Of divers crafts many more.
> Through his grace of Christ in heaven,
> He commenced in the sciences seven;
> Grammar is the first science I know,
> Dialect the second, so I have I bliss,
> Rhetoric the third without doubt,
> Music is the fourth, as I you say,
> Astronomy is the fifth, by my snout,
> Arithmetic the sixth, without doubt,
> Geometry the seventh maketh an end,
> For he is both meek and courteous,
> Grammar forsooth is the root,
> Whoever will learn on the book;
> But art passeth in his degree,
> As the fruit doth the root of the tree;
> Rhetoric measureth with ornate speech among,

And music it is a sweet song;
Astronomy numbereth, my dear brother,
Arithmetic showeth one thing that is another,
Geometry the seventh science it is,
That can separate falsehood from truth, I know
These be the sciences seven,
Who useth them well he may have heaven."

You may have noticed the order has been changed in this verse. You may also have picked up on the fact that Euclid apparently taught geometry through the grace of Christ – a fact I am sure he was not aware of!

I mentioned before that other jurisdictions make less of the Seven Liberal Arts and Sciences. Other aspects are usually emphasized instead. For example, the Grand Geometrician of the Universe is the usual title of Deity in the Fellowcraft Degree, and many grander Lodge rooms in the United Kingdom boast a zodiac on the ceiling. This reflection of the active and creative side of God (so beautifully realized by da Vinci on the ceiling of the Sistine Chapel in one of the most famous works of art created by man) again reminds us that the Third Degree leads the Fellowcraft away from the dreaming spires of academia and into the real world where, like our Grand Master, he will travel and spread his knowledge to man's benefit. We will see an interesting zodiacal interpretation by Foster Bailey shortly.

Now we see the introduction of the speculative masons into operative Lodges. These were educated men of their time, and we now know that their education was founded upon the Seven Liberal Arts and Sciences, including the Art of Memory as part of their studies on Rhetoric. The Seven Liberal Arts are already part of the education of an operative mason, as we have just seen. Should we therefore be surprised if these educated, speculative brothers expand upon the rhetoric elements and give a special place to the Lectures and instruction of Candidates, to give them the tools they need to understand the allegories, signs and symbols in masonry? Can we speculate ourselves that Elias Ashmole and other founders of the Royal Society, as they took over the decaying Lodges (for stonework was a dying art by them), really expected their new intellectual members to have a firm grounding in the traditional university studies in order to fully understand the lessons of masonry. I also wonder whether it was at about this time that the need for memorization came into play. Obviously there was a need to memorize certain work in the Operative Lodges – most masons would have been illiterate and they would therefore need to commit their Obligations, Charges and Passwords to memory. But I would be surprised if there was a need to commit the entire ritual to memory as we do today. Still, this is only my opinion.

By now the Middle Chamber Lecture was firmly in place in the Fellowcraft degree, and a key component was the reference to the Seven Liberal Arts and Sciences, the basis upon which all new members would have received all their education. Remember – not just part, but ALL of their education.

9.   Insights by prominent writers

Since that time, writers have uncovered many things in this wonderful passage. Insights have ranged from alchemy: seeing the seven arts as seven steps to create the Philosopher's Stone, through magical processes: circles, steps and invocations were beloved of Medieval theurgists, and several Continental Masonic Rites actually included magical practices, through Christian and Judaic mysticism: ranging from the seven lower Sephiroth of the Qabalah to the Seven Churches in Asia and the seven seals of Revelations, through Astrology: in the seven planets, to the idea of "The Quest."

In this interpretation, the First Degree symbolizes the realization that there is more to life than earthly pleasure, and the questor asks for light, which is eventually granted after obligations are taken and ancient penalties for infraction are lavishly described. The Second Degree symbolizes this quest for knowledge, and the Third Degree uses the journeying around the Temple as a microcosm of life and the world, as the now enlightened Master Mason uses his acquired knowledge for the practical purpose of benefiting mankind. W. Wilmshurst, in his book "The Meaning of Masonry", gives an eloquent description of this process: "The aspirant who attains proficiency in the work of self-perfecting to which the Fellowcraft grade alludes, has passed away from the North side of the Lodge, the side of darkness and imperfection; and now stands on the South East side in the meridian sunlight of moral illumination (so far as the natural man may possess it), but yet still far removed from that fuller realization of himself and of the mysteries of his own nature which is it possible for the…Master Mason to attain". In other words, a recognition of the God within himself, a mastery of the senses and a diligent application to the Liberal Arts and Sciences will provide the Mason with the building blocks for self-realization, but not the actual act itself. This will have to wait until the revelations of the Third Degree.

In the interest of time I will refer to two only of the many interpretations. Manly Palmer Hall never fails to inspire, while Foster Bailey, as mentioned previously, gives us an interesting astrological interpretation of the pillars of Wisdom, entirely in keeping with the Continental depiction of man's leaving the West and circumnavigating the zodiac in search of true Light.

"At the gates of the Temple of Wisdom. Bound with the cabletow of limitation, poor in spirit and body, man seeks admittance to the University of Understanding. In the Ancient Mysteries the order of the steps was seven, five and three – the seven liberal arts and sciences, the five sense and emotions, and the three steps symbolic of the Trinity of God in man." *The Lost Keys of Freemasonry – Manly Palmer Hall*

"Your attention is called here to the esoteric significance of the two pillars, B– and J–, when considered in connection with (the) zodiacal journey. Placed side by side in position these two pillars form the symbol used in astrology to denote the sign Gemini, and study of their meaning in this connection reveals perhaps more clearly than anything else the underlying subject of Masonry… In this sign, Gemini, the duality of man is symbolized by the Twins. Man – good and bad in his own nature, coming forth from darkness and seeking light; man – composed of two aspects or natures, for man 'is of the earth, earthy, and the second man is the Lord from Heaven'; man – the son of the Widow, but also the son of light. God and man conjoined – the two brothers, Castor and Pollux, shining forth together and signifying mortality and immortality." *The Spirit of Masonry – Foster Bailey*

10. Conclusion

The Seven Liberal Arts and Sciences have a long and venerable history. Reference to them is inevitable given the fact that they were the syllabus for all educated men, and Freemasonry, we are told, started to attract educated men like Elias Ashmole at the start of the Age of Enlightenment, who has an upbringing steeped in the Trinity, the Five Senses and the Seven Liberal Arts and Sciences. Although it was probably the speculative masons who embellished and developed these themes and lectures, we must not forget that they did not introduce them to Masonry: they were part of the Old Charges dating back to 1390.

To apologists of the 'ancient mysteries' school of Masonic origins, I am afraid the venerable history of the Seven Liberal Arts and Sciences neither lends proof nor contradicts an early start to the Craft. While they were practiced widely in some form in ancient Greece (and therefore in Ptolemaic Egypt), in their current form they were not finalized until the 4th Century C.E. in Italy. There is no indication that they were extant in Solomonic or early Egyptian society, and the likelihood is great that they were introduced into the early Charges to lend the Operative Craft Lodges, who were engaged at that time is building the later cathedrals and early Universities, a veneer of scholarship and respectability.

Since then, men of letters have never tired of seeing further symbolism in all parts of the Middle Chamber Lecture, and study of this Lecture will never cease to repay the effort with new insights and teachings.

MASONIC MEDITATION

1. Background

In the early days of Masonry, prior to being admitted to a Lodge, a Candidate had to undergo two trials. The first one was the 'Passage beneath the Veil', in which the blindfolded Candidate was led into the Lodge Room before the assembled members, who then proceeded to ask questions about his thoughts on art, philosophy, religion and politics, in order to gain a better impression of the Candidate. Note that this was not a debate, but a one-sided process of asking a question and receiving an answer from the Candidate. If his answers gave the Brethren confidence in his candidacy, he was then summoned to his Initiation. However, prior to receiving the degree he was placed in a Chamber of Reflection, in which there were emblems of mortality – such as a human skull, a half-burned candle, an hourglass – and a pen and paper, on which he was asked to write his Last Will and Testament, or answer three specific questions about his duty to God, to the Universe and to fellow man and towards himself. These traditions are still maintained in a number of Obediences.

The symbolism of all this should be readily apparent. By contemplating his death, the Candidate is symbolically dying to the old and preparing for the new. The 'walk of the dead' from the Chamber of Reflection to the Lodge Room represents the passage from one world to the next, and the cabletow the astral cord which holds him still to the material world (which is later cut, or removed, when he fully commits to his new existence by taking the Obligation).

So what is the Candidate meant to do in the Chamber of Reflection? What is the purpose of the emblems of mortality placed therein? How does he answer questions of a philosophical nature, the content of which he probably has never given a moment's though prior to this moment?

Interestingly enough, we find the answer in our own ritual[2]. There is a small italicized rubric which most people miss regarding the setting up of the Preparation Room. It reads as follows: "Proper

---

[2] That is, in New York at least.

decorum and a *meditative* atmosphere in the Preparation Room are vital to the mental preparation of the candidate. After properly clothing the candidate, some Lodges enhance the mood of the room by the light of a single candle or flashlight candle, thus creating what is referred to as a 'Chamber of Reflection'."

The Chamber of Reflection, or properly set up Preparation Room fulfill all the necessary prerequisites for meditation – and indeed we are exhorted to do so in our own Ritual. One of the problems most Lodges face is having the Preparation Room adjacent to the Lodge Room where the coats racks are, and trying to give the Candidates the peace of meditation we are asked to afford them is usually lost in the bustle of friendly chitchat, removal of coats and hats, joking and levity. As an aside, our Lodge had reintroduced the Chamber of Reflection and put it in another, more distant room, with a "Do Not Disturb" sign outside, away from the area where members congregate and chat, leading the Candidates into the Preparation Room only when necessary for their first entrance into the Lodge.

So what is meditation? What do we need to do it? What does it feel like? How does it help us in our 'daily advance in Masonic knowledge'?

In this talk I will explore what meditation is and what it is not, some of the types of meditation, how to do them, and we will end, naturally enough, with a meditation exercise.

2. What is meditation?

The most important thing to understand is that meditation is a very simple exercise, that anyone can do it, and that it can be done anywhere with no equipment necessary. The only basic requirements are some time without distractions, a comfortable environment (in terms of temperature and seating), and as little extraneous noise as possible. We can also add aids to meditation, such as relaxing music or a point of focus, such as a candle flame or picture, but these are not essential.

Although meditation had been practiced by a few Westerners in earlier times, it was virtually unknown in the West until the mid- to late-1800s, when groups such as the Theosophical Society under

Madame Blavatsky introduced Eastern ideas to middle-class English and American disciples, eager for new experience in an age of resurgent interest in esoteric and mystical subjects. However, it was not until the 1960s that meditation became known to a large number of people in the West. This was primarily due to *The Beatles*, who popularized the work of the Maharishi. The time was ripe for practices which encouraged self-actualization: the hippy movement was sweeping the young generation of baby-boomers, and a desire to understand the purpose of life led to a willingness to try any means available. This was the era of Woodstock, of Dr. Timothy Leary, LSD and Free Love. Into this heady mix, Transcendental Meditation was a new, drug-free means to experience an inner peace in a turbulent time, in which the Cold War was at its height, the threat of nuclear war ever present, public opinions was turning against the war in Vietnam, President Kennedy – and later his brother Robert – had been assassinated, and the atrocities committed against the black population in the Southern States had outraged the liberal Northern States.

Transcendental Meditation's time had come, for three main reasons. Firstly, it offered a means of escape from the stress of living in the late 1960s and early 1970s. Secondly, the advertising promised a host of benefits, ranging from peace of mind and relief from stress to increasingly grandiose claims of world peace…and even 'flying'! Thirdly, it was perceived as weird and new, and no doubt many were turned towards it because it unsettled and worried the older generation who did not understand it and equated it with mind control or brainwashing. This was also the time of the Hari Krishna movement (one can still see a few adherents on the streets, dressed in their saffron robes with topknot hairdos, often gyrating ecstatically down the street with their drums and finger cymbals, chanting "Hari Krishna, Hari Krishna, Krishna Krishna, Hari Rama" to the tune written by George Harrison of *The Beatles*. Many parents were terrified that their meditating children would soon be sporting shaved heads and saffron robes (of course, Punk Rock and Grunge was still nearly twenty years away!).

The colorful picture painted above is a reminder that it was only a very short time ago that meditation was seen as a weird, outlandish mode of behavior undertaken by people on the fringe of society and by gullible teenagers. Of course meditation was not a secret to those of devout belief in most religions, for whom meditation was a natural part of their spiritual practice; but these people were neither common, nor likely to stand up in defense of this very private means of inner contemplation.

For those who are new to meditation and who may yet harbor some concerns about the technique, you can rest assured that meditation is not harmful in any way. It is not hypnosis. You are in complete control at all times, and you decide exactly when to go into or come out of a meditative state. Above all, it is a perfectly natural process. I will now tell you the biggest secret of all. Meditation is sitting quietly and thinking about nothing in particular. There, the secret is out! Not so scary after all, is it? "But", you ask, "if this is all it is, then why bother to do it?" Ah, when you sit quietly and allow your mind to slow down and stop its incessant chatter: that is when you begin to *listen*....

3. Symbolism – the means to Meditation

The Oxford English Dictionary gives three definitions for the word 'symbol':

1. A mark or character used as a conventional representation of an object, function, or process, e.g. the letter or letters standing for a chemical element or a character in musical notation:
    'the symbol r in Figure 5 represents a gene which is ineffective'
    'the chemical symbol for helium is He'
    1.1 A shape or sign used to represent something such as an organization, e.g. a red cross or a Star of David:
    'the Red Cross symbol'
    'the Star of David, the Jewish symbol'
2. A thing that represents or stands for something else, especially a material object representing something abstract:
    'the limousine was another symbol of his wealth and authority'

In our symbolic world as Masons – or for that matter in any esoteric school of thought – symbols are usually categorized as falling
into one of three types: Natural, Artificial and Mystical. These equate
with the three listed in the Oxford English Dictionary. The first definition is the Artificial (being simple substitutions, for example 'He'
for Helium, and for that matter language in general, where each language has developed a seemingly random collection of letters to
substitute for objects or concepts). The second (1.1) is the Mystical,
where a symbol takes on what we might call an emotional quality, and
certainly one which draws on history, since contemplation of the symbol brings about a flood of ideas from all ages. The third include the
natural, for while a limousine might indicate wealth, smoke might indicate a fire, or in the case of early tribes, the approach of hostile
forces.

I will not labor the distinction of types of symbols here, as I will
cover this topic in more depth in the paper on *Symbolism & Freemasonry as a Mystery School*.

However, I think you will realize that the most potent type of
symbol to use in meditation is the mystical type. It is important that a
symbol be laden with an emotional connection as it is this which will
trigger a train of thoughts leading to new insights. Thus, all the symbols of Masonry are laid out before us for our contemplation: not to
be looked on in the Lodge Room and then forgotten, but to be pon-
dered, dissected, analyzed and thought about long after we have 'quit
the sacred retreat'.

Perhaps the most pertinent symbols for Masons, outside their ritual, is the Tarot. These ancient cards are also called the 'Book of
Thoth', and some believe they are the 'Book of Life', that book in
which, if one can understand it, the meaning of all things is revealed.
Anyone who saw the movie "The Ninth Gate" with Johnny Depp saw
one interpretation of many possibilities. However, the deeply Kabbalistic nature of the meaning of the picture cards – or Major Arcana –
would provide a lifetime's study, and indeed has. Even Carl Jung
wrote a book entirely devoted to meditations upon the symbolism in
the Tarot. These may be used to advantage either as a meditation on
the symbols themselves, or as a gateway to pass through in Path
Working, of which more later.

But whether you choose to use your mind's eye, or a Tarot card as an aid to meditation, the overall technique is broadly the same, with the exception that you will need a table and a stand for the latter. Of course, you are free to employ a picture of a symbol too!

4. Practicalities

We have explored some of the background to meditation, and we have also alluded to some of the requirements, such as a quiet place apart from others, and why symbols are used as objects upon which to focus. Now we will look at technique.

• **Environment**

Although the beauty of meditation is that it can be done any-where – at home, on a bus, on a park bench, at work – it is best to give oneself the best possible conditions when starting out. Find a quiet space where the temperature and humidity do not distract you. Cooler is better than too warm. The chair should be comfortable and have a back (try not to use a sofa or excessively padded seat – the aim is to meditate, not to fall asleep! Dress in loose clothing which does not restrict you. Sit upright with your feet a little apart, hands resting lightly on your knees, palms upward (not necessary on a bus – you want to look as natural as possible in public places). Try not to cross your legs or arms: for practical reasons this is a non-verbal posture of defense, and this will inhibit the openness required.

Try to avoid times of the day when you are stressed, or busy, or distracted. Do not try to meditate shortly after drinking coffee or an-other stimulant – it will not be effective. Similarly, if you try to meditate half an hour before an important meeting, you will not de-rive full benefit (although, once you have some experience of meditating, spending a few minutes in that quiet place before attend-ing to an important meeting or event can help to calm you and sharpen your focus). If you are too tired when you try to meditate you will probably just fall asleep! It is not recommended meditating in a prone position for the same reason.

- **Session length**

To begin with your session should last about ten minutes. Believe me, when you start you might want to give it five minutes: even ten will seem like an eternity! Later you can add to that, but in most instances you should not need more than half an hour. To begin with you can try it once a day or twice a day in the morning and evening. More proficient people find it so easy to go into the meditational state that they can do it at will, and so pleasant that they do it often. However, the idea is not to overdo it early on and then stop, but rather to build it into your daily routine. Do what you can, but remember it is as important to find time to exercise your subconscious as it is to exercise your body. What use is a temple that has a beautiful exterior, when its interior dirty, unkempt and not maintained? Remember the parable of the whited sepulcher!

Later on, once the basics of meditation have been grasped, we will build on this principle in later lessons to teach you how to use creative visualization, as did the saints of old, to effect real changes both in yourself and in the world around you.

When coming out of a meditation, it is important to allow some time to return to the 'real world' as well. Sit still and take a few breaths, then slowly open the eyes. Allow yourself a few moments to come back to yourself before getting up and going about your daily business.

If you have difficulty timing your sessions (and you can quickly lose track of time), you can use some kind of timer which has a soft alarm. If your alarm clock or timer is loud and intrusive try putting it in an adjacent room, or wrapping it in a towel.

- **Relaxation**

Before beginning a meditative process, it is important to give yourself some time to withdraw from the world and prepare the mind for meditation. Just as you would not want to start rigorous exercise without first doing some toning and stretching exercises, so you need to still the body and mind and give them a chance to uncouple from the pressures and troubles of daily life.

Therefore, close your eyes, and take several slow, deep breaths, feeling the cares of the world falling gently from your shoulders as you enter a calmer state. If you are at home and music helps, by all means use music. There are many so-called New Age CDs and tapes which are pleasant and undemanding to listen to. The music must be background music and not something which requires concentration. Sounds of nature work well: music should have no words or singing, although Gregorian Chant seems to work well – the early monks and nuns knew a lot about meditation.

- **Breathing**

Breathing has been used in a number of meditative techniques to enhance the experience. However, apart from taking a few deep breaths to begin, in order to flush out worldly cares and prepare yourself to meditate, it is recommended that you just continue to breathe normally until you have some success in learning to meditate and to switch from the mode of daily life into a contemplative state with relative ease.

- **Use of symbol or sound (Mantra or Nadam)**

As well as listening to quiet music, many traditions use the technique of vibrating a particular sound or word. Vibrating is a form of singing on one note. However, the effect is rather different: just as a note sung at the correct pitch can make a church or music hall resonate to that pitch (or ever shatter a glass!), so different pitches will tend to resonate or vibrate more in different parts of the body. If you experiment, you will find that if you hum at a particular pitch you will feel it strongly in the top part of your head. This is often used in Eastern traditions to awaken particular Chakras, or centers of energy in the body.

Mantra meditation is the constant repeating – vocally or internally – of a particular sound, word or phrase. The sound known to most Westerners is "Om" or "Aum". Phrases can be used as well: "Hail Mary, Full of Grace…" *Nadam* meditation is the use of a continuous sound, which can be recorded or imagined in the mind (examples include a waterfall, a rhythmic drum, high frequency sound).

If you have experience in meditation by all means use these methods. However, the approach we will be taking in the early stages is closer to *Nadam* than *Mantra*, if recorded background music or natural sounds are used.

- **Benefits**

It is important to stress the benefits of meditation. While we will later the using the technique for powerful intentions, the very act of calming the mind through meditation, of linking the subconscious to the conscious mind, will lead to physical relaxation and calm. You will learn to detach yourself from troubling thoughts and will have a powerful tool to help you remove yourself from the cares of the world, to allow yourself to recharge your energy. You will certainly find that the benefits you gain from meditation will spill out into your daily life. Do not be surprised if your friends and family notice!

5. Types of Meditation

There are many types of meditation and uses for the practice, all of which are pertinent to the Mason who wishes to expand his knowledge of the mystical side of Masonic teaching.

- **Greater awareness**

This is usually used to gain new insight into a common symbol. Common objects used are geometric designs, or objects from nature. It may be a stone, or a piece of wood, or a flower. It may even be a word or a phrase, or a prayer. The idea is to find time to contemplate the object in order to see new meaning, or find a new message in it. One particular example is meditation on each line of the Lord's Prayer, or each phrase of the Aaronic Blessing, in order to try to understand the profound message behind these often said yet rarely focused on prayers.

- **Self-awareness**

Similar to the previous exercise, this is intended to help you get to know and understand yourself better. You may choose to focus on a part of your body, or an attribute of your personality. This is often used to try to explore a negative trait with the intention that, by understanding one's problem, the subconscious will work to resolve it. For example, a fear (such as agoraphobia) or irrational behavior (such as anger) can be quietly contemplated and the reasons behind it explored – not by actively telling the mind what you think the reason is; but by passively letting the subconscious tell you of the cause that is *really* behind this symptom.

- **Awareness of God/Guardian Angel/Higher Self**
  At a higher level, many mystics believe that God is within them, and that this force – call it an angel, guardian or higher self can be communicated with. As the bible enjoins us: "be still and know God". Here, we still our minds and turn inwards to commune with the "still, small voice" which is our higher consciousness.

- **Solutions to questions**
  On a more mundane level many people use meditation as a way of finding an answer to a question. We will not go into the metaphysics of this here, other than to say that, as each human is a cell in the body we call the human race, so each subconscious mind is similarly linked, forming a global network of consciousness into which the individual subconscious mind can tap. People have used this to seek answers to questions, locate missing objects, spread peace and love throughout the world, and a host of other intentions.

- **'Reality' exercises**
  This is more of a training process than true meditation: calisthenics for the mind. In 'reality' exercise one focuses on a particular daily activity, such as eating lunch, or washing the dishes, and performs them with slow, deliberate actions, observing each action and recording the sensations minutely. This is an excellent activity to practice focus of the mind, and improving the level of concentration. This in turn leads to more focused meditation with less distraction, and the conscious mind unlearns bad habits and practices focus on a single activity to the exclusion of all else. This technique is taught in a number of mystery schools as a necessary prerequisite to meditation.

- **Pathworking**
  Pathworking (whether physically or in the mind) is a particular adaptation of meditation. Using the rosary is the clearest example. Through meditation one is led through a series of events in the life of the Christ, and is called to meditate upon what those events mean to

the person meditating. Jewish Kabbalists (and others) use the Tree of Life as a series of pathways and locations upon which to meditate. In this approach the meditation becomes a journey, a quest – possibly spiritual – during which people, objects and forces may be encountered. Bunyan's *Pilgrim's Progress* and Dante's *Inferno* are examples of such journeys committed to book form. One may even see the recent popularity of Dungeon and Dragons™ games, which use imagination rather than boards, as another manifestation of this type of meditation. We will find this form of meditation will recur later in our courses, which is to be expected as the way of the Knight Templar is a Spiritual Journey. A Pathworking usually involves a number of people with one person leading the visualization.

6. A Practical Exercise

For our practical exercise I suggest we use one of the secondary symbols from the Third Degree. It matters not whether we have Entered Apprentices or Fellowcraft present, as the symbol is not a Masonic secret. Besides, it is clearly visible in the stained glass windows in the Gothic Room of New York Grand Lodge and in many, many other Masonic buildings!

The symbol I am going to use is the beehive:

Relax – close your eyes – take a few deep breaths. Examine from outside its form and shape, and hear the low drone of the bees. Now shrink in size and enter the hive. Perfect symmetry – God's guidance, watch the beautiful dance by which the worker bees make sources of nectar known to the others. Feel the color, touch the walls of wax, smell the scent of honey, taste the honey, hear the incessant drone in the background, like a thousand monks quietly chanting to God. Make your way to the center down long, winding paths to see the Queen. Heart of their universe, this pulsating greatness pushing forth life, amid the Royal Jelly and murmuration of a thousand bees. Now depart and silently thank the bees for permitting you to enter their world in this spiritual sense, and sharing some of their teachings with you. Slowly open eyes – return to here and now – become conscious of present time.

Or perhaps you wish to pursue a more traditional form of meditation? Then sit quietly and contemplate the hive. You can consider its shape, the cylinder topped by a three-dimensional arch. A perfect edifice, containing many passages and rooms like the Memory Palaces of the Art of Memory. Or a shape reminiscent of the Holy Hill, or even Mount Abiegnus of the Rosicrucians. Or think about as bee, with its yellow and black banded coat, calling you to think about night and day, or the juxtaposition of opposites on the squared carpet of the Lodge. Or consider the mortality of the worker bee, doomed to die for the greater good of the collective, to die in order to be born anew.

You see: the moment you close your eyes and start to let your mind wander, you will be surprised where it takes you. The examples above are artificial, to you, for they are not *your* journeys and wanderings, but *mine*. So take the step, plunge into the unknown, and learn!

THE EGREGORE[3]

1. Introduction

Have you even walked into an old church or soaring cathedral, or a venerable mosque or ornate synagogue, and felt a *presence*? I am not referring to the all-pervasive presence of God, but rather that atmosphere which seems to be more than the sum of its parts? Take the illustration of being on vacation, or newly-moved, and walking into a local church on Sunday. Few of us have not had that strong emotion either of feeling welcomed, at home; or conversely, as if we are intruding on a private party, and more often than not, hastily leave for a more accommodating place. This feeling has nothing to do with the actual friendliness of the individuals who greet us at the door. Somehow it seems to transcend personal contact. It is as though the building itself contains an *atmosphere* with which we are either attuned or not.

While the term *egregor* or *egregore* was not coined until the latter part of the last century, the concept has been around for a long time. Certainly, it is most often strongly felt in places of great antiquity, where humans gathered to engage in a common purpose. While an *egregore* is not by any means a religious idea, it should not surprise us that it is very often associated with religious sites. After all, this was the time that people most often came together with a common idea. It is hard not to be moved, say, by the Church of the Holy Sepulcher, the Dome of the Rock, Notre Dame Cathedral, Stonehenge or Machu Picchu. But we can find *egregores* in places other than religious sites as well: the Coliseum in Rome, the Tower of London, the Giant's Stadium, Niagara Falls, the Grand Canyon…and this Lodge Room.

The *egregore* is not something out of the mind of a New Age devotee, or 'up there' with flying saucers and ghosts: it is something we have all felt. But what is it, exactly?

In this paper we will consider a working definition of an *egregore*. We will go on to discuss how one is created and maintained,

---

[3] Out of interest, a more generic version of this talk was first given at an esoteric conference at the University of Bucharest, Romania. It was the first time I gave a lecture simultaneously translated into another language!

and also how it can be destroyed. We will look at some examples of *egregores*, and from this deduce the primary functions of an *egregore*. Finally, we will consider the *egregore* in the context of Freemasonry.

2. Definition

Robert Ambelain, in his book *Practical Kabbalah*, said: "We give the name *Egregore* to a Force generated by a powerful spiritual current and later fed at regular intervals..." L. S. Bernstein offered the rather more prosaic term "group form."

An *egregore*, therefore, is usually something created by humans, not by gods, although some of us may believe that other entities can help to create an *egregore*. We should not be misled by the term "spiritual" in Ambelain's definition: he is using the term in contrast to 'physical'. It is not a physically created being, nor is it an independently living organism; but rather an artificial entity, which is not only brought into existence by a common idea, but needs to be fed regularly if it is not to fade away.

Ambelain gives us a particularly clear example when he talked of the *Body of Christ*, the *Celestial Jerusalem*, the *Mystical Church* – all of which have been used to describe the heart of the great spiritual current of Catholicism. Protestantism, Islam, Buddhism and Freemasonry have *egregores* as well. So do the great political ideologies. From this we can learn that an *egregore*, being itself a neutral creation, can be evil as well as good!

The great psychologist Jung proposed the idea of the *collective unconsciousness*, and to some extent the *egregore* is a similar concept, in that it suggests an unconscious linking of minds into a greater gestalt, or whole. On the other hand, this is a passive process; while the creation of an *egregore* most certainly requires a positive act, as we shall see. It may be closer to Jung's idea of *archetypes*, though once again this word has expanded over time to embrace almost any meaning we wish to attribute to it.

Perhaps a clue can be found in the title of Ambelain's book: *Practical Kabbalah*. Mirroring the Platonic idea that our ability to create a mental abstraction of an object, for example a 'chair', derives from our idea of a 'perfect chair' given to us by God, the Kabbalah suggests that there are several worlds of increasing perfection coexistent with ours. At the top, so to speak, is *Aziluth*, sometimes called the World of Archetypes where the perfect designs are to be found upon the celestial trestleboard. Way, way below this is the World of *Assiah*, the material world in which we live, where the works of man are infinitely inferior to those original plans, though we have a dim image of them within us, which we strive to emulate in our imperfect way. In his book *The Way of the Craftsman*, Kirk McNulty attempts to link these worlds to the three Masonic Degrees in an interesting – if not always entirely credible – manner. He places the Degrees as taking place on successively higher levels of the spiritual temple, and links these levels to the Kabbalistic worlds. It is certainly an interesting hypothesis for those looking for their daily advancement...

If we have, then, decided that an *egregore* is a human creation, a statement which we will shortly qualify, and that it may be created, maintained and destroyed, how then are such acts accomplished?

3. Creation, Maintenance, Destruction

An *egregore* comes into existence through the combined will of those who form it. This requires a single concept, directed effort, and much energy. Firstly, for an *egregore* to form requires the people forming it to be united in a common purpose. An *egregore* can be large or small: just a few people can create a true – if weak – *egregore*. Possibly the smallest unit would be the family. Indeed, Maurice Barrès said: "the shield of a very old family is its pentacle, the genealogical tree its magical chain. Immediately the descendants form but one single Being[4]". This, surely, is an eloquent description of a clan forming an *egregore*! The Eastern cult of family, and even the Roman Pre-Empire belief in the family unit and the *Lares et Penates*, or family household deities, give further examples of the family *egregore*. However, the usual idea of an egregore is of a much larger creation. As well as the single concept the effort needs to be given direction, and this is almost always accomplished by a leader who is usually a visionary. Thus the great religions, the great political and

---

[4] Source of the quotation is not given: this is from R. Ambelain's book "*Kabbale Pratique*", page 178.

philosophical movements, are initiated by a great leader – often succeeded by less than competent heads. However, this is less important, for once an *egregore* is formed and its image created, it requires far less effort to maintain than it did to create. If the Colossus of Rhodes required the vision of a genius to invent and erect it, once it was completed it became a focal embodiment of the power and authority of that nation, and thereby the image of the Rhodian *egregore* was set. Finally, we require the initial expenditure of much energy, for an *egregore* is not created by a passing whim. When we see images of St. Peter's Square in the Vatican filled with adoring believers, the well-ordered crowds in Red Square cheering the troops on Labor Day, the revelers in Times Square on New Year's Eve, or the Zeppelinfeld packed with Hitler's supporters chanting in unison, we can see the power of a common thought-form.

However, an *egregore* does not need very great numbers nor such great emotional outpouring to be created. Focus is more important than a general emotive atmosphere, and a few people providing the right focus is as effective as the hysterical outpouring of a highly-strung crowd. This is why the *egregores* of initiatory bodies are especially powerful, for little or no energy is 'lost'.

We stated earlier that *egregores* are mainly human creations. However, there may be exceptions to this. Remembering what we said about the *Mystical Church*, it is probable that other entities besides humans have contributed to its *egregore*. Is it not said by all the 'People of the Book' that angels and archangels fall down before the Throne and worship? Does the Song of the Great Architect not vibrate throughout Creation in the *Harmony of the Spheres*? Do not all these entities contribute to the *egregore* of, for example, the Catholic Faith?

Once built, an *egregore* needs to be fed in order to survive. As we have said, the energy required is much less than that required to initiate it, but nevertheless it needs to be fed from time to time to survive. This is why rallies are so important, be they prayer sessions, initiations, parades or mass gatherings. These are always directed by a few, for the maintenance of an *egregore* will always require an 'inner circle' to direct and focus the energy to the correct purpose. This is not to imply that this 'inner circle' necessarily understands the true nature of what they are doing – though this is more likely in initiatory groups – but rather that they instinctively ensure that the right energy is being produced. The most powerful means of providing energy is through ritual. We can see it in our own gentle Craft. But the *egregore* of all religions and even nations is maintained through regular ritual. Let us not forget that, when Communist Russia turned her back on the pomp and circumstance of monarchy and organized religion, they substituted parades and events every bit as ritualistic to feed their newly-created *egregore*. So long as people <u>believe</u>, the *egregore* will exist.

We will now turn to the destruction of an *egregore*. Why would one wish to do this? A mature *egregore* may take on a relatively independent existence. When this occurs, the results can be tragic. The phrase "the road to hell is paved with good intentions" has never been more true. When the visionary leader of a movement dies or is killed and the movement is taken over by others, we often see the original ideas compromised and in some cases completely perverted. Then we say that the people who took over bent the organization to their own ends, or that they were motivated by greed or evil. But is it possible that it was the *egregore* itself which was leading them in the wrong paths? Something to ponder.

The most effective way to destroy an *egregore* quickly is through the use of fire. If one can destroy all trace of the existence of the *egregore*, it will be most quickly eliminated. In ancient Egypt a way to eliminate a cult was to efface it utterly, as we see in the sacking of Al-Amarna and the erasing of the cartouches and monuments of Akhenaten. The Romans on the other hand had <u>not</u> learned that only immolation by fire destroys an egregore, and blood sacrifice only feeds it: a lesson known to most religions! Thus the spilling of so much martyred blood of Christians only reinforced the fledgling Christian *egregore* and ensured its eventual victory. On the other hand, the lesson appears to have been well-known to the Inquisition, who delighted in burning heretics along with their works, to ensure the destruction of the thought-form of the heresy. We see echoes of it in the burning of the library at Alexandria, and in *Kristallnacht*, the Night of Broken Glass, November 9th, 1938, when synagogues were destroyed throughout Germany and Austria, and 'subversive' works of art were burned on bonfires in the streets.

Perhaps the darkest example we have with us at the latter end of 2016 is that of ISIL. Who can doubt the power of a dark *egregore* when we see how easily people become polarized and indoctrinated, even at a vast distance, by the source of this potent negativity?

4. Examples

In history the *egregore* has been represented by many forms. In the religious examples above, we have seen the church as Bride, as a shining City, and as a pair of hands joined in prayer. The flag is a device common to many *egregores*, both religious and national. The Beaucéant was the banner of the Templars, showing that they were 'fair and favorable to the friends of Christ, but dark and terrible to His enemies'. We remember the Hammer and Sickle of Communist Russia and the Eagle and Backward Swastika of Nazi Germany – both signs of a black, stifling *egregore* born of fanaticism, conjured not out of the loving minds of positive thought, but evoked from the darkest recesses of the human mind. Remember Winston Churchill's chilling comment that "the lights are going out all over Europe", a reference to the dark cloud then hovering over that continent.

Often we anthropomorphize an *egregore*. We see this in Uncle Sam here, John Bull and Britannia in England, and Marianne in France. Even supranational ideals have their counterpart in an *egregore*. Think of Justice, the blind woman who holds the sword and balances. Think of Death, the shrouded skeleton on horseback with his scythe. Think of War, Liberty, National Pride, Love. Everything has its distinctive emblem or symbol, be it a person or a thing. In many cases this image is used as a protection or amulet, in the best tradition of a religious object. To look at it is to be reminded of one's attachment to it, to feel protection. In Freemasonry the forget-me-not was worn in Europe during the Second World War both as a sign of belonging and as a sign of defiance. Even now, we don our Square & Compasses for reasons which, if we are honest, go beyond merely wearing a badge.

There is a darker side to this. While a person suited to an *egregore* will indeed feel welcomed in and cared for, we must remember what we said at the beginning of this paper about walking into a new church or synagogue and instantly feeling unwelcome. The *egregore* can also <u>reject</u> people. This can be for two reasons. The first is that the *egregore* feels threatened by the new person, and will make them feel unwelcome, the better to hasten their departure. It will do this especially if it feels the person is not functioning on the same wavelength as the other members, and therefore may try to change the character of the *egregore* – or even that the person may not be joining for pure motives, and needs to be expelled. The second reason is more common, and it simply that a person is not spiritually or emotionally mature enough to be ready for that *egregore*. I point this out to remind our Brethren that, when a new and promising Candidate goes through the Degrees, never to be seen again, despite all attempts by the Lodge to retain him, it is not necessarily the fault of the Lodge, and the members should not recriminate themselves over this. In all probability the person was not ready for Freemasonry and could not handle the importance of its teachings. Manifestations of this may be gentle, such as the person finding non-Masonic distractions to be of greater interest, or where the violation is severe, the rejection will be more dramatic, as can be seen in Masonic jurisprudence cases.

As an aside here, one common manifestation of this is the former member who leaves, and then seeks to vilify Freemasonry. More often than not they both break their vows (proving themselves a dishonorable person and worthy of contempt) or even invent and embellish facts at the prospect of a lucrative book deal or television appearance (a worse moral crime, since they often claim they are doing this for religious reasons, whilst their very actions illustrate their hypocrisy). The biggest disservice Freemasonry does to itself is to answer these allegations, deny these charges, or, worst of all, cave in and publicly change its Constitution, Rules, Regulation, Ritual or Passwords to accommodate public sentiment. If it remains aloof it will survive; but if it capitulates, it will go the way of all weak and timorous organizations.

5. Freemasonry & The Egregore

We have outlined and examined the *egregore*, its definition, history and creation. "But", I can feel many of you thinking, "what can it do for me? Why do we bother to create this thing?"

Up to now I have delivered what might be classed as a theoretical or academic paper on the *egregore*. Now we are going to turn rather more practical. The answer is both simple and profound, if you are prepared to meditate on its implications.

The *egregore* is a battery, and we are its cells.

When we join an initiatory Order we are linked to the *egregore*, and become one of its constitutive cells. We add to the power of the *egregore*, which is essentially a store of energy, and in exchange the *egregore* provides us with a sense of belonging, and isolates the member from the external world, and, being the sum of the collective power previously received, provides a source of strength to that person in time of need, if he knows how to tap into it. This is why we feel the most in harmony with our Brethren in the Lodge room. This is why, when we see a Square & Compass, our hearts leap within our breast in a sense of pride and belonging. This is why many Masonic bodies include a moment where the Brethren form a circle and join hands. The *egregore* is the central point of projection and a source of energy, and we form the circle which surrounds it. The image of the circle is powerful for it suggests a circuit, protection, unity and infinity.

In our Craft we have not created an anthropomorphic being, but rather a force for good. So long as we adhere to our Landmarks we will maintain this *egregore* much as it has been maintained since Freemasonry was invented. Ours is a special *egregore*, for it is not limited by language, political or religious persuasion: indeed, it is fed by people who make a particular effort to leave these thoughts outside of the space in which they unite to feed it. If we could see it – even in our mind's eye – we would perhaps be disappointed. It is not <u>entirely</u> filled with a golden luminosity, for even in our Craft there are many people who join for personal gain, who seek power over others, who glory in their status and who do not understand the meaning of Truth. But these, though many, are nevertheless a small minority, and clearer colors shine through the temporary haze. Remember also that if these people did not have our best interests at heart they would be rejected by the *egregore*: but the *egregore* is big enough to handle a few people whose focus is a little misguided

When we are down, when we are in need of strength, when we are lonely and feel the need to belong, how do we tap this wonderful source of energy created to our use? We do it by the same method man has always used: through symbol.

So when we need to borrow that little bit of energy which will help us through, just take a moment to be calm and take yourself away, either physically or mentally, from the cares of daily life, focus upon an image of the Square & Compasses, that symbol par excellence of our *egregore*, and ask it to lend you its beneficial healing energy. You may want to reflect a physical posture which attunes you to this source as well, for all squares, horizontals and perpendiculars are, after all, signs of an upright man and Mason. So put your feet in a square, stand or sit with body erect and recall the time you stood in the North-East corner of the Lodge, as new 'cell' in the great battery of Freemasonry, and be once more that link to the Spiritual Temple, that Temple not built with human hands…our *egregore*.

SYMBOLISM, & FREEMASONRY AS A MYSTERY SCHOOL

1. Introduction

Freemasonry has been called "a system of morality, veiled in allegory and illustrated by symbols". I need for once to stress the term "Freemasonry" over "Masonry" since, in the words of the Canadian Charge to the Brethren: "Masonry, my brethren, according to the accepted usage of the term, is an art, founded on the principles of geometry, and directed to the service and convenience of mankind; while Freemasonry, embracing a wider range and having a nobler object in view, namely the cultivation and improvement of the human mind, may with more propriety be styled a science". Morality and allegory we will leave to a later date. Here we are going to consider symbols. Now, I need not tell you that one can spend a lifetime studying and finding new meanings in the rich encyclopedia of symbols we use. Just as when attending a religious or national ceremony the very familiarity with the event allows us to go beyond focusing on the immediate activity to discover new treasures beneath; so one can see, for example, the First Degree, the Royal Arch Degree or the Royal and Select Master Degree a hundred times and still come away from the ceremony both profoundly moved and with new thoughts to take home for private meditation.

This paper considers a definition of what constitutes a Masonic symbol, and then goes on to consider a working definition for the requirements of a Western Mystery School, and considers whether Freemasonry can be considered as such.

To begin, if Freemasonry, then is "illustrated by symbols", the first question we need to clarify in our minds is: what is a symbol?

2. What Is a Symbol?

It is commonly held that the conscious and subconscious minds communicate by the use of symbols. Why not language? Language is an artificial series of symbols created by humankind to communicate ideas to one another. Unfortunately, language is also incapable

36

of fully communicating thought, as it is limited, by its rules, syntax and structure, from fully expressing the wholeness of all the thought, ideas and corollaries which a thought engenders. Language serves a purpose, but the alphabetical symbols in modern Western language only represent sounds. Poetry, of course, attempts to recapture some of this lost emotion in words; but then, daily conversation is hardly held in iambic pentameters!

The ancients understood this concept, and their languages were far richer for it. A perfect example of this is the Hebrew language. In this language a letter had several meanings. It had a sound, but also a numeric value. It could also represent an object, a concept and, when conjoined with other letters, new concepts. It also had a magical or talismanic quality. For example, the letter Aleph (א), the first letter of the Hebrew alphabet, signifies the sound 'a'. However, it also bears the numerical value of '1', a direction in space, an object (the Ox), and this leads to the fact that the letter now has three numerical values – for 'a', 'aleph' and 'ox' in Hebrew. Astrologically it is associated with Air. And so forth. Thus, their language functioned on a number of different levels, as people could simultaneously communicate sounds, values, concepts and pictures. Similarly, the ancient Egyptian language had its hieratic (or holy), hieroglyphic (or symbolic), and demotic (or graphic) forms of writing, and possibly of pronunciation. Even in Western religion until recently Latin was used by the Roman Catholics (and, it could be argued, even now the King James English of the 17th Century is similarly employed in the Anglican tradition) as the hieratic religious language, separate from everyday language. and in itself creating a sacred space of sound, away from the modern language of work, business and bar. This, I always think, is a potent argument against the endless attempts to 'modernize' our rituals, for part of the atmosphere which separates our rites from the mundane is the very other-worldliness of its archaic language. Most of us have heard brave attempts to update Shakespeare by translating his poetic words into modern vernacular, or dressing his characters in modern day clothing. To my mind, neither is successful.

It is perhaps interesting to note that modern studies on the functioning of the brain have identified that the left hemisphere is used for language and analytic processes, while the right hemisphere is used for visual and conceptual processes. In other words, language is seen even in our own bodies as being a separate process from symbolic communication.

What, then, are symbols? In one definition, symbols are classified under three headings: Natural, Artificial and Mystical.

Natural symbols are those which were first noticed by primitive man. For example, if we see smoke, we deduce that there is a fire. If we hear splashing, we assume water must be nearby. If we see flashing in the sky, rain cannot be far behind. Thus, early man learned to associate these natural symbols directly with their source – cause and effect. As an aside, I find it interesting to note how early in our primitive history man decided he was central to the entire process of Nature. To cite an example, we can see in the early glyphs that man believed the sun would not rise without his active participation in rites, which sometimes led to human sacrifice. Man's somewhat arrogant belief that everything revolves around him, and that even God and Nature cannot accomplish their tasks without his active participation, seems to go far back in our psyche.

The next development is artificial symbolism. The most obvious is an alphabet, though as we have seen, this is a special instance of symbolism. Other examples are road signs, where icons instantly remind us of our direction and alert us to possible dangers or hazards. A flag is another example of a straightforward symbol which usually elicits a far from straightforward response.

Finally, mystical symbols are those which attract the most complex thoughts, and are usually loaded with the most complex of emotions and reactions. In Christianity the most obvious example is the cross; in Judaism the Star of David. Thinking about or meditating on the cross is going to fill a Christian with far more avenues of thought than, say, meditating on the letter 'A'. Likewise, a moment's thought on the Star of David will conjure up for a Jew a vast array of simultaneous thoughts of ancestry, theology, astrology, Qabbalistic interpretations and, of course, the tragic use of that potent symbol on the uniforms worn in the concentration camps.

Every religion and every esoteric group has symbols which have a particular, special meaning. It is useful to explore the potency of symbols in your own tradition before beginning to look at the symbols of other traditions.

The key here is to realize that symbols are open to a host of interpretations. Nobody can arrogate to themselves the exclusive
understanding of a symbol, for the very nature of symbols is that they
are mirrors which reflect the individual's experiences and belief system. Sadly, certain symbols can be tainted by a national or
supranational usage. I will give two examples. The fylfot cross or
swastika was for thousands of years a symbol of good luck to the Hindus. Indeed, in my old church in England, there was a most exquisite
altar cloth bearing the swastika as a motif for the edging. Naturally
enough it is on display; but never used. Another example is the All-
Seeing Eye. Now, many Fundamentalists and Conspiracy Theorists
in general have used these symbols to link us to the Illuminati and
claimed that we are therefore a dangerous and subversive organization. However, remember where the All-Seeing Eye made its first
appearance (at least to my knowledge): ancient Egypt! The R_x on
prescriptions takes its origins from the same root: the Eye of Horus.
This is the watchful Hawk's Eye of the Son of God who supervises
mankind with benevolent love. Surely, then we may translate the All-
Seeing Eye into the kindly Eye of God, watching his children with
love and compassion. The fact that the Illuminati – whoever they
were, and don't believe most of what you read in sensationalist novels
– appropriated this symbol for their organization no more makes the
sign intrinsically evil or tainted than the fylfot cross.

We should draw two conclusions from this. Firstly, symbols are
neutral in themselves, and have no one, unique meaning. Secondly,
we can therefore use symbols to communicate ideas which cannot be
communicated by language; and this second point leads us to realize
that the same symbol can mean different things to different people. I
stress that, while my observations of symbols generally follow the
opinions of respected authors, our pronouncements are not law!

Finally, and perhaps the most important point: why do we bother
with symbols at all? Kirk McNulty opens his book *Freemasonry – A
Journey through Ritual and Symbol* with these words: "Throughout
all times and in all cultures men and women have sought to acquire
knowledge about human nature and the purpose of human existence.
In their search they have made use of an enormous variety of disciplines which have promised to penetrate the mystery of human nature
and give them greater insight into themselves." If symbols are seen as

a key to unlock the inner person, and this is certainly a central idea of psychology, then it is not surprising that every culture relies on the use of symbols to unlock these mysteries. And if mankind believes further in the Hermetic saying: "As above, so below", then it is hardly surprising that man also seeks to find links and correspondences between symbols observed in nature, in the heavens, and in his inner experiences, be they through meditation or in dreams.

In fact, this link between the higher and the lower is one of the very requirements for an educational process to be called a Mystery School, as we shall now see.

3. Key Aspects of Western Esotericism

I admire the oldest university in the world, the Sorbonne in France, for inaugurating the first professorial chair in 'Esoteric Studies", previously occupied by the redoubtable Antoine Faivre, whose scholarly books are well worth reading (although published in French, they are almost immediately published in English by the State University of New York Press). In his book *Access to Western Esotericism*, he summarizes the thesis of "The Esoteric Origins of the American Renaissance" by Arthur Verslius, as follows:

There are four primary aspects of Western Esoteric Traditions:

1. **Correspondences** – between nature, humanity and the divine;
2. **Living Nature** – not a dead cosmos consisting of discrete objects to be manipulated;
3. **Imagination & Meditation** – the imagination represents a means to human inner knowledge; meditation refers to the symbols and other means that offer or reveal this knowledge;
4. **Experiences of Transmutation** – as of lead into gold, or of essences into an elixir.

To these four Faivre adds two more:

5. **Praxis of the Concordance** – an approach that unifies various currents of thought, that is willing to join various traditions and see them as one.

6. **Transmission** – meaning from a master to a disciple, in an initiatic chain.

As we can see from the above categorization, symbolism is key to all of these steps. In order to see correspondences, we resort to symbols, as contained in the most famous axiom of all: "As above, so below". Similarly, the philosophy of the stars – astrology – and belief in the Hermetic axiom led man to observe the heavens for predictions of fate on earth. Imagination and meditation alone could be employed as a bridge to study the inner being, that spark of the divine (or Holy Guardian Angel as many traditions style the higher self). And alchemy used extensive symbols both to protect its science from profane eyes and to show the link between outer transmutation and inner transmutation – the perfection of the human soul as the creation of 'gold' from 'dross'. Antoine Faivre's additions also require a sense of the symbolic, both in the desire to condense several systems into one (he is, of course, referring to the Egyptian, Hebrew, Greek and Roman Mystery Schools, Neoplatonism, Templarism, Rosicrucianism) and to identify the symbols which were common to more than one School, or which affected later manifestations. Finally, the transmission of an essence from one generation to another is not something that we can observe according to the Laws of Physics, but nevertheless we accept without question, for example, when a bishop lays his hands upon an ordinand and says: "Receive the Holy Spirit for the Office of Priest".

4. Is Freemasonry a Mystery School?

I hope you have realized that one of the main currents of the Western Mystery Tradition is Freemasonry! So how do we fulfill Faivre's requirements to be an Esoteric Tradition or Mystery School?

We recognize correspondences between what we do and what exists above. Consider the symbol of the Temple. Our ritual is shot through with references to "that house not built with hands, eternal in the heaven" and the fact that the working tools with which we build a physical temple are to be interpreted in a more rarified manner. We naturally believe in a well-ordered universe, for we call the Mason's God the "Grand Architect of the Universe", which implies an active, sentient force at work which harmonizes all and sees that all operates according to a grand design. We use Imagination and Meditation to understand the lessons and allegories seen in Lodge and learn to apply them to our inner life. We learn these lessons through the use of symbols. We celebrate Praxis of the Concordance: after all, we have most certainly claimed every Mystery Tradition in Western history as our antecedents! And we believe that a Worshipful Master can create a Mason (for the Charter or Dispensation empowers him to work, but does not contain the transmission: the Charter or absence only dictates whether or not the transmission has been performed clandestinely).

This leaves us with Experiences of Transmutation. And perhaps this is the very fact which separates Freemasonry from other Fraternal traditions: for we believe that if a man lives and acts as a Mason, then he will indeed transform himself into a being more fit for the service of God and man. He is a man who lives by a different set of rules to other men, who "towards himself is a severe judge, but is tolerant of the debilities of his neighbor."

If we have, perhaps, established that Freemasonry is a Mystery School by Faivre's standards, and that, as in the Mystery Schools of old, it uses symbol and allegory to teach its members, what is it trying to teach us? Kirk McNulty makes an interesting observation in his book *Freemasonry – A Journey through Ritual and Symbol*: "The objective was to train people to live in consonance with natural laws as they operate in the non-material domains. Although the laws were considered to be of Divine origin, the Mysteries were not usually religious. Generally speaking, they were more concerned with philosophy and morality than with theology and religion."

While this talk does not cover any theories on the origins of Freemasonry, I find this comment a fascinating statement. Surely this description of the Mystery Schools could be precisely describing Freemasonry?

5. Conclusion

This talk will, perhaps have delighted the scholar and frustrated those who were expecting the 'Cliff Notes' answer to life, the universe and everything. However, as all true students of the Mysteries know, nothing comes easily or quickly, for as the art of alchemy teaches, the transformation of understanding is a process and not a blinding light of inspiration. These flashes may come, but not from nowhere: they occur only when all the pieces are in place and understood as individual contributors. Then the magical alchemical transformation can take place, as it were with the introduction of a catalyst; and then all the pieces built slowly and painstakingly over time meld together into a wondrous new whole, which has been given many names, from the Philosopher's Stone, Azoth, to the Pot o' Gold at the end of the Rainbow.

It has been necessary to set the ground work before we begin the process of studying the symbols themselves. Why else would we study symbols and believe we have anything to learn from Freemasonry, unless we see the symbols and allegories as having value beyond being quaint little whimsies from a bygone age, and our Fraternity as offering more than an opportunity to give generously to charity and to enjoy the companionship of friends united in a common bond?

We know that Freemasonry is influenced by many esoteric schools of thought, for even the most conservative of theories about our origins states that men of culture and high philosophy entered the dying guilds of stonemasons, and adapted their tools and craft to symbolic interpretation, thereby making 'Speculatives' out of 'Operatives'. But what philosophies interested these learned men? Why, Neoplatonism, the Kabbalah, the Mystery Schools, ancient Egypt – in fact, all those very currents which the more outrageous theories insist we are descended from. So one may ask, do we really care whether our Fraternity was descended from Egypt, or Eleusis, or Mithraism, since like it or not, these very influences came to shape our Craft whether it be through ancient roots or the conscious acts of educated men? Either way, the symbols are there, the allegories are there, and anyone who studies them cannot for a moment deny that our rituals are shot through with these mysteries.

McNulty points out that: "Freemasonry is a very old, secular, fraternal society which requires the belief in a Supreme Being as its principal qualification for membership and which is dedicated to the practice of tolerance, respect and understanding of others; the encouragement of high standards of morality among its members; and the performance of charitable works. Freemasonry certainly is and does all these things; but in some hard-to-define way it seems to be 'something else' beyond these things. One looks for this additional dimension, in part, because Freemasonry has survived for almost three hundred years while other apparently similar fraternal organizations have disappeared; and, also, because it has drawn members from the best minds and the most idealistic leaders of the day. If a contemporary Mason were asked about that 'something else', he would probably say that it is an indescribably quality related in some way to the very rich and complex symbolic structure that is characteristic of the Craft."

My Brothers, it is this 'very rich and complex symbolic structure' that we should be studying.

THE PURPOSE OF INITIATION IN FREEMASONRY

Nasrudin used to take his donkey across a frontier every day, loaded with baskets full of straw. Because he freely confessed to being a smuggler when he came home every night, the frontier guards would search him again and again. They used to strip him, sift the straw, steep it in water, sometimes even burn it. Meanwhile, Nasrudin was becoming more and more wealthy.

Then he retired and went to live in another country. Here one of the frontier guards happened to meet him, years later.

"You can tell me now, Nasrudin," he said. "What on earth were you smuggling all that time when we could never catch you out?"

"Donkeys," said Nasrudin.

From *Perfume of the Desert – Inspirations from Sufi Wisdom*, ed. A. Harvey & E. Hanut, 1999, pub. Quest Books

*   *   *   *   *   *   *

1. Introduction

What is Freemasonry *for*? By what measure of success are we judging ourselves? If the indicators are number of members, sums donated to charity, or speed of advancement to Master Mason, then indeed we are achieving all our goals. But this can be claimed of almost any society, club, fraternity or union who has members and collects money for charity. Ah, we say, but ours is a fraternity with rituals and education, and this is what makes us unique. If this is so, we have a problem: if our rituals are so important to us, why do they become a secondary consideration against the desire to attract large numbers of members? Some have been concerned with *quality*, and by this they mean the quality of candidates being attracted to the Craft. Far fewer members seem to be concerned about the quality of the experience we offer to these candidates.

In Europe, every effort is made to ensure that the rituals are special for the candidate, and only one person – two at the most – is advanced through a particular degree at one time. The focus on education is on the meaning of the rituals and their application to daily life. The ritual is everything: it inspires, educates, and binds its members together in fraternity.

Here I have heard reports of Masters – even of Lodges meeting at Grand Lodge – who say that it would be much easier to attract new members if only we got rid of "those boring rituals". Many Grand Lodges, including ours in New York, have held One Day Classes in an attempt to bolster membership numbers in one go. In several instances one could become a Third Degree Mason in one morning, and follow it up with membership in the Shrine (with an optional side serving of Scottish Rite if you wanted to get all the way to the 32nd Degree in one day). As the French press printed when New York did this in the early 2000s: "How to become a 32nd Degree Freemason at the speed of sound – American Style!" That the experiment has not been repeated may give a clue as to its long term efficacy.

Is this an Initiation?

Of course, you can also become a priest overnight if you pay the express mailing fee when you send you check or give your credit card number to an online 'instant' Church. However, ask yourself this: would you go to such a priest for confession, or to receive advice on major life issues or theological questions? Would you consider him as one who had traveled the long and arduous road to realize his vocational calling as a servant of Christ? The journey *is* the process: being bopped on the head (or not in the case of a mail order 'priesting'), is only the arriving. The entire process – and point – has been missed.

To put this more bluntly, conversations with a number of new members reveals the following telling comments: "I joined Freemasonry to learn"; "I can go to business meetings all day at work – I didn't join Masonry to attend yet more business meetings"; "I have friends and an active social life – why do I need more dinners?"; "I choose to give to charity, but I didn't join Freemasonry because of its charities". Most tellingly: "My father joined Freemasonry many years ago in the Caribbean and the whole family saw the transformation it worked in him. I see nothing of that process here." More importantly, we are clearly seeing a resurgence in the Craft due to books such as those by Brent Morris and Chris Hodapp, and most especially that veritable Masonic 'love-fest' which is the "Lost Symbol" by Dan Brown. These well-read young men are not seeking to be-come 'Fast Food' Masons. They understand – apparently far better than many of our Grand Masters – that the journey is more important than the destination. They realize that Initiation is not about sitting in a room with hundreds of other people and watching a few elderly men putting on a play.

However, this talk is not meant to be a polemic against how not to initiate a person: it is more concerned with trying to identify some of the key elements which set an initiatory experience apart from other activities. In doing so I will be basing most of my talk on ap-plying a theory in fact derived from anthropological studies, which were actually focused on ecclesiology. But then, since I am sure we all understand the commonality between ritual content – be they held in fraternities, mystery schools, churches, synagogues or tree-houses – the lessons drawn from this theory can be applied equally to a group which performs rites of initiation.

Ritual – and especially the act of Initiation – is key and central to Freemasonry, and if the Fraternity is to have any relevance in modern society, it must accept that this is truly its 'Mission Statement', and that the time spent in organizing mass rallies, charitable donations and filling the evenings with committee meetings and dinners, while wor-thy, is not central to its purpose and function.

Whatever might be going on in the minds of those who wish to remove rituals from Freemasonry altogether, or reduce them to plays in which those being initiated are reduced to little more than an audi-ence, rituals are far, far more that pretty little plays to be learned by rote and put on for the satisfaction of a group of actors, or an annoy-ance that gets in the way of charitable works and delicious (?) dinners. So in this talk I will use the term 'ritual', which for our purposes is in-terchangeable with 'initiation'.

2. Tom Driver's Theory (Summary)

In his book *Liberating Rites*, Tom Driver sees ritual as resulting from the tensions arising from two dimensions. In the first, a perfor-mance must balance the modalities of ritual – where efficaciousness is paramount; and theater – where entertainment is paramount. This is logical, as seeing a play with no teaching is simply that, an evening's entertainment. On the other hand, a ritual which only serves to promote a particular message or state of mind with no eye to keeping the attention through beauty, pageantry or spectacle will soon lose our attention.

The second dimension is that of Confession versus Ethical, or the personal aspect versus the public aspect. Again, this makes sense, since all ritual is a balance between what we either do in private or within ourselves, and what we carry from what we have learned into public life, be it to improve ourselves, to change the world, or to perform little acts of kindness.

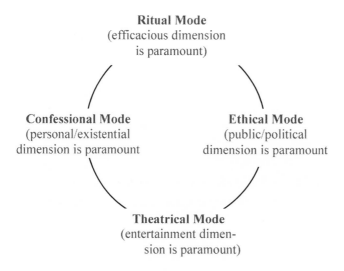

Ritual Mode
(efficacious dimension
is paramount)

Confessional Mode
(personal/existential
dimension is paramount

Ethical Mode
(public/political
dimension is paramount

Theatrical Mode
(entertainment dimen-
sion is paramount)

Fig 1 - MODES OF PERFORMANCE (after Tom F. Driver)

This theory, although developed for religion, is applicable to Masonry. No I am not implying that Masonic ritual is religious. I <u>am</u> categorically stating that much of religion is ritual, in that it uses symbols, repetitive action, separation of space and time to convey emotional states and teachings.

The Masonic Degrees are an exquisite tension between Ritual, Theatrical, Confessional and Ethical modes. The allegory of meaning is concealed within a formalized method of delivery which, nevertheless is intended to be communicated in a highly absorbing and entertaining environment. The wearing of unusual clothing, and being divested of anything which might connect one to the outside world is removed, and the neophyte enters a new dimension outside of time and space (this should mean no clocks, no alarms, no cellular phones, and no profane signs of any kind. If we find our illuminated Fire Exit signs jarring in a Lodge Room, in some countries Lodges are required to make a public announcement about all Fire Exits prior to every meeting! It must be particularly hard to separate the sacred space from the profane under such draconian circumstances... In truth, this list should include "no artificial candles", for the symbolism of three 'natural' luminaries describing a triangle is very profound and worthy of a paper in itself...). And yet we do not intend to bore him to death with dry, dull teachings. We present him with a kaleidoscope of sensations and symbols which he will study with pleasure throughout his Masonic career. The two opposing modes of Confession and Ethics are also superbly balanced in our inspired Rites. The ceremony itself balances the things the Candidate must do for himself, including his first spoken words upon entering the Lodge, and his Obligation both to conceal and *to study* the teachings he will receive; and those actions which this new community – the parts and characters within this symbolic Temple – will do to and for him.

We will consider three aspects of ritual and relate them to the Masonic experience: ritual as subversive, ritual as teaching, and ritual as transcendence.

3.   Ritual as Subversive

History has shown us that kings, presidents and the church alike have been terrified of the power of ritual, and those of Freemasonry in particular. From the Morgan Affair and the Papal proscriptions of the 18th and 19th Century, through the persecution of Freemasonry under both Fascism and Communism earlier this century, to the recent enforced public declarations of membership by judges and policemen in England under the Labor Government, Masons have been singled out for attack. Why is this? And why should this be a good thing for Freemasonry?

Ritual takes us away from Society, even if only for a few hours. It allows us, for a period, to overcome social alienation – in the famous wearing of white gloves – and affords us an opportunity to talk with intelligent, informed people about the state of our nation, without concern that our words might be carried back to inimical forces by spies – our traditional cowans and eavesdroppers. This might not seem a big thing to us in the United States, but ask a Mason in Spain in the 1930s or occupied France in the 1940s for his opinion, and he will tell you that a poorly chosen Candidate meant more than a disrupted Lodge – it probably meant a firing squad. What we stand for is contrary to any Society which seeks to control, segregate, repress or persecute its habitants; and sadly that is the state of affairs in many countries of this world. Our Masonic meetings allow us to rehearse and debate teachings from an earlier time, and many books have been written about how these deposits of mystical learning were bought at the price of blood, and are a sacred heritage which it is our duty and our joy to preserve and, in succession, to pass to the next generation.

This state of existence beyond the threshold of daily Society has been described as "liminality", which comes from the Latin "limen" meaning threshold. Arnold Van Gennep described these rites being flanked by 'pre-liminal' or separation rites, and 'post-liminal' or reincorporation rites. Having been separated from conventional reality through darkness, enclosure and androgynous clothing, the candidates or "threshold people" are ambiguous entities which float passively through the liminal rites which take place outside of time and space, before being reintegrated by the post-liminal rites to take their place among the new community. Van Gennep described liminal ritual as being "frequently linked to death, to being in the womb, to invisibility, to darkness, …to an eclipse of the sun or moon." Masons will recognize many of these allusions.

It is hardly surprising, therefore, as Tom Driver suggests: "As the powers of nation-states have grown in modern times, so has the desire on their part to eliminate as much liminality as possible from ritual performance, because liminality can lead to a weakening of state control over people's ideas, emotions, and behavior."

He continues: "Much goes on in rituals that would not be tolerated at other times: hand-clapping,...rhapsodic speech, cross-dressing, speech-song recitations, direct address to invisible beings...public exchanges of affection, mystical union with other participants...The liminality of rituals means that they are informed, on the one hand, by a greater than usual sense of order and, on the other, by a heightened sense of freedom and possibility."

So ritual in general – and Masonic ritual in particular – is a process which separates the man from normal Society, and places him in a position in which to analyze that Society with the symbolic tools he is given, and, if he finds Society wanting in its stand on charity, fraternity, rights, God and nature, empowers him to go out into that Society in order to change it for the better. No wonder Masons are seen as subversive.

And herein lies the paradox. According to Driver: "...Ritual stands in contradiction to society while at the same time being a part of it." Our ritual empowers us to live, act and work within society but empowers us with the mission to change it for the better. This empowerment given through the liminal process of ritual internalizes this drive to a far greater extent than a debating society or business meeting possibly could, for though internalizing the symbols we become those symbols ourselves, symbols of what man can achieve by right thinking, right acting and right saying. We have only to look to George Washington to see those great Masonic symbols in action...

4. Ritual as Teaching

Our rituals are full of symbolic teachings. We do not lay out the secrets of our deposit like pearls before swine. We protect them, even from the 'casual' Mason, for only those who are prepared to work at understanding the meaning behind the parables and allegories is truly worthy of that deposit. Ritual allows the deposit of knowledge to be passed from generation to generation, unchanged, so that if one generation fails to understand the true pearls therein contained, the message is transmitted intact to the next generation, when someone might then discern the wisdom within. Woe betide the ignorant Custodian of the Work who decides to 'modernize', 'abbreviate', or 'amend' the ritual:

he commits a capital offense in the eyes of the early members who placed this sacred deposit in the cure of our Mystery School!

As an aside, I remember a story – I think a Greek myth – being told in my early schooling, of an old man who appears before a great king, carrying twelve books. When the king asks what he has in those books the old man says: "Sire, they contain all the wisdom of mankind". "How much will you sell them to me for?" asks the king. "For half your kingdom", replies the old man. The king laughs and says this is a ludicrous price. The old man then asks for a brazier. Intrigued, the king has a servant fetch a lit brazier. The old man solemnly places six of the books into the brazier and burns them, to the horror of the king. Then the old man asks the king if he would like to buy the remaining six books. Shrewdly (for he is a wise king) the king asks how much. "Half your kingdom", the old man replies. The king shakes his head. Solemnly, the old man places another three books in the brazier and they burn to dust… The king promptly purchases the remaining three for half his kingdom!

Let not our great deposit be squandered in like manner, for if a generation destroys some of the great symbolism in the name of 'progress' or 'expediency', the next generation cannot go back to the dead to ask them what they meant!

There is a second reason we communicate our teachings through the use of symbols. While allegories and parables tell a story, it is only through the use of symbols that we truly become a universal Brotherhood. Language divides us, but ritual reassembles.

Roy Rappaport wrote: "The distinctions of language cut the world into bits – into categories, classes, oppositions, and contrasts. It is in the nature of language to search out all differences and to turn them into distinctions which then provide bases for boundaries and barriers." And further: "It is…in the nature of (ritual) to unite, or reunite, the psychic, social, natural and cosmic orders which language and the exigencies of life pull apart. It is of importance in this regard that representation in ritual are often multi-modal, employing at one and the same time words, music, noise, odors, objects and substances."

A ritual can act like a mantra or meditational exercise. It is not to be seen once and forgotten: it is to be seen again and again, whereby different messages and nuances are perceived and understood. In Masonry, this effect is enhanced considerably through the possibility of seeing the ritual through the eyes of different participants, as the Brother takes first one then another part in the mysteries as he progresses in the Lodge. This lifetime of learning opens like a rose to reveal the beauty within, to the intelligent and seeking eye.

Sadly, this value breaks down when, as Driver writes, people: "do not see the necessary correspondence between what they signify and the reality of the ...community in the world". Religion makes the same complaint. There is little value in going to pray, then coming back into the world unchanged, and continuing the same negative behavior as before. To return to Driver's model, the confessional mode should drive us towards the ethical mode: charity, right thinking, right acting and right saying. While these are not primary concerns of Masonry and its rituals, they are a visible and confirming sign that the ritual has achieved success in communicating its lessons; that they have not fallen on stony ground, but indeed have been internalized and have become an unconscious part of the Brother's daily behavior. This is when learning transforms us.

In light of these ideas, when we consider the One Day Classes held across the country, I would offer the personal comment that they are not effective, and do not accomplish the purpose for which they were originally envisaged. It is critical that the neophyte undergoes the experience of transformation, of *liminalization* himself. While the side degrees are often run as theatrical experiences, in which the candidates watch the drama unfold by means of a proxy, or exemplar, the first three Degrees of the Holy Saints John are too important to be conferred *en masse*. If I might give an extreme example, it is rather like a row of Jewish babies at a *bris* watching one of them being circumcised on their behalf; or a group of Confirmands watching the diocesan bishop laying his hands on an exemplar for the class. How about those to be initiated into the Mysteries of Eleusis sitting outside the cave and being given a brief summary of what is happening to the one allowed into the cave to undergo the Rites? Or one which has been seriously debated: the personal effectiveness of a papal blessing when watched on television? Ludicrous examples, certainly! But do they apply to Masonic initiation as well? I believe so.

5. Ritual as Transformation

Ritual can transform us in two ways: internally, in the way we learn to think and to perceive things in a new way; and externally, in making us part of a new community.

This external community has been called a number of things. It is not strictly a 'club' or even a 'Fraternity', for undergoing a transforming ritual is a far more powerful than going out for a few drinks, or sharing in some community project. In mystical groups the term often applied is "egregore", or the collective thoughts and inspiration of previous generations. If that is a little too esoteric for some, the term used by Driver is "communitas", which he defines as: "a spirit of unity and mutual belonging not existing outside ritual". In other words, charitable giving, a dinner, business meeting or coach trip do not confer this common bond which transcends Lodge and even continent, for any well-traveled Mason will tell you that the welcome received from those who share this sense of "communitas" is as warm and sincere in a Lodge in New York as in Bamako. Those who hold out the hand of Brotherhood are not doing so on the strength of a dues card or a common set of passwords and grips: they are doing it out of a sense of *common experience*.

This transformation takes place at a number of levels. There is nothing which can describe the excitement and joy of making that link between symbol and the external world which opens up a whole new area of understanding to the perceptive Mason; that momentous instant when the interior and exterior worlds link, and the Hermetic axiom "as above, so below" is once more realized. In turn, this realization or understanding leads the experiencer to enact that part of the ritual with a greater understanding, with the result that those who also understand that particular teaching will immediately realize that this Mason, too, has the key to its interpretation: while those who still seek its inner meaning will marvel at the depth of feeling and command that Mason brings to his role.

I like to give the reader a means in my papers to experience what I say on a practical level, and this is no exception. One means of opening up one's uncritical mind to the power of the symbols which surround us in our ritual is through using what is called 'creative visualization'. When the reader next takes part in a Masonic ritual, I would ask him to spend a few moments before the ritual begins sitting quietly in his place or station, preferably with his eyes closed, and imagine himself transported back to the historical time in which the ritual is set. While any Officer in anybody can do this exercise, let us use the example of the Master in this Blue Lodge. Let him imagine with all his power of concentration that he is indeed King Solomon. He should feel the crown upon his head (the top hat being magically transformed into its prototype!), the rich red and gold robes enfolding his body, the scepter of power (for us the gavel) lying to his right, the sensation of the opulent throne pressing against his body. Hear the muffled sound of workmen and their subdued cries all around this great building site (for remember, no sound of metal was to be heard). Feel the heat of the noon day sun beating down; the acrid, drying sand assailing the nostrils. Now the eyes are opened and I guarantee the words uttered by this new King Solomon will thrill the most experienced ritualist in the room. At the Obligation he will step down from his throne, leaving the triple dais and walking across the great flagstones of the Temple floor, aware of the eyes of all his courtiers upon him. He walks between the pylons formed by the Senior and Junior Wardens and enters the holy place, to administer the vows to the faithful workmen kneeling in awe and love before him, in the simple white vestments of the Apprentice who has earned the Great Master's approbation. See the members of the 'living temple' arrayed on either side in the shadows, huge and dread as the great statues of the Assessors in the Egyptian Temples from which this Great Temple took its design. Then the Great King takes his position before the massive altar, and opens his mouth to speak...

6. Conclusion

In order to survive, Freemasonry must be a society which offers more than making as many members as possible, giving more money to charity, and organizing yet more committees, dinners and events which the same dwindling number of stalwarts doggedly support. To those who say that our society would attract far more members if we didn't have Degrees, I would ask: then what do we have left to offer? Where will we find Candidates who do not seek the Light, and who yearn for long business meetings, relentless collations and endless calls for charitable donations?

We are a Mystery School. Our gentle Craft is a place which imparts important – and relevant – lessons about the nature of our relationship with God, with each other, and with the earth. As with all Mystery Schools these lessons are not poured out at the feet of the new student, but are revealed over time to the true seeker of meaning in today's fast and dangerous world. Our message has never been more relevant. It is taught through the allegory and symbolism of ritual. Ironically enough, after every possible experiment in making membership in Freemasonry as quick, easy, and convenient as possible have apparently failed, it takes a book by a non-Mason, Dan Brown, to start them talking about the fact that there is something in Freemasonry. Perhaps now, instead of saying: "there are no secrets in Masonry", they will learn that the way to attract new members is, *au contraire*, to raise the bar, to make it harder to join, to become more mysterious. Perhaps then they will enjoy a deluge of young men seeking such secrets, who will boost the memberships of Lodges in their Grand Lodge jurisdictions and take Freemasonry, the 'Mystery School' rather than the 'Old Boy's Club', forward in this new millennium.

Finally, as I am sure you have realized, in the Sufi parable which began this paper, the straw which occupied the border guards so completely is all the chaff and secondary attributes of Freemasonry – the pomp, the titles, the dinners, the charities, the meetings, the business, the committees; while, buried under all this superficial activity is the true way to wealth of the spirit. The donkeys, under the very noses of the guards, who failed to appreciate their value, represent the *ritual*!

SPIRITUAL HEALING

1. Introduction

This paper is not intended to be an academic treatise on the history of Spiritual Healing. Although it will take a little time to trace its possible origins, the main focus of the paper is on its relevance to us in the present time, and how we can use this precious gift from God to help ourselves, our family, our friends and mankind in general.

The latter part of the Seventeenth Century saw the rise of modern science and so-called rational thinking, when Astronomy was born of Astrology, Chemistry from Alchemy, and Medicine from Herbalism; and Empiricism overtook Experientialism as the acid test. The development of powerful telescopes and microscopes, the mapping of the periodic table, the discovery of the circulation of the blood: all these things led to a culture of materialism and the belief that, if a thing couldn't be observed, measured and repeated, it didn't exist. This, combined with an increasing estrangement from the established church, led to a culture of cynicism and censure of all things not scientifically observable. It is interesting to note how quickly this attitude took hold – at least in public – against people who had only a few years before studied the old traditions alongside the new teachings. Newton wrote more books on Astrology than Astronomy, yet how many schoolchildren are taught *that* fact? And yet, even as the philosophy of this Age of Enlightenment sought to free mankind from the tyranny of tradition and superstition, applying the same kind of systematic thinking used in Newtonian physics to all aspects of human existence, another definition of the word 'Enlightenment' – "being spiritually illuminated by acquiring new wisdom or understanding" – was being implemented, and often by the very people who were making such strides in providing the keys to unlock the secrets of the material world.

Alongside the very materialistic movement which drove the great advances in medicine and the sciences, and which brought about the Industrial Revolution, the philosophy of enlightenment which overthrew the power of kings, pontiffs and states, and saw nobility in every man, woman and child on God's good earth, we find a deep search for the non-material, a higher understanding of the meaning of life, and the relationship of man with his God. Indeed, it is interesting timing that at the very beginnings of this rise of Reason, one of the most influential alchemical, spiritual and certainly subversive books in history should appear: the *Fama Fraternitatis* in 1615.

Alchemy, astrology, herbalism had never truly died – they simply went underground for a time, and changed their emphasis to suit a newer world. For they will always be relevant. Even now the extraordinary field of quantum mechanics is forcing die-hard scientists to admit that their cast-iron theories are imperfect, that there is room for the invisible, the magical, the unexpected. Indeed, they are truly coming to realize that there truly is "more in heaven and earth than is dreamed of in their philosophy."

The main purpose of the paper, however, is to not to study these currents in detail – writers such as Francis King and René Le Forestier have covered this ground in far more detail than I could hope to – it is rather to reawaken us to the fruits of this labor, the importance of this part of our ministry and mission, and most importantly to consider ways to bring the Rosicrucian injunction to heal back into the heart of our practice.

2. Early Signs of Spiritual Healing

Mankind has always wondered why people get hurt, become ill, and how and why some appear to recover while others succumb to their wounds or ailments. A long-held linguistic theory states that the third earliest color distinguished by humans – and therefore which they named – after black and white (night and day) was red (blood). As the need to appease the forces which controlled thunder and lightning, inundation and harvest led to the creation of a people apart – a proto-priesthood or proto-shamanic tribe (remember that Melchizedek, the first priest, was a priest of the harvest, offering leavened wheat and fermented grape), so their powers extended to the cure of people as well as the appeasing of the gods. Even now the title 'curate' is used in many churches.

It is rare to find a religion or cult, past or present, where the roles of god-appeaser and healer were not combined. Even in the Catholic Church I can, as a chorister, cite the Feast of St. Blaise on

Fig. 1 - St. Blaise

15th February, when singers go to church to have their throats blessed by the priest, using two lit candles in a 'V' shape. Incidentally, is this so far from the New Age practice of ear candling and smudging? Yet the priest would laugh at these superstitions even while putting on his specially set aside robes, take up and bind the candles, place them either side of the kneeling person's neck while reciting incantations for health, and see no irony in this.

Early Civilizations, for example the Egyptians, have left us abundant clues to the importance of the priest-healer in their society, in the form of hieroglyphs, statues, medical instruments, and even Imhotep – doctor, high priest and architect to King Djoser, around whom a cult sprang up was deified, and had followers in Greece, where he was identified with Asclepius, another deified healer.

On occasions the ability to heal has also been associated with kingship. For example, the touch of the anointed monarchs of England was believed to cure the 'King's Evil', or scrofula. The Fisher King of the Grail Legends is often identified as a demi-god, upon whose health rests the well-being of the kingdom, and who guards the Grail, containing 'the precious blood of Our Lord'. Which brings us naturally enough to the King of Kings – the King of Israel who made the lame to walk, the blind to see. Here we see the triple currents of priesthood, kingship and healer combined in one.

3. The Christian Avatar

In Exodus 15:26 God says "I, the Lord, am thy physician." In Exodus 23:25 God says "I will take sickness away from the midst of thee." And there are two quotations which Christian tradition at least tells us refer to the Christos: "He sent his word and healed them, and delivered them from their destruction" (Psalm 107:20), and "with his stripes we are healed" (Isaiah 53:5).

Jesus, then, was a spiritual healer. One thing to note – and this is important for what came later – he worked many of his healing miracles as a man: and he would call upon God to work through him. Now Jesus used three techniques to heal. Sometimes he used words, sometimes touch, and sometimes he used simple herbs and medicines (for example, when he smeared mud and spittle on the eyes of a blind man (see John 9:6 – 7).

It is interesting to note that the means of healing – word, touch and elemental materials – were the very methods used by God to create mankind. He fashioned man out of clay (using spiritual 'touch' and the elements) and breathed the Word into him. Just as Adam Kadmon was tasked with creating the lesser creatures (God fashioned them but Adam was given the distinct privilege of naming them), so knowing the name of a person, angel or demon is to control them, as the ancient *grimoires* point out. Clay has the curious property

Fig. 2 – Jesus healing the blind man

of containing all the elements – it is composed of earth and water and air, and certain types generate heat, or fire when used on the skin in facial masques, a property long known by healers and cosmetologists.

So placed it dries and draws out impurities. And when we spit into it, we introduce a part of ourselves – a living element – into the compound. And God did not think it beneath Him to breathe – or Jesus to spit – into this clay, in order to create something new which contained a part of himself, be it Adam or a healing poultice.

He healed for love of mankind and the people he healed. He did not charge for this service. Likewise, he could not heal everybody, but he did what he could within his sphere of influence. He lived among mankind – specifically among the Hebrew tribes in a small country on the East coast of the Mediterranean. He dressed like them, followed their customs, and spoke the Aramaic language. He healed the sick, and that gratis.

4. Superstition and Healing

The Middle Ages saw some of the most bizarre interpretations of the Healing message, and as we can see with totalitarian governments of our current times, a power without a counterbalance, like the pillar of severity in the Tree of Life, is inherently unstable and will eventually topple over. Sometimes, however, it can take many centuries for such an unbalanced power to fall. The Catholic Church was no exception, and a body which existed for nearly twelve hundred years virtually unchallenged from within was going to develop some weird ideas. One of the more bizarre in the realm of healing was the Trial by Ordeal, a semi-magical way to determining guilt by trials of fire or water. The trial by fire usually required the defendant to walk over nine red-hot ploughshares or grasp a red hot poker: if their wounds vanished then God had shown them to be innocent; if the wounds remained or festered after a given period they were clearly guilty. The trial by water had the defendant placed in cold water: if they floated they were deemed guilty and burned. If they sank, they were deemed innocent – but did not live to enjoy the verdict! Even the Holy Church could not support this almost pagan interpretation of God's influence on daily life for long, and the practice was banned by Edict of the Lateran Council in 1215.

Medicine was at its most primitive. The Dark Ages had seen most of the ancient knowledge lost, and the Church encouraged the

Fig. 3 – Early 'Treatment'

proletariat to focus on their spiritual, rather than their physical health. The Classics had been proscribed and were unavailable to any but the wealthiest or the monks, whose large libraries were not subject to the same strict censorship. All empires grow stagnant, and Europe was no different under the rule of the Catholic Church. With the exception of architecture and armaments, and perhaps those arts which were allowed to flourish under royal and church patronage, there was little development in any field of human endeavor. Indeed, it was this atmosphere of rot and stagnation which provided the perfect breeding ground for the tiniest of creatures which eventually began first loosening of the Church's stranglehold. In 1347 the Black Death, a flea-borne plague, swept across Europe, striking good and bad, rich and poor alike. The Church promised cures for those who prayed, who gave to the Church, but it was all to no avail. The people wanted to know why they were being afflicted, and the Church had no answers. Priest and bishop alike abandoned their posts and fled into the country to avoid the plague. After twelve hundred years, the people began to question the power – and the purpose – of Christ's earthly Bride.

What better way to divert attention from one's own shortcomings than to direct the fear of the people in another direction. Politicians have been doing it for time immemorial, and fickle mankind is so easily led down false paths. In 1260 the pope authorized Inquisitors – those who are tasked with rooting out heresy in the church – to absolve one another of irregularities in the pursuit of their duties. This was essentially a license to torture, and now this body could act with impunity. Christianity was maintained by the aristocracy, but it was a veneer on the poorer classes, who still held strongly to the more ancient traditions which existed long before Christian proselytism. Local priests maintained an uneasy truce with villagers who would attend services in church, but still followed their 'old ways' out of it.

Local and national festivals were absorbed into Christian feast days. There were even instances of the Church allowing pagan celebrations within their portals – the Fool's Mass is an example.

In this nether-world ambience, locals saw no conflict in attending church and pouring blood on their fields to encourage a good harvest. Nor did they see any harm in trying the Church's repertoire of oils, anointing and blessings to cure ailments, and if they did not have an instant effect, visiting the local healing women for one of her potions. These herbal practitioners, often inheriting generations of 'old' knowledge, were in a difficult position. If their cure worked they grew in reputation, which brought them in conflict with the Church outside whose bornes they worked: if they failed the irate visitor was likely to

Fig. 4 – the "Fool's' Mass"

denounce them to the local Church as practicing witchcraft, and give witness against them. Loners were always a source of suspicion in those days. The Church recognized as saints the early Hermits, Anchorites, Stylites and other 'holy loners'; but that behavior was no longer tolerated by a power which insisted on blind obedience and conformity. A person without a social or supportive network is an easy target. There was probably more than an element of jealousy, too, in the eyes of the local priest who could not understand why people went to the 'old woman' for help, rather than to him. The money she earned was similarly money not being spent at <u>his</u> door on masses or indulgences.

It wasn't until the Renaissance, and the gradual loosening of the stranglehold of the Catholic Church, that the several currents of neo-Platonic thought, access to ancient texts, the increasing sophistication of astrology, the more general acceptance of theurgy, and the acceptance of medicines as a valid means of healing independent of the Church, that the stage was set for the next step.

5. The Rosicrucian Manifesto – Spiritual Healing Gets a Name

The *Fama*, *Confessio* and *Chemical Wedding* are so well known to those who claim Rosicrucian beliefs, it would be pointless to discuss their historical context or their content here. The environment had to be in place for the seed to take hold, and grow into the blooming rose which still amazes and delights our senses nearly four hundred years later.

Fig. 5 – Title Page of the 'Fama'

Setting aside all the other teachings of these books, there is one point which is expressly stated to be the main purpose and function of the members of the Invisible College, without which their existence, their studies, their travels and their message would be in vain: "Their agreement was this: "First, that none of them should profess any other thing, than to heal the sick, and that *gratis*." (Fama Fraternitatis, 1615). Surely this goes back to the heart of Jesus' mission. He spoke through words; he taught in parables; he worked miracles. But the actions which really got the attention of the people and the priests was his ability to "heal the sick, and that gratis."

At this time there was a particular fascination with the grimoires, and also the seminal Kabbalistic texts. One legend, not unlike that of the 'Lost Chord' was that of the 'Lost Word'. This, like the Holy Grail, took several forms. It was the word uttered by God to create the universe and the same word would end it. It was the word or breath – the Logos – uttered by God to give life to Man. It was His

64

sacred name, Yahweh, which could also be any of the above. The idea that Jesus similarly used a word of power to bring about miracles, was a common belief. This brought a particular fascination with the Seven Words from the Cross, specifically the last one, which is a form of 'So mote it be', or 'So it is', or 'Amen'. Jesus said 'It is accomplished', or in the Greek 'Tetelestai'. And so the word, spoken with confidence, accomplishes the fact. In 'The Art of Rosicrucian Healing" (1947, pub. The Society of Rosicrucians) Dr. Winslow Plummer says: "Christ always used two processes. He required *some effort* on the part of the one desiring to the cured. Then he "*spoke the WORD*." He elaborates: "(Speak the WORD) is *not so simple* when the practitioner understands the force that must be back of the WORD. The "WORD" consists of not more than three words. Christ used a formula which we can accept as an example. "Be thou healed." "Receive thy sight." "Arise and walk."

Similarly, the obsession with meaningful and symbolic gestures and materials are rife in the *Chemical Wedding*. Take, for example, the following passage: "We were to moisten the ashes with our fore-prepared water till they became altogether like very fine dough…we having opened our little forms, there appeared two beautiful, bright and almost transparent little images." Note the similarity to Genesis and the healing of the blind man. Similar stories of 'homunculi' or

Fig. 6 – The Golem

beings created by the Alchemist (as we shall see later), as well as the biblical description of the 'teraphim', and the 'golem' of the Kabbalists have similar echoes. Also, given the preoccupation with healing in this epoch, from stories of the Holy Grail to alchemical allusions to the Elixir of Life and the Philosopher's Stone, it is interesting that the hero of the *Wedding* is dubbed a Knight of the Golden Stone, an al-chemical goal which has its foundation and origin in the most common and reviled of materials…mud, perhaps?

The effects of this manifesto and the interest it stirred in some of the most influential and intelligent minds of Europe is well known – even at the time the Age of Enlightenment was knocking at the gate.

6. The Nineteenth Century Revival

While the currents continued through the Eighteenth and early Nineteenth Centuries, they were largely underground currents, as the people who indulged in esoteric pursuits either feared ridicule before a public weaned on the God of Science, which had apparently re-placed the Church as the master who required total obedience; or believed the masses unworthy of their labors and therefore worked in secret. Others used accepted Orders in which to practice their more occult interests.

Freemasonry was a prime example of this. And yet this was about to change.

Given the above, it should not be surprising that the first signs of the esoteric revival were to be found in the family of Masonic Orders. In the end of the eighteenth Century we find Martinez de Pasqually hiding his peculiar form of Gnosticism within a Masonic Order; Saint-Martin proposing esoteric spirituality as the Unknown Philoso-pher; German Orders of Rosicrucianism and Baron von Hund's Rite of Strict Observance.

Many believe the Rosicrucian current continued unabated in Eng-land, and in 1866 Robert Wentworth Little established the *Societas Rosicruciana In Anglia* (S.R.I.A.), a body which drew its members from regular Masons, but was not in fact a Masonic body itself[5].

The latter part of the Nineteenth Century, together with a back-lash against the excessive materialism of the time – especially in England where the burgeoning Empire of Queen Victoria both

---

[5] I was rather saddened to learn, on a visit to England in August 2016, that this is no longer the case. If I understand it correctly the reason for including it as a 'Masonic' Order after nearly 150 years of proud independence of the Grand Lodge, while accepting only Christian Master Masons among its ranks, has more to do with politics than necessity…

brought about a greater understanding of foreign cultures and a stronger focus on money, as well as in the invincibility of man and his

inventions which lessened the hold of the church – some people began to seek more out of life than a purely materialistic and jingoistic existence. In this *fin de siècle* atmosphere, it is not surprising that a significant number sought a greater meaning to their daily lives. The S.R.I.A. was a good example of this early spiritual yearning, and in its fourth Grade of Philosophus the Philosophy to be studied was in fact comparative Theosophy, and the Philosophus was enjoined, from a Christian background, to study the other great world religions, which now included Judaism, Hinduism, Brahmanism, Buddhism, Islam, Confucianism, Zoroastrianism, Shintoism, and the religions of an-

Fig 7. – Martinez de Pasqually

cient Egypt, Rome and Greece. – most of which would have been unknown to a majority of the English a century earlier.

In the last part of the Nineteenth Century there was an explosion of societies, groups, phenomena and scandals associated with the esoteric and the occult. Modern Spiritualism began in Hydesville, New York in 1848 with the Fox sisters. Faith Healing enjoyed new currency, and during this time Mary Baker Eddy founded the Church of Christ Scientist at Boston in 1879, following an experience she had in 1866. Their theology was strongly based on the idea that man is perfect, being made in God's image, and therefore all illness is but man losing his way, and through prayer – with no need for medical treatment – man can reestablish the close bond with God and in this close relationship illness cannot exist, for it is not of God. Among the many orders of Spiritualism, perhaps the two best known were the Theosophical Society of Madame Blavatsky and the Hermetic Order of the Golden Dawn. The former tried to graft Eastern spirituality on Western tradition, and the latter attempted to recreate the entire mystery tradition into one holistic system. Even the church itself was not immune, and in England, for example, attempts at reform resulted in the Oxford Movement in 1840, which saw the reintroduction of Catholic practices into the Church of England, which proponents claimed had been hi-jacked by the Protestants; and what became the Liberal Catholic Church, which simplistically began as the church of the Theosophical Society, with Charles Leadbeater's extraordinary books reinterpreting the mass and its accoutrements in terms of angelic powers and esoteric currents.

Alongside the return to spiritual values, the Christos was now revisited as Avatar. Whether or not one saw Jesus as a historical figure, or God incarnate – and the rediscovery of early Gnostic texts was beginning to raise questions on this point – the idea that Jesus was actually a mortal who discovered God within himself and by this act became God, was a powerful one at this time, and it is interesting to note that one of the earliest 'heresies' of the Christian faith which the 'winners', the Catholics, stamped out mercilessly at that most political of meetings known as the Council of Nicea, became one of the more fashionable ideas at the turn of the Twentieth Century.

Fig. 8 – McGregor Mathers, a leader of the Hermetic Order of the Golden Dawn

As well as the more extreme adherence to ideas of Spiritual Healing seen among Christian Scientists other, gentler interpretations could also be found. Indeed, Dr. Winslow Plummer lists them in The Art of Rosicrucian Healing: "Homeopathy, Allopathy, Hydrotherapy, Osteopathy, Chiropractic." He points out that the treatments balance the four elements – Water as in hydrotherapy, or the use of water; Fire, or the use of light and cauterizing techniques; Earth, or the use of muds and physical contact; and Air, or specializing breathing techniques and the exposure of the body to solar rays.

Fig. 9 – Dr. Winslow Plummer

One thing to understand from all these approaches was that they wanted to treat the human as a total being, as a spiritual as well as physical entity. They also wanted to treat the underlying cause rather than the symptoms alone. What these techniques had in common was that they saw an underlying spiritual cause to the problem, and whether they thought this should be treated by prayer alone, or by other methods, the intention was to cure the whole person and bring him or her back into harmony or vibration with God.

Finally, in this whistle stop tour of Rosicrucian or Spiritual Healing types, we find the schools of Homeopathy and Bach Remedies, both of which hark back to the early days of herbal medicine derided by the scientists, because it relied not only upon the physical constituents of the herbs, but also in the living force contained in them and the efficacy of harvesting them at precise times when the planets were said to be auspicious. Both Homeopathy and Bach use minute amounts of the substance macerated in alcohol or water. The term "homeopathy" was coined by the Saxon physician Christian Friedrich Samuel Hahnemann (1755–1843), and the method treats like with like – or minute doses of poison to treat a problem; while Bach remedies use dilutions of plant "essences", extracted by the sun's rays or by boiling, to treat emotional and spiritual conditions, including but not limited to depression, anxiety, insomnia and stress.

7. Examples of Rosicrucian Healing

We need look no further for the esoteric revival of Rosicrucian Healing than to the North-Eastern United States. We have already mentioned the work of Dr. Winslow Plummer in the American *Societas Rosicruciana In America*, an offshoot of the *Societas Rosicruciana in Fœderatis Civitatibus*, founded in 1879, and who was a practitioner rather than theoretician. The opening words of his work of healing follow: "The Rosicrucian system of healing differs from all other systems in several notable particulars. It has a remarkable lineage and an honorable record of achievement that occupies a permanent niche in both secular and arcane history. Its methods have been studied by initiates and sought by those outside the pale of the Fraternity for many centuries, but few have been willing to undertake the necessary labor and study required for attainment of proficiency in the Art."

In England, the SRIA was largely a theoretical body devoted to giving lectures and the pursuit of knowledge. However, according to Dr. D. G Williams, many of its founders were practicing homeopaths, who were therefore disposed to this way of thinking. The Golden Dawn contained at least one alchemist – the Rev. W. A. Ayton. Dr. Felkin's fascinating pamphlet on Rosicrucian Medicine, claims that Rosicrucian Medicine began with Paracelsus in the Fourteenth Century. He goes on to outline a number of practical techniques, with particular emphasis on light and the 'photo-dynamic remedies' of Dr. M Ritter. He continues by listing a large number of ailments and their cures. The point is expressly made that, although Culpeper, the famous herbalist, advocated drying herbs prior to use, this destroyed the life force which was as important as the medicinal aspects; so only living, green herbs should be used.

The flurry of activity in Eighteenth Century France, which had gone quiet during the revolution of the early Nineteenth Century and the subsequent upheavals, broke forth again in the latter years of that Century. In parallel with the esoteric revival in England, France was also undergoing an esoteric renaissance in the resurrection of ancient traditions and their grafting onto more modern vehicles. A number of churches arose based on either Gnostic or Cathar teachings. Jules Doinel founded his Gnostic Church following a vision in which he claimed to have been spiritually consecrated as "Bishop of Montségur and Primate of the Albigenses" by the 'Eon Jesus', and later contacted a number of Cathar and Gnostic spirits in séances at the salon of Maria de Mariategni, Lady Caithness, Duchesse de Medina Pomar. At an early stage Doinel joined the fledgling Martinist Order of Papus, while Papus and Paul Sédir were, among others, consecrated bishops (Tau Vincent and Tau Paul) in the Gnostic Church.

Fig. 10 – Jules Doinel

While the Gnostic Church certainly contained rituals of Spiritual Healing, as Gnostic they could not strictly be called "Rosicrucian", and the 'Consolamentum' was more a spiritual preparation for union with God through death than an explicit act of 'healing the sick, and that gratis'.

While most of the Orders united under the general Martinist banner, including the revival of the Elus Cohen, the Chevaliers Bienfaisant de la Cité Sainte, the Rites of Memphis-Mizraïm and the Church, none of these Orders could be said to focus upon Rosicrucian Healing as a major part of their philosophy. In Martinism the objective is to perfect oneself, as Saint-Martin called it, to become a 'Man of Desire' by lifting oneself above the 'Men of the Stream' living in the 'Forest of Errors'. Again, the objective is to heal oneself spiritually and there is little direct focus on physical healing. However, we will return to this point later! There was, however, an exception to this focus in the family of French Rosicrucian Orders of the late Nineteenth and early Twentieth Centuries. In his book *Templiers et Rose-Croix*, Robert Ambelain informs us that: "This particular lineage has given us what in some occult Masonic circles, is now called the "Rose Croix d'Orient" …this lineage came from the "Orient" (no doubt more simply from Syria and Armenia) through Greece." Also: "Before 1916 only two people possessed it in France. Georges Lagrèze, who had received it in Cairo, and Papus, to whom he had passed it."

This Order was apparently promulgated by Demetrius Semelas, who was also responsible for founding the Order of the Lily and Eagle in Greece. This is one Order within the esoteric family whose main purpose is that of empowering the ability to heal the sick, and there is a specific ritual to be used to this end. I had the wonderful good fortune to accompany my dear friend and mentor, Gilbert Tappa, to Marseilles a few years ago, where he introduced me to an extraordinary man who had devoted years of his life to 'healing the sick, and that gratis'. He worked in his converted garage, which contained a small central altar. Every wall was covered with pieces of white paper which, on closer inspection, proved to be identical. Each one had a pentacle in a circle drawn upon it, and within the pentacle was a lock of hair, a small photograph or other link with the sick person. He received requests for help from all over Europe. He would take a piece of paper, place the personal object within the pentacle and say his special prayers over the paper. Then he would hang the paper on the wall. The letters of thanks for miraculous cures were as numerous as the letters for assistance. I know not whether he worked within the confines of the Rose Croix d'Orient or had his own empowerment, but he was a shining example of what we mortals are capable of if we put our mind to it.

Fig. 11 – Demetrius Semelas

Similarly, in Italy in 1896 Giuliano Kremmerz, an alchemist who was interested in healing, founded the Therapeutic and Magical Brotherhood of Myriam. This Order believed in 'sacred materialism', or the idea that all things are linked and therefore one may act to effect change in others, even at a distance. The use of magic circles and meditation is prevalent in this school of magical learning.

Finally, we should mention that greatest of healers of these times, Maître Philippe Nizier, as well as his disciple and successor, Jean Chapas. On Palm Sunday a few years ago I stood in miserable weather in the cemetery in Lyons and participated in a healing circle formed by Martinists from as far away as South America, who had traveled there to remember the Maître on his special day. The power of a humble man to attract nearly seventy people to his graveside to perform a ritual in the pouring rain speak much for the love and respect in which he is held. He believed so fervently in the

Fig. 12 – Maître Philippe Nizier

power of prayer, and knew his prayers would be answered, just at Jesus knew when he prayed to His Father that He would be heard, and his requests would be granted. Maître Philippe showed inspirational confidence as he continued to heal, despite the persecution and ridicule of so-called professional doctors, who were terrified by a man who had no need of chemicals and poisons and operations to heal: after all, how <u>dare</u> he lay his hands on people and cure them without a doctor's certificate and ten years' learning how to dispense prescriptions and cut people open! It was he who raised the veil between the material and mystical worlds and showed to his followers – and many skeptics – that the invisible forces were just as important in curing the whole person as physical medicines. He reminded us not only that our bodies contain a spiritual element but also that to heal the symptoms one must focus on the whole person; that we must make ourselves in tune with God as well as see to our temporary discomforts. For no cure endures when the person is out of sorts with God and Nature.

In a way the tenets of the Rose Croix d'Orient were influenced by Gnostic thought, which was quite prepared to see Jesus as a man. Indeed, one of the more prevalent theologies of the mass of beliefs called 'gnosticism', particularly the work of Valentinus, argued that Jesus was indeed a man upon whom the 'Christos' force descended at the time of his baptism, and which left him, mission accomplished so to speak, when he hung upon the cross. They argue that the desperate words "Eli, Eli lama sabachthani" reflect this desertion, before the time when the calmer vehicle of the Christos, a Jesus finally endowed with wisdom and understanding, commended his soul to God. One of the so-called Gnostic texts – the Second Treatise of the Great Seth which – goes so far as to have the Christos sitting on a hill watching the crucifixion of the man Jesus and laughing. However, if we hold to this Gnostic idea that Jesus was a man, who was having a dialogue with his inner self when he asked permission to heal, then we have the powerful argument that if Jesus could heal while he was mortal, so can we. This newer thinking sees Jesus as Avatar or even Exemplar rather than the Son of God: and as we are all sons of God we all contain the divine spark, and we can also achieve divinity and be reunited with God through our own free will.

8. Modern Texts

Perhaps most pertinent to modern day Rosicrucian Healing are two books written by that doyen of mysticism, Robert Ambelain, called *Spiritual Alchemy* and *The Sacramentary of the Rose & Cross*. Both books he claims to be inspired by the teachings of the Rose Croix d'Orient, which seems appropriate given the healing tradition of that Order. The first book is more like a theoretical primer, and the second the practical application.

Spiritual Alchemy is dedicated to Georges Lagrèze, the man credited with bringing the Order to France. The basic premise of the book is that the alchemists of old, far from idly seeking instant wealth by converting base metal into gold, were in fact trying to implement the Hermetic axiom "As above, so below" in a practical manner, seeing their material experiments as a means of learning lessons to apply to themselves. In other words, the transmutation from base substance to philosopher's gold did not occur in a crucible: it occurred in themselves. The elaborate symbolism used and the cryptic descriptions of their activities were intended to keep the profane and the idly curious away from their true research. *Hekas, hekas, este bebeloi!*[6] However, like the 'gutter press' of today, as the alchemists would not write clearly about what they were doing, then someone else was there to do so, and to make up anything they didn't understand! And that person would not be a fan! It is interesting to note that the nascent scientific community – so determined to observe and test every theory – was so keen to ignore their own principles in their condemnation of the 'old ways', dismissing them wholesale without applying any of their 'scientific techniques' to determine if there was any currency in their teachings. So alchemy and the ancient arts were driven underground, which was probably no great hardship to the already secretive community of alchemists, until the twentieth century, when it became more popular again under such contemporary apologists as Jean Dubuis and Adam McLean.

What is Spiritual Alchemy? Well, alchemy can be defined as being mineral, vegetable and animal. The mineral type is that of observing the transmutation of metals into gold, through a long process of refinement which takes the raw material from base substance to sublime state. From which are produced the Philosopher's Stone and the ultimate panacea. Minerals being the densest of the three levels of existence, harsh chemicals and strong heat are used in what are often dangerous processes involving acids and crucibles. Vegetable alchemy is called 'spagyrics', and focuses on the extraction of the life essence of vegetation in order to create the Elixir of Long Life. In such a way the higher force is extracted from the base material and

---

[6] The Greek Mystery Schools used this cry, later adopted by the Hermetic Order of the Golden Dawn: 'Be far from here all profane things!'.

concentrated. The heat or light source most often used is that of the sun or moon, and spagyrics is considered a gentler path, and may have given birth to homeopathy and the Bach remedies, among others. Finally, Spiritual Alchemy is by logical deduction the art of the transformation of man. This is the subtlest process as it involves the most developed substance of the material plane: after all, man is closer to God than the angels, as the saying goes.

While practice and study of the mineral and spagyric forms of alchemy is most educational, the practice of spiritual alchemy, or self-transformation, can be practiced without previous experience in the other, more material forms. The fire which is referred to in all alchemical texts (a well-known Anonymous Text contains the following instruction: "I only command you to cook at the beginning, cook in the middle, cook at the end, and do not do any other thing…") is, according Ambelain, clearly prayer, which is the only human activity which should underline, underpin and continue through the entirely of any spiritual operation. Using diagrams developed from "A Open Entrance to the Closed Palace of the King", attributed to Philalethes, he takes the reader through the four elements (earth, air, water, fire), the three principles (sulfur, mercury, salt), and the two philosophical metals (Philosophical Silver and Philosophical Gold) to create the *Summum*

Fig. 13 – The Rose upon the Cross, an image appropriated by a number of Rosicrucian Bodies

Bonum. He then interprets this diagram in terms of the four Cardinal Virtues, the three Theological Virtues, and to the two Sublime Virtues (Wisdom and Understanding). He also interprets this powerful image in terms of the mortification of the senses, and also the seven deadly sins and their progeny – Error and Blindness, which lead to spiritual darkness. Through these strong analogies he breaks the process of self-purification down into clearly understandable steps: and this is an excellent manual for anyone who wishes to work the process of spiritual alchemy upon themselves. His book also contains a virtual Sacramentary of prayers – well known to Elus Cohen – which he reminds us should, like the Philosopher's athanor, permeate all our undertakings. Thus prepared, the practitioner is better prepared to work the Rosicrucian Healing outlined explicitly in his 'Sacramentary of the Rose & Cross'.

This final book is fascinating – and from extensive practical experience, it works! At first glance, one might be put off by the Medieval tone. It reads as though it is claiming to be hundreds of years old, and yet there are enough clues to suggest it is of modern composition. Despite the quaint phrases and anachronistic situations, for example, 'prayer before drinking water from an unknown or doubtful source', 'prayer for the discovery of a spring', 'prayer to obtain the pardon of one condemned to death', 'prayer to protect the fidelity of a wife or the chastity of a young girl', the book is a veritable treasury of Rosicrucian Healing prayers: for women in various stages of labor and for their children, for general healings, prayers over herbal remedies, the healing of burns, healing at a distance, heart troubles. The list is long and involved, though again, occasionally quirky (for example, prayer for the healing of leprosy, prayer for the healing of madness – both easily adaptable to more practical use, but couched in mock-medieval terms. I particularly like the 'Prayer Against Elephantiasis'!). These prayers are not sufficient of themselves: they are to be used in rituals: and remember Dr. Plummer's injunction, that the actual moment of healing should involve The WORD, or a short and simple command to heal. This in no way negates the importance of prayer and the use of the preparatory orisons to prepare the healer for the actual task – but neither is efficacious without the other.

The important thing to note is that a prominent Rosicrucian, Alchemist, Martinist, Mason and Mystic has enjoined us to use these techniques, and in doing so we will rediscover a major part of our Rosicrucian legacy, as well as fulfill the prime objective: 'to heal the sick, and that gratis.'

9. What We Can Do Today?

One of the oldest forms in magic is the circle. In Church services the circle is a regular feature of movement and censing. In our Martinist traditions the cincture about the waist links us to our initiatory chain and also provide a protective circle about us. Almost every esoteric ritual has included the drawing of a circle of protection about oneself. Perhaps this comes from a primitive desire to define a boundary which was taboo for others to cross. If so, it is easy to see how this simple defensive mechanism was developed to include non-human beings and ultimate nonmaterial worlds. So, the circle we draw in Assiah resonates in Yetzirah, too. And the material limit we draw on Earth provide an equally impenetrable barrier to spirits of higher realms.

Circles are found in almost every culture (with the interesting exception of Aborigines, who apparently did not know the form when they were first encountered). In America there is a popular household ornament called 'Circle of Friends' which comes from the indigenous Indian culture, and which depicts a circle of primitive terracotta figures holding hands or resting their arms upon each other's. The legend says that if the people seated around the fire

Fig. 14 – Native American Circle of Friends

shared their good memories and stories, while the embers faded their friendship was sealed, bringing them ever closer together. A candle was placed in the center of the terracotta form, within the circle of friends, and lit to bring good luck to the owner and those who sat with them.

In Lodges, if we form a Chain of Union or Fraternal Chain at the end of our meeting, we can use this to strengthen the sense of unity between our members, and also with those members of our Order who are spread across the world. If we are feeling brave, we might even consider using this battery to send healing vibrations to our absent Brethren, especially if they are not present due to sickness.

The form of a circle is used in almost all groups who come to-gether for a common purpose. If we consider a group coming together for the purpose of performing a healing, let us consider some of the elements which need to be present.

The circle limits the bad and also contains the good. By forming the circle, whether drawn upon the ground or formed by our joining of hands, we keep dark forces out by our combined will and focus and channel the good. And in the center, according to many traditions, is God. Here, in harmony with the Indian tribes of North America, we may place a candle at the Closing Ceremony. As the light of that can-dle radiates out beyond us and into the faces of those Masters of the Past who crowd around us in this most solemn of ceremonies, so we join hands in the ancient way and recite prayers celebrating the divine forces, as so many have done before us. Remember the importance of the prayer, the Pater Noster, given to us by the Christos. Never un-derestimate its power. The many, many members of the exoteric Church of St. Paul recite it without feeling as a jumble of words on a daily basis, and it has a soothing effect as a mantra, perhaps. But we, who are of the esoteric Church of St. John better understand its eso-teric nature, and we say it with feeling and can sense the power it generates. I commend you to read the works of Papus, Sédir, Chapas and others on the esoteric meaning of the Lord's Prayer.

We, the inheritors of the Rosicrucians, form a living battery, a positive charge of good as we bathe in the light of the flame and join with countless past generations of Rosicrucians in that still, silent mo-ment, an endless link of strength and power which can be harnessed to such good ends.

We should be proud to be inheritors of the Rosicrucian tradition. It is imperative that we follow their prime directive. We must not let the divine energy generated at this moment evaporate into the æther with a casual shake of the hands!

There are so many uses to which you can put this energy. You can pray for the health of an individual – it matters not if you are concerned with physical or spiritual health – or a relative; friends; a group known to you; or another member of the circle; the community; or the world. Be sure your prayer is focused – vague hopes for 'world peace' will elicit a warm, comfortable feeling, but do little to change the planet. The light needs to be focused. The prayers of attunement need to be followed by a clear statement of the intent of the circle, and then when the object of the healing has been clearly identified, the energy needs to be centered and focused, and then projected to the person or people needing it, with a short command (remember the words of Dr. Plummer). If the person is present they can be put into the middle of the Pantacle (I recommend moving the candle first, or have the person hold it. The circle can then generate a powerful vortex of energy and, moving their joined hands forward to touch the person being healed, force the white light into the recipient by means of strong visualization.

Now visualization is an important part of the exercise, and many Orders devote much time in training this important skill. There is no harm to be had in following the practices of other Rosicrucian Orders, either, for there are many roads to the summit of Mount Abiegnus. Feel absolutely free to use the Middle Pillar exercise of the Golden Dawn, the prayer techniques of the

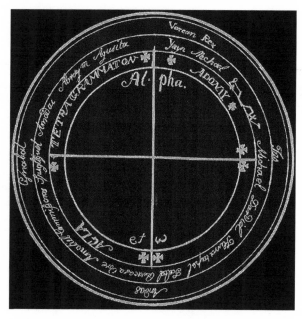

Fig. 15 – A Magic Circle

Theosophical Society, or any method with which you and your circle feel comfortable.

This is a wonderful practice, and we can bring a genuinely useful aspect of our beliefs to the service of mankind. Here we can give something back. I enjoin you never to hold hands in a circle of prayer without using the energy for a good intention. Because we are all Rosicrucians, because we are all spiritual healers, because we all contain the Light, what better way is there to employ it, than in following the injunction of our forebears: 'to heal the sick, and that gratis'?

To end, I would like to give you a practical example of what can be achieved.

Following a meeting in which I was discussing these thoughts, I was approached by a friend who told me his wife worked as a teacher. That very day one of her young students had been attacked in the playground, and as a result he was lying in a coma in intensive care in hospital, limbs broken, and with a poor chance of pulling through. He asked me if we could try the technique I had just described. There were about fifteen of us of Rosicrucian persuasion present, attending a Masonic conference in Washington D.C. I asked the group to stand in a circle, lit a candle and placed it in the center, then asked everyone to hold hands, close their eyes and breathe rhythmically. After several minutes of calm, we recited the Lord's Prayer and the Hail Mary, and then I asked those present to visualize a golden child forming above the candle. As the child grew I asked that we all imbue it with health and vitality, robust and strong. At length, when the child was fully formed, we filled it with the energy from our circle, and felt it vibrating with positive energies. We then sent it to the hospital and to the child. We felt drained but very positive after this experience.

The end to the story came the following day. I was sitting with a few colleagues, when my friend sought us out, beaming from ear to ear. He said the boy was out of danger, out of intensive care, and was now sitting up and communicating. He still had a long time to heal and his bones were still broken, but his family were overjoyed. The story becomes even more powerful when I tell you that his father is a priest. My friend's wife told him that a group was praying for his son, and he said: "I know. In fact, I can even tell you when they were praying, because I felt a presence in the room and at that moment my son woke from his coma and looked at me; and we know then that he was out of danger." I am sure I do not need to tell you that the time he gave for this miracle was precisely the time that we were gathered together in that hotel room to send him our powerful ray of healing.

"HEAL THE SICK, AND THAT GRATIS!"

RAPHAËL

1. The Guide

This topic, I should immediately clarify, refers to the archangel, and not the artist!

Why would Raphael be of any interest to a Mason? To be honest, the reference in Freemasonry occurs in only one ritual, and is so slight and fleeting, probably only those who have participated in the ritual and learned the words would know where it occurs.

Towards the end of the 18th Degree of the Ancient Accepted Scottish Rite, there is a catechism between the Most Wise Master and the Neophyte, taken directly from the Book of Tobit, which goes as follows:

MWM	Who was your conductor?
Neo	Raphael.
Orator	"He found RAPHAEL that was an angel... and he said unto him, 'Canst thou go with me?' To

> whom the angel said, 'I will go with thee and I know the way well.'"

Without giving too much away, it identifies the third letter of the Word of the 18th Degree. Of course the intelligent Rosicrucian – and Mason – will recognize that the four letters of the Rosicrucian password map onto the four letters to the Tetragrammaton, or the Lost Word rediscovered in the Holy Royal Arch Degree. This profound truth is worthy of a completely separate paper, of course! However, for now let us note that, if Raphael maps to the third letter of the Rosicrucian name, the third letter of the Tetragrammaton or Great and Sacred Name of God is 'Vav', or the 'v' in 'Jehovah' to those less familiar with the Hebrew alphabet. Since the Hebrew language uses letters as numbers, from which the whole of Gematria, which is an Assyro-Babylonian-Greek system of assigning numbers to letters, later manifested in the Jewish art of linking words with similar numerical values, I will throw in a quick 'bone' to those who are more esoterically inclined, by pointing out that 'Vav' bears the numerical value of '6'; and Tiphareth, to which Raphael is assigned on the Qabbalistic Tree of Life, is the sixth manifestation of God from Kether, as He manifests His will in the universe.

We will return to this point later.

It is interesting to note that, in the English version of the 18th Degree, the title of the person who leads the Neophyte through the journeys and answers for him through most of the ceremony is Raphael; while here in the United States it is more prosaically the Master of Ceremonies. I was curious about this, and contacted Brent Morris and Jeff Croteau of the House of the Temple and the AASR Library in Lexington, respectively. Both confirmed that, when the ritual was transmitted to England by the Northern Masonic Jurisdiction in 1847, the title of the guide was Master of Ceremonies. So the substitution of Raphael is a purely English invention. Still, in this instance I rather prefer the English name for this character, and it completely reflects the catechism towards the end of the ritual. One might go further and suggest that the image of the Conductor who leads a blindfolded Candidate in *any* Degree as that of an angel is both profound, and fits quite happily with any of the religions of The Book, all of which recognize angels as God's messengers and servants.

84

So in this pivotal Degree, the one responsible for guiding the Neophyte through the trials and tribulations, as did Virgil in Dante's Inferno, and finally delivering him for reward for his perseverance, is Raphael. In Milton's Paradise Lost, it is Raphael whom God sends to Adam to tell him of Satan's infiltration of Eden, and to warn him that Satan is going to try to curse Adam and Eve. Raphael even has a long discussion with Adam, who is curious about creation and the events which transpired in Heaven.

This talk will focus on the identity of this enigmatic character who, while he merits only one reference in our 18th Degree, is nevertheless one of the most important characters in the Degree. We will trace his origins, what he symbolizes, and how he became one of the most important images in contemporary esoteric imagery.

As a brief aside, this is not the first time Raphael appeared in the embryonic Scottish Rite. In his book on the history of the Scottish Rite in England, written in 1987, A. C. F. Jackson attributed the authorship of the Rose Croix Degree to Jean-Baptiste Willermoz around 1765. Willermoz was part of a group of Freemasons in Lyon, France, who produced a prolific output of esoteric Masonic rituals, many of which bear titles which eventually found their way into the present day Scottish Rite system. One of his friends and teachers, Martinez de Pasqually, had established a unique Order titled Knight Mason Elect Priests of the Universe, or Elus Cohen, which built a magical degree system around a framework or early Lodge of Perfection Degrees in Bordeaux. It is interesting to note that in the central Degree of his system, which Willermoz joined around 1766, the Candidate symbolically underwent a creation broadly following the story of Adam's creation in the Book of Genesis, but with a distinctly gnostic flavor, within a magic circle which the Operator invoked, among other powers, the Archangel Raphael.

2. His Place in The Old Testament

Raphael is one of three archangels mentioned in the canonical Bible, along with Gabriel and Michael. And yet he only appears in the Book of Tobit, which is not even in the canon of the Protestant Bible. The Angel Gabriel, meaning God is My Strength, we meet for the first time in the Book of Daniel, when he comes to explain the meaning of a vision to Daniel, and later to deliver a message from heaven; and in the New Testament he is a messenger and a revealer of truth, visiting both Mary and Anne to inform them of their fates in delivering Jesus and John who became the Baptist. In Islam Gabriel, or Gibril, is also the angel who recites the revelation of the Koran to Mohammad. Michael, or Who is Like unto God, also appears to Daniel, described as "Michael, the great prince", and reappears also in Revelation, where he leads God's armies against Satan.

So where does Raphael come from?

He first appears in the Book of Tobit, which was approved for inclusion at the Council of Carthage in 397 C.E. However, it was rejected from the Protestant Bible, and for this reason, Tobit is not found in most Protestant Bibles, although it is contained within that section which resides between the Old and New Testaments, called the Apocrypha, in the original King James Bible. However, the Apocrypha was removed from it in 1885 C. E., so it will be included or not depending upon the age and version of the Bible gracing your altar in Lodge or Chapter.

In the Book of Tobit, we learn that Raphael was sent by God to help Tobit, Tobiah and Sarah. Tobit was a virtuous man, who in the manner of many of the moral tales of the Old Testament was struck by misfortune – in his case by blindness. At the same time in another town Sarah, daughter of Raguel, was similarly afflicted. She had married seven times, and each time a demon, Asmodeus, killed her husbands before they could retire to the matrimonial bed. Unusually the story tells us the outcome before the narrative. We are told that God hears both their prayers, and decides to send His angel Raphael to heal Tobit of his blindness, see his son Tobiah married successfully to Sarah, and to bind the demon Asmodeus.

In the text we find Raphael depicted as a guide (indeed, in Orthodox iconography he is often depicted with a staff). He is hired by Tobit's son Tobiah to guide him, as we learn in Chapter 5: "Therefore when he went to seek a man, he found Raphael that was an angel. But he knew not; and he said unto him, Canst thou go with me to Rages? and knowest thou those places well? To whom the angel said, I will go with thee, and I know the way well."

Raphael is also shown to be a healer, for on the journey he teaches Tobiah to catch a fish and remove its gall, heart and liver. Tobiah will use the heart and liver to flush out Asmodeus, whom Raphael then battles and overcomes; and later he will use the gall, on Raphael's instructions, to cure his father's blindness.

This is one reason that Raphael is associated so strongly with the Rosicrucian movement.

The story of the fish is one of the reasons a number of people were strongly against including the so-called apocryphal books in the Bible. There is no doubt that Tobit Chapter 6, verse 7 contains what amounts to a magic spell: "As regards the fish's heart and liver, if you burn them so that the smoke surrounds a man or a woman who is afflicted by a demon or evil spirit, the affliction will leave him completely, and no demons shall ever return to him again" (I've used the New America Bible translation here as it is very clear to understand). Why would magic spells be included among the sacred texts which includes such injunctions as: "Thou shalt not suffer a witch to live." (Exodus 22:18). A good question indeed!

One noteworthy aspect of the tale is the fact that Raphael instructs Tobiah to perform these actions: he does not perform them himself. In fact, a close inspection of the story will reveal the fact that at no time does Raphael physically come into contact with anything. This point is explicitly emphasized towards the end, when Raphael says: "All these days I did appear unto you; but I did neither eat nor drink, but ye did see a vision." Finally, he reveals himself: "I am Raphael, one of the seven holy angels." Note in passing that this is one of the reasons why the seven angels have long been associated with the seven days of the weeks, one ruling over each, as well as the lower seven Sephiroth of the Kabbalistic Tree of Life.

According to the Talmud he is one of the three angels who visited Abraham following his circumcision. If you recall your scriptures, they turned their faces towards Sodom and Gomorrah, and determine to travel there to mete God's judgement upon them, upon which Abraham argues with the Lord that if even a small number of righteous men should be found there, the cities of the plain should be spared. In the following Chapter it says that two angels arrive in Sodom. I personally like to think this implies that Raphael had left the other two during that journey; for he is the healer, not the destroyer nor the bearer of harsh messages from God.

3. Other Non-Canonical Sources

For another book not found in the traditional canons, but enduring in the canon of the Ethiopian Orthodox Tewahedo Church, we turn to the Book of Enoch. This book is considered to be a very early writing, quite possibly developed at the same time as or even predating the verbal Torah. However, although it was clearly known to the authors of the New Testament, it was neither included in the biblical canon of the Jews or Christians, with the exception noted above. Attributed to Enoch, grandfather to Noah, who was bodily taken up into heaven according to tradition, this extraordinary series of writings includes a details account of the descent of the Watchers, the angels who fathered the Nephilim; Enoch's ascents into heaven and his account of its organization; a series of parables and dream visions; and an astrological description of the heavenly luminaries.

In the Book of the Watchers he names the seven archangels as: Gabriel, Michael, Raphael, Uriel, Raguel, Ramiel and Sariel. It would be logical to assume this quotation influenced the line in Tobit in which Raphael refers to himself as one of the seven angels. His explicit function in the book is found in Enoch 10:4, "And again the Lord said to Raphael: Bind Azazel hand and foot, and cast him into the darkness." Azazel was the fallen angel who taught mankind how to harden and fashion metals, thus bringing the art of war to mankind; also interestingly he also introduced mankind to cosmetics (if you wonder why I don't say 'to womankind', think of the pharaohs!). Some scholars have noted that his punishment is not unlike that of the scapegoat ritual on the Day of Atonement (two goats, one for Yahweh and one of 'complete removal' or Azazel).

It is interesting to note Raphael's battle with and binding of the demon Asmodeus in the Book of Tobit recalls his battle with the demon Azazel in the Book of Enoch. Asmodeus later crops up in the building of Solomon's Temple. A legend taken for the Book of Solomon says when Solomon prayed to God for help in building the Temple, God answered with the gift of a magic ring, which was brought to their king personally by Raphael. It was engraved with the five-pointed star, and had the power to subdue all demons. It was also Raphael who was credited with writing the ten books on healing which was given to Noah, after the flood, entitled the "Book of the Angel Raziel."

In other non-canonical stories, Raphael guards the Tree of Life in Eden, and is one of the seven angels who stand before the Throne. Elsewhere, in the Talmud he is one of the three angels to visit Abraham after his circumcision.

In Islam, Raphael is called Israfil, and according to the Hadith, Israfil is the angel who will herald Judgement Day. The first blow of the trump will destroy the world, while the second will call all humans back to life in order to face judgement.

So Raphael is seen to be close to God, a guide, a warrior and a healer. Yet almost everyone sees him in his most popular manifestation, as healer. This is because his name in Hebrew, רפאל, Resh-Peh-Aleph-Lamed, means 'God Heals', or 'Healer of God'.

4. The Guide in Masonic and Esoteric Degrees

In our Degree we find him in his role as a guide, or psychopomp, leading the Neophyte who can only see dimly due to the veil before his eyes on the path which leads to revelation, both symbolically in the virtues he is to learn, and actually before the Book of Seven Seals upon the altar. He is also the Neophyte's Higher Self, sometimes referred to in Rosicrucian circles as the Holy Guardian Angel. We see this in his role as the person who speaks on behalf of the Neophyte. His role diminishes as the Neophyte learns the lessons, and as the external Higher Self increasingly fuses with the Neophyte himself. By the end of the ritual, the Neophyte has symbolically gained full knowledge of his Higher Self, and can now answer for himself, leaving the Master of Ceremonies – or Raphael – either mute, or reduced to the role of prompter.

If you wonder why I was coy in explaining the Rose Croix ritual in more detail earlier, it is because Raphael's role as psychopomp and higher self goes beyond the Scottish Rite in Masonry. He appears under different guises in many Orders. He is the Junior or Senior

Deacon in the Blue Lodge; he is the Principal Sojourner in the Royal Arch; he is the veiled Guide in the Order of Knight of York; the Conductor in rites too numerous to mention: in fine, he is present in every ceremony in which the candidate is blindfolded and therefore needs both a guide and one who will speak for him. Further, he is present is many esoteric orders, too. He is the Hegemon in the Hermetic Order of the Golden Dawn; and the *Hodos Chameleonis* of Rosicrucian Adept Grades; the Assistant in Martinism; and the Conductor of the Sat B'hai. He is even in the Ninth card of the Major Arcana of the Tarot, the Hermit, who holds open the door of knowledge and illuminates the path with his lamp of wisdom.

Remember that the role of Raphael is therefore reflected in the roles of Deacon in Blue Lodge, and Principal Sojourner in Chapter, where the blindfolded candidate is led by another who guides him and speaks on his behalf, offering comfort and courage during the ordeals. Surely it is no coincidence that, regarding the two just listed, both carry staffs.

So we have considered Raphael's roots and biblical history – both canonical and apocryphal – and identified some of his powers. However, we need to give him a personality: otherwise it is really like thinking of Penicillin as a small white tablet, or Viagra™ as a little blue one. We can see what they look like – but that gives us no idea of what they can do!

5. His Qualities & Powers

Given that Raphael was given to us by the Hebrews, and they probably received a version of this powerful archangel via the Assyrians or other early Middle Eastern cultures, it is hardly surprising that he features strongly in the Kabbalah. And this is where I intend to look. One clue is that, for most people, Raphael is the most loved, the most personable of all the angels. There are lists of angels for the planets and constellations, and great hierarchies which have been bashed out over the centuries. But even of the four best known archangels, Uriel seems hard to pin down, Michael seems aloof and stern, and Gabriel is that messenger who delivers news which none but the most devout really want to hear. But it is Raphael, the kind healer, who garners our attention and our love. Why is this? I think by the time we have finished considering his Kabbalistic credentials, we will understand why we love him most of all.

The first questions we need to ask is, in the cosmic filing cabinet which is the Kabbalistic Tree of Life, where do we find Raphael? This great Archangel is associated with Tiphareth. Raphael is central on the Tree of Life. Tiphareth is the invisible sun, the sun behind the visible sun which vivifies all. Tiphareth is also referred to as the Christ center, and all systems of Rosicrucian advancement see the path to this Sephira as requiring a symbolic death, a parting of the Veil of Paroketh, in order to attain the title of Adeptus Minor, or Lesser Adept. Here one learns and grows in knowledge of one's Holy Guardian Angel, one's Higher Self. And this is exactly how we have already identified Raphael, our guide, psychopomp and internal prompter. He redeems us, he heals our soul, he makes us worthy of the ascent towards the One. He raises us up from the lower levels of reality, from the earthly realm of Malkuth in Assiah.

We are reminded of the seven churches in Assiah – or Asia – of Revelations, to whom the seven angels are referred. It is a thrilling visual image to imagine the prayers and incense rising up from these churches to their intercessors, the seven angels about the Throne of God. This recalls the Four Worlds of the Kabbalah, from the material world of Assiah through the angelic world of Yetzirah, to the archangelic world of Briah, where Raphael may be found, before ascending to the ultimate realm of Atziluth, where God lives behind the Great Veil. In Tiphareth, balancing the Pillars of Boaz and Jachin, or Severity and Mercy, for this balance is required for healing, we find that, given his role as guide, Raphael is also associated with Mercury. Alchemically this affords him the volatile nature of Quicksilver, which is associated with Wednesday (mercredi in French – from the planet Mercury). Once again he is found in the middle of the week, and mediating between the alchemical qualities of salt and sulfur.

In the Tarot he is linked through his association with Mercury to the Magician, who wields the four elements while combining them, like the Quintessence or the Spirit element, the 'Shin' in the word 'Yeheshuah', creating the Son proceeding from the Father (Yod-Heh-Vav-Heh, or Jehovah). He is also found in the 6th card of the Major Arcana, spreading his arms in blessing over The Lovers, while behind the man the Tree of Life, with which he is personally associated, flourishes.

Through these correspondences he is identified with the Hebrew letter Beth, which means House. He is associated with the colors yellow and purple, both colors of sovereignty, and stands in the East representing the Kerub with the aspect of man of Ezekiel's vision; and therefore Air, the aspirate representing Life. Through Air he is associated with the air signs Gemini, Libra and Aquarius. Note again that all three Astrological signs emphasize the unification of duality: Gemini, the twins united above and below; Libra, the balance of the scales which measure Good and Evil with the feather of Ma'at; and Aquarius, who pours the contents of her vases on earth and water alike.

Finally, his Hebrew name, given that that alphabet, in common with Greek, assigns numbers to letters, sums to 311. Curiously, though Gematria, where words with the same sum have a correspondence, 311 is also the number of Man (Ish: Shin-Yod-Aleph, remembering Hebrew writes from right to left).

What do we learn from this avalanche of associations?

6. A True & Trusted Friend

I believe the reason we identify with Raphael before all the other angels, is because he identifies so closely with us. He heals us, he tends us, he guides us. He is Air, he is Man, he is Tiphareth. He is our Christ consciousness. Perhaps if there was any power in heaven God wished to send to us, to suffer upon the cross, to die, and to live again, it was Raphael, the Man, the Healer, the Repairer? He represents balance. He did battle with demons, perhaps even with Satan himself during forty days in the desert? He bears the trappings of monarchy, purple and gold. He is the House not made with hands. He is the Magician. He is the Hermit. He is Holman Hunt's Light of the World, the very human image of Jesus as prophet, priest and king, who knocks on the door of our hearts, and asks us: will you let me in? Will you let me heal you? Will you accept your Higher Self, your Holy Guardian Angel, to guide you?

I would like to end with a Catholic prayer written to invoke the Archangel Raphael into our lives, a prayer which I believe would not offend those of other faiths:

"Glorious Archangel Saint Raphael, great prince of the heavenly court, you are illustrious for your gifts of wisdom and grace. You are a guide of those who journey by land or sea or air, consoler of the afflicted, and refuge of sinners. We beg you, assist us in all our needs and in all the sufferings of this life, as once you helped the young Tobiah on his travels. Because you are the "Medicine of God", we humbly pray you to heal the many infirmities of our soul and the ills that afflict our bodies.

"Saint Raphael of the glorious seven who stand before the throne of Him who lives and reigns, Angel of health, the Lord has filled your hand with balm from heaven to soothe or cure our pains. Heal or cure the victims of disease, and guide our steps when doubtful of our ways.

"Grant us the great grace of purity of soul, and prepare me to be the temple of the Holy Spirit. Amen."

DIFFERENCES IN ENGLISH AND NEW YORK MASONRY

__NOTE__: This paper was initially written to educate Brethren of my New York Lodge on some of the differences between the way the two Nations practice their Freemasonry. It was not intended to be a comprehensive study; and it was also practical, in that I took along a number of pieces of paraphernalia, demonstrated signs, steps, etc. It proved popular, and I have given it in a number of Lodges both across the State and in other States, where it has elicited lively discussions. One gratifying fact is that a number of English Masons have attended Lodges in which I gave the talk, and their input added considerable color to the events.

1. Introduction

The subject matter we will investigate together is vast, and one which has filled many, many books over the centuries. To make the evening manageable and I hope, informative, I have limited my scope according to three constraints. Firstly, I wanted to ensure that our new Entered Apprentices could attend, and this requires that I focus exclusively on the ritual of the First Degree. Secondly, I wanted to give a general talk which would have something of interest for everyone, and which would cover history, ritual and symbolism, and interpretation. Thirdly, I wanted to keep it short, though our definitions of 'short' may differ!

Another observation which I have made over the years is the different focus of research given to Masonry by what I call the 'Anglo-Saxon' school and the 'Continental' school. Walk into a Masonic bookstore in England or America and you will find the shelves groaning with heavy tomes about 'Famous Dead Masons', and the 'Glorious History of Freemasonry'. If you visit the Masonic bookstores of Paris, Vienna or Brussels, however, you will find the inventory pays little heed to history but focuses more on the interpretation of the ritual and the meaning of its symbols. It is not my task to argue the relative merits of these approaches. However, I believe that balance is good, and I will strive to mix history with interpretation. I may even be able to throw in the occasional 'Famous Dead Mason'...

To put the talk in context, I will first give a little history of the early days of Freemasonry both in England and New York State, which will help us to understand how the differences in ritual came about. I will then give you some, I trust, interesting and practical examples where the ritual and furniture differ in our traditions, and how these affect our respective understanding of the First Degree. Finally, I will go completely 'European' and consider the hidden symbolism of a common article used in the First Degree. I will challenge you to perform a simple exercise at home which, if sincerely practiced, will open your eyes to a new way of learning about our Mystic Craft.

2. Historical Context

There are two types of information presented to the inquiring scholar of Masonic history, according to Mackey: history and tradition. In our rituals we are usually told "Masonic tradition informs us…", which alerts us to be cautious in taking what follows literally, and to look for the allegory instead. However, in trying to determine the origins of Masonry it can be harder to distinguish fact from tradition. Indeed, in Mackey's book on the subject, he outlines no less than forty-three theories extant at his time. However, Freemasonry – that speculative Fraternal Order, which claims to take its primary symbols from the failing medieval guilds and old operative Lodges – is accepted to have 'officially' come into being on St. John Baptist's Day in 1717, at the Goose & Gridiron Ale-house in London, England, when four existing Lodges assembled and elected Anthony Sayer to the new office of Grand Master. It must be remembered that the idea of central rule did not come into force instantaneously – indeed, the first Grand Lodge saw its jurisdiction as extending no further than a total of three square miles from the heart of Old London Town. Initially this allowed several bodies to set themselves up as Grand Lodges with claim to regularizing the existing Lodges which had hitherto functioned independently, by issuing charters and proclaiming them 'duly constituted'. Indeed, in the second half of the 18th Century there were no less than six Grand Lodges, including those of England,

Scotland, Ireland, York and the 'Grand Lodge of England South of the River Trent', as well as the Grand Lodge of Antient Freemasons, of which more later. Initially this caused little friction, as their jurisdictions did not overlap. Soon, four of the bodies commenced issuing Charters to Lodges in other countries. New York Lodges existing in the first half of the Seventeenth Century received their Charters (and their Provincial Grand Masters) from the so-called Premier Grand Lodge in London. I have been to the United Grand Lodge of England & Wales and seen the old record books, in which St. John's Lodge is listed – albeit with a number in the 200s – as being duly constituted in 1757, although the entry has a line through it, which symbolizes the time when it was struck from the rolls for non-payment of Grand Lodge dues following the War of Independence.

Nevertheless, there are scholars who now believe organized Masonry now goes back far earlier than 1717. We obviously know there were Lodges prior to this time. There had to be existing Lodges to establish the Premier Grand Lodge, after all! And records show us that there were Lodges who accepted such Speculatives as Elias Ashmole and Robert Moray many years earlier; and in Scotland there is considerable indication that the Stuart family were not only patrons, but members of the Craft. This is the authority under which James II and his successors signed Patents and Charters in France for many years following James' expulsion from England. This 'Stuart' or 'Ecossais' form of Masonry is far more explicitly esoteric than our modern day variety, and there appears to have been considerable communication between Sweden and Scotland, among other masonic groups, which is surprising when you consider the face that one was staunchly Protestant and the other Catholic! But that is a subject for a different paper.

At this time, therefore, the rituals practiced in London and New York would have been broadly similar, but variations would easily have crept in as many Lodges were still irregular, in that they still believed that a copy of the Ancient Charges were all a person needed to allow him to 'make masons'.

However, the seeds of dissention were beginning to spread in England as the number of Lodges grew rapidly and with them, more opinions and disquiet, which finally led to the Craft being split in two with the creation of a rival Grand Lodge 'under the Old Institutions' who were called the 'Antients', and those who remained loyal to the existing Grand Lodge based in London, but which now saw itself as exercising sovereignty over the whole of England and Wales, who were known as the 'Moderns'. If the terms seem contradictory, remember that the newer Grand Lodge of the Antients claimed that they were going back to what they perceived as the 'roots' of Masonry, saying that the original body had grown lax, and had allowed modern practices to taint its purity. While part of the reason was the weak administration and the ineffectual Grand Masters, much of the dissent focused on changes in custom and ritual. The five main objections were as follows: Firstly, the opening of the Lodge to men of non-Christian faith (although Jews rose to prominent positions in both Grand Lodges). The second objection was the neglect of St. John's Days as special Masonic festivals. Thirdly, the modes of recognition in the First and Second Degrees had been transposed, and this was viewed as the destruction of an important Landmark. In addition, passwords in the Second and Third Degrees were altered, and we still see the remnants of that in the alternatives given in the Third Degree. The Moderns' Grand Lodge also refused to recognize the Royal Arch Degree, which is not a focus of this talk but mentioned for completeness. Fourth, the removal of the catechisms – the Questions and Answers – attached to each Degree. Fifth, the abandonment of the esoteric part of the Installation of the Worshipful Master.

In 1771 the Antient Grand Lodge fell under the rule of the third Duke of Athol, and was succeeded by his son who ruled, with one ten-year interval, until 1813. Thus the Antients came to be known as 'Athol Masons'. Perhaps a little impertinently, despite the fact that a Grand Lodge of York existed, albeit more often dormant than active, the Athol Masons arrogated the popular tradition of 10th Century lineage to their cause, and their Charters included the words: "We, the Grand Lodge of the Most Ancient and Honorable Fraternity of Free and Accepted Masons, according to the old Constitutions granted by his Royal Highness Prince Edwin, at York, Anno Domini Nine Hundred Twenty and Six…". This was based on documents going back to 1390 which said that Prince Edwin, son of King Athelstan, called a meeting of the Masons at York in 926 and revived the Institution, giving the Craft a new code of laws. Thus the Antients became

associated with York Rite Masonry, which encompassed far more Degrees than those recognized by the Moderns' Grand Lodge, and
included Degrees which both extended the basic Masonic histories
and included Orders of Chivalry in its portfolio.

In New York State, meanwhile, with the tide of battle turning in
favor of the new Americans, the Provincial Grand Master, who favored the English side, fled to Canada, taking with him his letters
patent. Had he turned these over to his Deputy, the history of Masonry in New York State may have been very different. Now, the
majority of the English Regimental Lodges on American soil had
been warranted by the Duke of Athol, and these gained the upper
hand in the ensuing years until, in the fall of 1782, a Charter authoriz-
ing the creation of an Antient or Athol Provincial Grand Lodge was
received from England. Remember that New York City remained in
English hands until November 25th, 1783. I recall this document being proudly exhibited in our Masonic Library until a few years ago.
At the secession of New York, those remaining Englishmen who
served in Grand Lodge resigned and took affectionate leave of their
fellows. The Provincial Grand Lodge became, de facto, the Grand
Lodge of New York State. On February 4th, 1784, Hon. Robert R.
Livingston, Chancellor (and future Governor) of the State of New
York was nominated Grand Master. Despite being faced with a variety of unaffiliated Lodges, Lodges under Athol warrant and Lodges –
including St. John's and Royal Arch – under Moderns Charters, the
dissent between Antients and Moderns was not as fierce as in England, and St. John's and Royal Arch duly surrendered their Charters
and received new ones. I do not wish to imply that the birth of the
Grand Lodge of New York was painless, though it was certainly less
painful than that of the United Grand Lodge of England and Wales!

In England the twenty-one Articles of Union would be signed in
1813, creating the United Grand Lodge of England and ending a
sixty-year feud. This of course meant nothing to the State of New
York, which had founded its ritual and structure on the body under
whose Charter they had operated – that of the Athol, or Antient Masons. Now we see England and New York pursuing two different
courses, and that is why the rituals differ. We have covered some
Masonic history, and also met a few Famous Dead Masons, as promised. Now let us focus on some of those differences in ritual.

II. Examples of Differences

Let us now transport ourselves back to the early seventeen hundreds in London, England, and look in on a Lodge meeting, when Lodges met privately in the upstairs rooms of the ale-houses, before Grand Lodges and schisms. I am indebted to Pick & Knight's Pocket *History of Freemasonry* for an imaginative description, from which this is taken:

"The Lodge would be graced with an oblong-square table down the center. Shortly before the opening of Lodge two Brethren enter and unlock the Lodge box with two, sometimes three, keys. They take out the properties and place them on the table around which the working is to be done; these include a tinder box for striking a flame to light the candles. They also see that the punch bowl and firing glasses are properly arranged, together with the long clay church-warden pipes, for throughout this century Lodge work was accompanied by smoking and drinking. They would also put out the chamber pots and spittoons in the corner of the room, for the door would be locked and much drink consumed.

"The Brethren do not enter in procession but just stroll in (*aside*: note, that in England Masons now process in and out of the Lodge in reverse order of seniority, standing in two lines to welcome the Master with rhythmic applause), habited in their white aprons. When the Master enters, the members take their seats after he is seated. The Master takes off his hat on declaring the Lodge open and the other Brethren follow suit, but do not replace their hats as the Master does his (*aside*: nowadays nobody, even the Master, wears a hat).

"The Master and Wardens then chalk the 'Lodge' on the floor according to which ceremony is to be performed, filling in the outline with a few simple figures, such as two pillars, square, level, plumb rule and the letter "G" (the last being introduced after 1730; it then signified "geometry"). Later in the century the Tyler was paid to 'draw the Lodge' – the precursor of the Tracing Board. When a Candidate has been initiated he has to take mop and pail and wash out the drawing before taking his seat.

"A lecture (in the form of a catechism) is then worked, the Master asking the questions of the members in turn. When it is concluded, there is a very simple closing – the Master giving his command and the Senior Warden saying, 'It is our Master's will and pleasure that this Lodge stand closed.'

What an evocative picture! While much is common to both Antient and the Antient-Modern hybrid which is English Masonry, let us examine a few instances where the differences are clear.

3. Membership

We should remember that, initially, the Entered Apprentice Degree was sufficient to make you a full member of a Lodge, with voting rights and the ability to attend all meetings, save those in which the Fellowcraft or Master Mason Degree were being conferred. This was the same in the Colonies as well. So why are only Master Masons permitted to attend business meetings and vote, given that an Entered Apprentice can attend and vote in just about every other jurisdiction in the world? The main reason was exposés! Almost as soon as modern Masonry came into existence there were account written in books and newspapers claiming to divulge what went on in the tiled Lodge room. Many were little more than the fevered imagination of the author; others were downright salacious, no doubt with the intent of selling more copies. Still others were remarkably accurate, and are even used by scholars to get a good idea of what went on at meetings in those days.

There was clearly a need to find a better way to prevent cowans and eavesdroppers, and, worse, unfriendly authors from gaining admittance.

In Britain and France, the main approach was to reverse the passwords of the first two degrees, and in some jurisdictions to change some of the password altogether. However, in the United States, a different tack was taken. Following the damage done by the Morgan Affair and the subsequent anti-Masonic backlash, at the Masonic Conference held in Baltimore of May 8, 1843, with representative from 14 jurisdictions then in existence, attempts were made to harmonize the Ceremonies across the States and bring about greater cohesion among the Grand Lodges. While this was not particularly successful, one of the proposals was: "The Committee considers it an 'impropriety' to transact 'business in Lodges below the Degree of Master Mason, except as such that appertains to the conferring of the lower Degrees and the instruction therein.'" The rationale behind this was to prevent anyone who had not been proven a loyal member from gaining access to the inner workings of the Lodge, its finances, politics and business. While most Grand Lodges still conducted business on the First Degree, as they began to adopt the recommendations of the so-called Baltimore Convention, the Grand Lodges fell in line with this recommendation, which the majority of Grand Lodges follow to this day.

4. The Lodge Room

As the Lodges started to meet in places set aside for their exclusive use, the need to 'draw the Lodge' was replaced by an industry which grew up around the provision of Lodge furniture. Even Lodges who meet in multipurpose rooms, such as community centers, will more likely have a room full of Masonic furniture than a small Masonic box. The first thing most people notice is the mosaic floor of alternating black and white squares. This arose from the early printed and illustrated bibles of the sixteenth century, which depicted both the Temple and King Solomon's palace with these checkered floors. Of course, illustrations were in black and white in those days: who knows what colors the illustrator of the Geneva Bible had in mind for these floors! Once the furniture became permanent the same design was woven into the carpets. In English Lodge rooms the carpet expands almost to the seats, leaving a thin passageway for the Candidate to be led around the room before taking his Obligation, and only after this voluntary act does he symbolically step onto the hallowed ground of the carpeting. This feat is considerably easier in our Lodges, as the checkered portion is reduced to a small area in the center.

An interesting feature of the larger carpets are the four tassels woven into the corners, delimiting the corners of the sacred space. These are thought to derive from the skirret lines which were tied to corner stakes, indicating the limits of the future building, and which marked out the straight edges along which the brick or stonework was to be laid.

Similarly, the dining table of old became the Altar, while in the English tradition it ended up as a pedestal in front of the Master, for with the removal of the dining table as part of the Act of Union in 1813, in which incidentally the practice of eating and holding ceremonies at the same time was forbidden, it was recognized that the Master, Wardens, Secretary and Treasurer still needed places to put their papers. In either case, the fixed lights are universal, the Holy Bible representing the Divine Word, the Square the Great Architect, and the Compasses His created Universe.

5. The Three Lesser Lights

On being brought to Light we behold the three lesser lights representing the Sun, Moon and Master of the Lodge. In our Lodge Rooms the three lesser lights stand in a triangular shape about the central altar. However, in English Masonry they have been moved, along with the Tracing Board, Working Tools and Altar (which becomes the Master's Pedestal). The Preceptor found these items tended to get in the way, and so they were sidelined – in the case of the three lesser lights to stand beside the Master and Wardens.

If you visit Independent Royal Arch Lodge you will also find another tradition from across the pond – that of the Columns on the Wardens' pedestals. These are smaller representations of the two larger columns between which you pass when entering the Lodge through the Inner Door. As the Junior Warden rules the hours of refreshment and the Senior Warden the hours of work in the quarry, so when the Lodge is at work the Senior Warden's column is in the vertical positions while the Junior Warden's lies flat; and vice versa when at refreshment. There is much esoteric symbolism in placing the Candidate between the two pillars, but as I must limit myself to matters an Entered Apprentice may hear, I will save that for a later talk.

6. The Apron

One of the reasons the Antient model survived in the New World was its insistence on the egalitarian nature of Masonry. As Ossian Lang, the notable New York Masonic historian, states: "their principal merit was that they kept close to the humanity of the Craft and saved Masonry from becoming an aristocratic institution, or a fraternity of snobs." The same, sadly, cannot be said of English Masonry, where the tintinnabulation of the many jewels can sometimes be deafening! While we have Grand Honors, in England there are variations of salute for every level of vanity, from the Provincial Officer to the Grand Master, and which also differ depending upon the Degree the Lodge is working at the time. Yet this is not a criticism of the country which gave us the most impressive pageantry the world perhaps has even known, and the close association of British Freemasonry with the British Empire well explains the carry-over of pomp and circumstance into its Lodges. By the time an English Mason receives his third Degree he is resplendent in an apron which bears little resemblance to the original plain, simple lambskin worn in the past, as can be seen by the splendid examples worn in this Lodge in honor of its colonial roots. This elaborate garb is replete with symbolism of its own – the rosettes incidentally are formalized buttonholes, the top one indicating the manner in which the Entered Apprentice should wear his apron, with the flap up as the new operative Mason was more likely to make errors and soil his clothing with mortar and flying shards.

In England a Mason owns his apron and carries it in a distinctively deep briefcase to all Masonic meetings. The elegant simplicity of the white apron, and the fact that these are freely available to members and visitors alike at the door of any New York Lodge, is a legacy of the Antients, who wished to preserve this egalitarian custom.

However, I recently learned from Bro. Patrick Craddock, that excellent purveyor of bespoke and exquisite aprons, that the real reason we now wear these simple aprons was in fact due to the Great Depression, prior to which most made up their own designs and had all kinds of elaborate aprons made. In an effort to keep their businesses open, and in order to save the Craft from severely depleted membership, and realizing that Masons had been hit as hard as everyone else by the downturn in the economy, making it hard to pay dues and even to purchase aprons, Masonic supply companies offered Lodges boxes of white aprons made of the cheapest stuff possible, so that they would both the affordable, and kept outside the Lodge for any Brother who couldn't afford his own apron to be able to attend Lodge. Sadly, by the time the economy turned upwards once more, this was the only thing most Masons remembered, and to this day, we still put on old, grubby off-white pieces of 'stuff' in order to attend Lodge (as a re-minder to Lodges, *please* wash your visitors' aprons at least once a year)!

7. The Due Guard and the Steps

In England there is no Due Guard, but there are a series of elabo-rate steps taken to reach the Master's Pedestal in each Degree. In America there are no special steps beyond the act of moving towards the Sacred Altar of Freemasonry, as the Candidate, having affirmed his faith in God, takes a bold, regular step towards his God in order to take upon himself that most sacred and binding Obligation. In Eng-land's First Degree, this is achieved through three steps. Let us remember that the Latin for step is 'gradus' or grade; also 'degree'. The three steps differ from one another (demonstrated). Apart from the significance of the number 'three', we can also note that the steps are of varied and therefore irregular length. Only after the Candidate has taken upon himself the Obligation can he be taught the true square step of the regular and accepted Mason.

The English Candidate kneels before the Master's pedestal, and is placed in a position which is particularly disconcerting. Believe me when I say that this position is far more uncomfortable than our Due Guard!

I can find no explanation as to this difference between the two rit-uals. The penal sign of the First Degree is similar in both countries, so I can only offer my theory, and would welcome feedback. If you remember I said earlier that one of the reasons the Antients split from the Moderns was over the reversal of the signs of the First and Second Degrees. As the Antients were effectively reabsorbed back into the Moderns some sixty years later, one may conjecture that the 're-versed' signs ended up being retained. If we substitute the Due Guard of the First and Second Degrees we have an interesting progression, in which, if you think about it, we become increasingly intimate with the Sacred Word. We progress from one hand, through one hand on the text and one on the back binder, to... and so forth.

8. The Missing Officer

The final difference I want to mention it that of the missing Officer. In the ritual finally agreed in the Act of Union, there are not five but six Officers, excluding the Tyler. Given our interest in the number seven this makes sense. Remembering that there is but a single means of entry to an English Lodge, and not two (the Inner and Outer doors of our tradition), the duties of the Junior Deacon are limited to conveying messages between the Senior and Junior Warden, leading the Candidates in the First Degree and assisting in the Second and Third Degrees, while the task of guarding the inside of the door is given to the Inner Guard who, armed with the appropriate implement to the Degree, challenges the Candidate upon entry. This newest position was ratified in the Act of union of 1813 – some years after New York had removed itself from English rule.

Note that the Charge of the English Ritual contains this phrase: "Monarchs themselves have been promoters of the art; have not thought it derogatory to their dignity to exchange the scepter for the trowel…". This refers to the old custom of the newest Entered Apprentice Mason to be charged with guarding the door armed with a trowel or sword. For remember another signal difference: all meetings in England are held on the First Degree, and all Entered Apprentices are considered full members of their Lodge. As we learned earlier, in most American Lodges the fact that the meetings are held on the Third Degree was in answer to a peculiarly American problem.

9. The Significance of Symbols

Time prevents me from a detailed analysis of all the symbols both unique and common in the rituals. However, those of you who know me well know it is a mission of mine to get people reading and thinking about these symbols.

I lie – I am not limiting myself because of time, but because I do not intend to deny you the sheer pleasure of discovery in working out for yourselves your own understanding of the lessons contained in our wonderful rituals, and the pleasure of exploring the insights of other eminent writers in this field. You have the pieces of the jigsaw. They will describe the picture on the box. But only by assembling the pieces yourself can you experience that joy of completion. For now, I will content myself with the cabletow, a common enough piece of Lodge Room equipment.

The cabletow is placed about the candidate's neck prior to entering the Lodge for the first time. Following the Obligation, it is removed. I will not say more in a public book: Masons will be able to remember the working and explanation of this symbol in their own ritual. When it is finally removed, in most rituals we are told we are now bound by a stronger tie, which is of course the 'Mystic Tie'.

But what does this mean? The cabletow represents the umbilical cord, or the tie which binds us to the material world of earthly pleasures and idle distractions. By entering the Lodge and voluntarily undertaking, like the Knights of old, a binding Obligation to learn and keep the arcane secrets of this Degree, we renounce worldly things and dedicate our lives to the pursuit of such knowledge as will benefit and improve ourselves (the First Degree), mankind (the Second Degree) and help us to know God (the Sublime Degree).

The cabletow is removed and its rough, vegetable fibers replaced with a living cabletow – the Master's hand as he seals the initiatic succession with the handshake of welcome and gives the grip in order to communicate the secrets of the Degree.

10. Afterword

I cannot decide which is the more enjoyable – to take part in the ritual or to write a paper. They both offer so much. By learning a part by heart you move the words to the mouth, and allow the mind to rise above the verbal formulae and recognize the message buried within the phrase, which then speaks to the soul. By preparing for a talk you have an opportunity to read and improve your knowledge of a particular area of Masonry, and you can be sure to find a precious jewel of learning which you did not know existed before.

My Brothers, and especially the newer members: learn the ritual and study your Craft. Your enjoyment of this unique organization will be repaid a thousandfold!

THE ORIGINS OF FREEMASONRY: UK TO US

OR THE FOUNDING OF THE PREMIER GRAND LODGE OF ENGLAND, SOME RIVALS, AND THE ARRIVAL OF FREEMASONRY IN THE AMERICAN COLONIES

NOTE*: This talk was given at the Annual Communication of the Grand Lodge of Nebraska, as the first of a series of talks tracing the origins of Freemasonry, its exportation to the colonies, and its spread across the United States until the Grand Lodge of Nebraska was formed. I was invited to give the first talk. Given its common roots I have put it next to the previous paper.*

1. Introduction & Welcome

Brethren, welcome to the first in a continuing series of talks on the founding of Freemasonry and its expansion from the United Kingdom to the American Colonies, its own 'Declarations of Independence' from its founders, and its spread across the United States, as those intrepid explorers and pioneers struck out for pastures new across this vast land.

This paper does not intend to set out a brand new academic theory: rather, it takes its ideas from a number of books and papers, and attempts to assemble them in a coherent and understandable manner. Because of this, I have not cited specific passages in this paper (in the original delivery I provided a list of sources and a Bibliography for those interested in reading further). The good news is, instead of sucking the life out of this Workshop by presenting you with a list of dates and cold, dry facts, I will instead try to give you the Masonic equivalent of an early opera or oratorio: I will use the recitative to push us forward through the factual parts, then linger like an aria on interesting and anecdotal stories which emphasize a particular event or key part of history.

That said, I intend to put forward a theory about the practical founding of the Craft in England, and by this I mean how the organization might have got started, rather than the origins of its teachings and rituals. I am surprised nobody has put this series of facts together before, since the building blocks are all out there. I hope you find it interesting.

I will limit myself to England – the topic is vast enough as it is – and a few anecdotes about the early days of Freemasonry in what were then Crown Colonies. Next year you will hear about the founding of the first Grand Lodges in the United States, and since that will be the end point for 2014, I must allow my successor to speak of how Lodges organized in the first place, from whence they derived their Charters, and what steps they took to secede from the Premier Grand Lodge of England, The Grand Lodge of the Most Ancient and Honourable Fraternity of Free and Accepted Masons, the Grand Lodge of Ireland and the Grand Lodge of Antient, Free and Accepted Masons of Scotland. I will assume some knowledge of Masonic history, and we can fill in any gaps during the Workshop moments. Basic history you can read: it is the debate and the theory which makes this kind of event meaningful.

I invite questions at any time during this talk, but I neither promise to know the answers, nor the ability to quote precise dates and names from memory: I am a devotee of Masonic history but I am not a computer! Since this is a Workshop, that means you have to work just as hard as me, so if any of you know the answer to another Brother's question, please feel free to shout it out. A Workshop is meant to be, after all, a moderated exchange of ideas, rather than a talking head and a passive audience!

I would also like to thank my host, the M.W. Rex Moats, for inviting me to your Annual Communication to share some of my thoughts with you at the first of this inspired series of Lectures. These, I am confident, will renew your interest in your State's history, and in the extraordinary and exciting Masonic timeline of which you are all a part.

2. Fact versus Fiction – Some Caveats

When I talk in some locations, I have to remind the audience that an enormous amount has been written about Freemasonry. This may seem odd for a group who lives so close to the world-famous Iowa

Masonic Library & Museum, and indeed I am fortunate to have access to the Livingston Masonic Library in New York. But for those who do not, often the only access they had was through bookstores which, if they stocked anything, were invariably limited to books about 'Our Glorious History', 'Famous Dead People', or 'Our Mysterious Origins'. Books with these titles inevitably tend to be quite free and casual with the facts, leaving our Brethren either wildly misinformed, or, worse, providing our detractors with a host of incorrect details with which to attack us. Indeed, the problem has worsened considerably with the advent of the Internet.

Another unfortunate consequence of such claims as: "so many signers of the Declaration were Freemasons that they could have held a Lodge Meeting", or "Freemasons were directly responsible for the American Revolution", is that serious historians have avoided studying the role of Freemasonry in the development of the United States, both because they (rightly) see that many of our so-called history books contain poorly researched details or outright fantasies; and because they don't want to associate their hard-earned reputations with what they perceive to be a poorly-perceived organization. Perhaps the two Masons who did the most to create a sense of pride in our Fraternity, while making it a poison pill to any serious historian, were Doctor Anderson and Chevalier Ramsay. Dr. Anderson was responsible for composing the Constitutions of the Grand Lodge of England, and in his first edition of 1723 traced our origins back to Adam himself! His second edition of 1738 contained a list of previous Grand Masters, including Moses, Nebuchadnezzar, Alfred the Great, Cardinal Wolsey, and Sir Christopher Wren. In 1734, Benjamin Franklin reprinted the 1723 Constitutions of Dr. Andersen in Philadelphia, and so the myths of our origins were preserved in the New World. Similarly, Chevalier Ramsay's great Oration of 1737, which tried to link Freemasonry to the Knights of St. John of Jerusalem (not to the Knights Templar, as is sometimes claimed), enhanced our self-image, but did nothing for our reputation among historians.

Both claims were classic manifestations of the Age of Enlightenment. The leaders of that time seemed to straddle two worlds. We know that Sir Isaac Newton, in addition to his theories on Gravity and his profound monograph *Philosophiæ Naturalis Principia Mathematica*, spent as much time absorbed in alchemy and a lifelong study of the potential codes hidden in the biblical description of King Solomon's Temple. It was traditional at that time, when establishing a new society, to claim it had descended from ancient roots. We must also remember that at least the speculative branch of Freemasonry was attractive to men of fashion and quality, and it is hardly surprising, therefore, to find that alongside the traditional claims of a descent from operative Masonic sheds and lodges, there were more exotic claims to descent from mysterious organizations which were long dead and who therefore couldn't disagree, such as the Crusading Knights, the mysterious Rosicrucians, and the Ancient Egyptian, Roman and Greek mystery cults.

From the earliest days, Freemasonry was associated with religious free thought, and even Deism. The First Charge of Dr. Andersen's Constitutions of 1723, states: "'tis now thought more expedient only to oblige them to that Religion to which all men agree, leaving their particular opinions to themselves." It is now known that in 1721 two members of the Jewish faith, Nathan Blanch and John Hart were admitted into the Lodge of Antiquity, then No.1, and it is likely Dr. Andersen included this phrase so as to give them retrospective coverage. These were the early years of emancipation from the clutches of the church. We should remember that both Protestants and Catholics had suffered from extreme forms of persecution – as well as the wars fought regularly across Europe in the name of religion. Edward Wightman had been burned at the stake in Lichfield, England for heresy in 1612, and of course the beheading of King Charles I in 1649 was seen as much a religious execution as a political one. The Catholic Church had its Inquisition (the last recorded death was that of Cayetano Ripoll, a teacher who was garroted as late as 1826 for allegedly teaching Deist principles!). If we put these dates in the context of English Freemasonry, King Charles was executed only 68 years prior to the founding of Grand Lodge. To put that in perspective, that's like us looking back to 1945. The Second World War is still a living and painful memory to many. Ripoll's death by strangulation for teaching Deism took place 109 years after the founding of Grand Lodge. Something to think about!

Another problem we face is that, in the absence of facts, it is all too easy to project our own wishes and simply fill the gaps with our own inventions. It is a simple fact that the records documenting early

Freemasonry, both in England and here, are almost non-existent.
Sure, we have occasional letters and charters, a few references in local
newspapers or broadsheets, and the sporadic exposés: but that is about
it. On the other side, Lodge minutes, where they exist from that time,
are concerned with the minutiae of the Lodge, and not the great historical events of the day. So there is no two-way flow of information
allowing us to link ourselves directly to key moments in history. Indeed, even the Grand Lodge of England didn't start keeping minutes
until 1723, with the appointment of William Cowper, some 6 years after its foundation!

And so the academic historians have given us a wide berth. I
think that is a great pity. If we could set aside our sometimes outrageous claims about our roots and our overblown role in overt history,
I think there is a very powerful story to be told about our covert role
in that history. We may not have sparked the Revolution; but we
made it possible. A CBS reporter recently asked an academic historian about her opinion of Freemasonry. Her response was interesting.
She said, to paraphrase, that there were three powerful influences on
pre-Revolutionary society in the Colonies: there was the Church,
there were the Politicians, but apart from these, Freemasonry was really the 'only game in town'. This was the only organization apart
from attending church, where men could get together to talk about
politics and the key subjects of the day, rub shoulders – as equals –
with the most influential people in their town or village, and learn a
system of morality and thinking which would profoundly affect the
way they saw the world. One academic, Professor Steven Bullock,
had begun to redress this imbalance by writing specifically about the
social effects of Freemasonry before and during the formative years
of this country. But his last book on this subject was published 18
years ago, and there has not been an avalanche of other respected academics following his lead. I sincerely hope that this will now begin to
change.

For now, I will put forward a theory of mine regarding our origins, touch briefly on some English history which impacts the
development of Masonry in this country, and end with an anecdote of
Masonic life in this country around the time of the War of Independence.

3.   The Practical Origins of Freemasonry

I think we can live with a compromise solution to our roots. We have little documentary evidence, but that hasn't stopped worthy – and occasionally scurrilous – authors from suggesting a descent from Operative Masons, Scottish Lodges, the Knights Templar, the Mystery Plays, the Rosicrucians, the early Mystery Schools, or all of the above! Personally, I think the answer is much simpler. Freemasonry was modeled on a romantic idea of the builders who erected the great cathedrals and castles, and this vehicle allowed them to include anything and everything which took their magpie fancy. The great libraries gave the literate access to the ancient religions, cults, sects and the teachings of their mystery schools, and all this was grist to the mill for the great men who sat on the cusp of the old world of alchemy and religion, and finally had the religious freedom to study previously hard to find or even forbidden texts, such as the Kabbalah and the theurgical works of Paracelsus; yet in this Age of Enlightenment wished to pursue true science, and learn what made everything tick. The speed at which religious tolerance gained ground in this country, for example, can be seen in the fact that, in Massachusetts, the Salem Witch Trials took place in 1692, yet by 1733, Henry Price possessed a Warrant to establish Lodges – only 41 years later.

In 2004 the Prestonian Lecturer, Bro. Trevor Stewart, visited St. John's Lodge No. 1 in New York to give the Prestonian Lecture, perhaps the most prestigious lecture in all Freemasonry. In this well-researched and very insightful paper, which attempted to identify the sources of the themes, rituals and early development of Freemasonry, it was actually an aside which particularly caught my attention. He mentioned there were minutes indicating that some members of an early Lodge were sufficiently interested in the new sciences to arrange for a doctor to dissect a cadaver in their presence; and that a party also attended an execution by firing squad to try to answer the question: did a person being shot hear the sound of the bullet which killed him?

So here we had men who were well-steeped in the Classics, many of whom would have received the traditional education of the Seven Liberal Arts and Science at University, who harked back wistfully to a magical time when alchemy and superstition held sway, and yet who were fascinated by the progress science was making in a world freed from the edicts and strictures of formal religious control. But for me the key question is not so much what they learned, as how they got together in the first place! We know that by 1717 there were at least four Lodges, made up of the mixture of operative and speculative Masons, and that, within a couple of years, they had royal patronage, and the upper middle and ruling classes flocking to join them. Other than patting ourselves on the head for finding vague references to operative Lodges in Scotland a Century earlier (with no real indication of what they did), and the now infamous 'I was made a Freemason' diary entry by Elias Ashmole in 1646, none of this really tells us how we got from one man being made a Freemason to a group of men running four Lodges in London, in which membership was sought and valued by everybody who was anybody!

It was a chance comment in Pick and Knight's book, The Pocket History of Freemasonry, which really got me thinking about this. And this hinges not, as so many researchers have done in the past, on Sir Isaac Newton, but rather on Sir Christopher Wren, despite a common perception that he was never a member of a Lodge. Born in 1632, becoming a Professor of Astronomy in 1657 and of Mathematics in 1661 (hardly surprising, given that universities, as mentioned above, taught the Seven Liberal Arts and Sciences in the trivium and quadrivium syllabi), after the Great Fire of London in 1666 he was entrusted with the reconstruction of the city of London. Remember that most of London was built of wood, and that the Great Plague of 1665, when the bubonic plague primarily affected London, so vividly recorded by Samuel Pepys in his famous Diary. King Charles II, his Royal Court, and most of the aristocracy, wealthy merchants and professionals fled to the countryside, leaving the plague to be endured by the poor and those few noble aldermen, including the Mayor of London, who elected to stay to run the city.

The Great Fire of London started in Pudding Lane, allegedly in the baker shop of Charles Farynor, baker to King Charles II. While it had the benefit of virtually eliminating the plague which had begun the previous year, with minimal loss of life (some accounts say as few as 16 perished) the wood and pitch houses were devastated, and central London was flattened. Sir Christopher Wren was tasked by

Charles II with rebuilding some 50 churches, including St. Paul's Cathedral, which began in 1675.

Now, Pick and Knight mention, almost casually (on page 66) that "An Act of Parliament was passed encouraging all manner of building trade workers to settle in the city of London and promising their freedom on the completion of seven years' residence and work there. At the same time, King Charles II exercised his influence with the corporations of other towns for the rehabilitation of those who had lost their homes and businesses in the fire.

"The move brought hundreds of masons flocking into the city. We have no records of their organization but operative masonry must have been given an enormous impetus and, following the tendency of the time, 'accepted' masons were no doubt admitted into the lodges."

No doubt, too, those masons who had served their 7 years were now Freemen of the city of London, and likely called free-masons as opposed to indentured, or entered Apprentices.

If we add to this the fact that all the aristocrats and wealthy businessmen would have been moving back from their country estates into a flattened city following the fire. They would have been far less likely to have lost their London residences, since they had almost assuredly been built with stone rather than wood. So we find London a melting pot of practical industry and educated observers, mixing cheek by jowl. The town was awash with masons rebuilding the churches and those parts of the new city that were not simply being replaced with more wooden structures; and the wealthy and intelligent would have been fascinated by all this work going on all around them. Whether or not Dr. Andersen was fabricating history when he claimed Sir Christopher Wren as a Grand Master of Masons, we find an account by Sir Christopher Wren's son, of his father's building of the great Cathedral of St. Paul, which states: "The highest or last Stone on the top of the Lantern, was laid by the Hands of the Surveyor's Son, Christopher Wren, deputed by his Father, in the Presence of that excellent Artificer Mr. Strong, his son, and other free and Accepted Masons, chiefly employed in the Execution of the work." The Cathedral was completed in 1711. Further, one of the four Lodges which formed the Grand Lodge in 1717, six years later, was the Lodge "that met at the goose and Gridiron Ale-house in St. Paul's Church Yard." In a very brief paper written for the Ars Quatuor Coronati in 1996,

Bros. Williamson and Baigent cite a manuscript classified as MS Aubrey I and MS Aubrey II, in which appears in the margin, in John Aubrey's hand: "This day (May 1691 the 18th being Monday after Rogation Sunday) is a great convention at St. Paul's church of the Fraternity of the Accepted-Masons [the word Free had been written but was struck out] where Sr. Christopher Wren is to be adopted a Brother..." Now, in my opinion it would make sense for the word 'Free' to be struck out and substituted by the more specific word 'Accepted', since as I pointed out above, a free-mason at the time may simply have referred to any operative mason who had served his 7 years. Now John Aubrey, a famous English Naturalist, was one of the founders of the Royal Society, and as such not given to fantasy. The researchers, despite certain scholars arguing the possibility that Wren didn't attend the initiation, point to the fact that the Clerk to the Royal Society copied this document, including the margin note, after the date of Wren's initiation, they suggest that both Aubrey, Cramer, Wren himself and the Royal Society in general had agreed with this addendum to the original script, and therefore it was a truthful statement.

The rest is so well documented I can do little more than repeat the highlights here. In 1717 four pre-existing Lodges including the Lodge associated with St. Paul's Cathedral, which apparently still 'met in St. Paul's churchyard' (for what operative purpose if the Cathedral had been completed 6 years earlier?), came together to form a Grand Lodge, exercising control over quarterly meetings and occasional banquets. Within a very short time they had grown to a number of Lodges, attracted a member of the Royal family to be their Grand Master, attracted a multitude of wealthy and influential men to their ranks, and had expanded their purview into exercising the right to issue warrants and determine the existence of future Lodges. Within a few years their powers were codified by Dr. Andersen into a set of Constitutions, and the Mother Grand Lodge was well established.

One minor note: a number of people have suggested the mysterious appearance of four existing Lodges in the public arena in 1717 to form a Grand Lodge and attract the patronage of the house of Hanover was at least in part due to the fact that Freemasonry was seen by King George I as closely associated with the House of Stuart, and therefore not necessarily loyal to the new Crown. The Civil War had only ended in 1651, within some people's living memory; and the Jacobite Rebellion of 1715, when the Old Pretender, or James Edward, son of former King James II attempted to overthrow King George I, was only two years past. Further, Sir Christopher Wren, having been appointed to his position by King Charles II, was hardly a favorite of King George I. Fortunately, the House of Stuart had not yet got into the business of issuing Masonic Charters to all and sundry in France. Nevertheless, it is probably that the leaders felt that Freemasonry had to reinvent itself as a new organization, loyal to the Hanoverian rulers. How better than to begin again, with the formation of a body which, within a few years, could count a Hanoverian Prince as its head? Indeed, by his second edition for the Constitutions, Dr. Andersen was confident enough to include Sir Christopher Wren as a former Grand Master (no doubt under the Stuart throne), without fearing censure from the King.

Recently, popular theories have sought to link Sir Isaac Newton, and more generally, the Royal Society, to the founding of Speculative Masonry. Both may be true in part. However, I personally believe that Newton's obsession with the sacred geometry of Solomon's Temple, which some have cited as a link to our Craft, was in fact just that – a personal obsession. In this he may have been influenced by Villelpando's book, *Ezechielem Explanationes*, a popular book which had been published a couple of decades earlier, and which contained his thoughts of Ezekiel's vision and his elaborate reconstructions of Solomon's Temple. Incidentally, noting that a commonly accepted time for the first appearance of the Third Degree was around 1730 (for at the time of the Grand Lodge of 1717, only two Degrees were worked), one can perhaps attempt to seek a catalyst for its invention. As Masons we know the first two Degrees reference the Temple in a somewhat abstract sense; and it is only in the Third Degree that the building really becomes a three-dimensional reality, especially in the Hiramic Legend. According to an interesting article in Wikipedia, titled Isaac Newton's occult studies, "Around 1692, Gerhard Schott produced a highly detailed model of the temple for use in an opera in Hamburg composed by Christian Heinrich Postel. This immense 13-foot-high (4.0 m) and 80-foot-around (24 m) model was later sold in 1725 and was exhibited in London as early as 1723, and then later temporarily installed at the London Royal Exchange from 1729–1730, where it could be viewed for half-a-crown." Given the proximity of the presentation of this enormous model of Solomon's Temple in central London exactly prior to the alleged appearance of the Third Degree, might we be tempted to ponder the possibility of a connection between the two? This can only be conjecture, since we neither have documentary proof, nor could we know if the appearance of this possible catalyst inspired the Degree or reawakened previous memories of a ritual associated with it. Still, it is a most interesting coincidence.

As for Freemasonry being founded by the Royal Society, it is certainly possible, but not very likely. It reminds me of mathematical Set Theory in a way. I may be a Mason, and I may be a golfer; but the chances of a group of Masons coming together to buy a golf club are remote. I may have a group of Masons who are fond of golf, and we play golf in clubs. But would I really go to the lengths of founding a very expensive golf club, employ staff, professional golfers, just to have only my Masonic friends join? Similarly, I can see how there may be a high intersection of members who belong both to the Royal Society, which is focused on the latest science and technology, and also to a Masonic Lodge, where they can debate more liberal arts, and indulge in pleasant communication among friends of a more esoteric bent. But neither would be required to create and maintain the other. Naturally there would be overlap, at least in one direction. I would probably talk about Masonic topics while playing a round of golf (but probably wouldn't bore everyone with golfing stories in Lodge). Similarly, as we learned from Worshipful Bro. Trevor Stewart, the Masons who went to watch the firing squad may well have included a number of members of the Royal Society, for whom the speed of sound was of interest; on the other hand, it is rather less likely that those same members would have discussed the finer points of spiritual alchemy in a Royal Society presentation!

4. Rival Grand Lodges, and the 'York Rite' Myth

Life for the Grand Lodge of England did not progress smoothly for long. As with any club which is perceived to be exclusive, it attracted ridicule, for it is human nature to belittle and ridicule anyone or anything one doesn't understand, as we can see in any school playground. Then came the purported exposés, as some managed to penetrate its meetings and leaked what they find out for reasons of personal vengeance or financial gain. Finally, in this inevitable pattern, we saw the act of emulation, as those excluded from the club set up rival organizations and fraternities.

One example of this was the Gormogons, which appeared in 1724, only 7 years following the public announcement of the founding of Grand Lodge. Hogarth's satirical print The Mystery of Masonry Brought to Light by the Gormogons tells us both how well-known Freemasonry had become at that time, and also just how absurd the public processions in workmen's attire through the streets of London by the overfed gentry must have looked to real operative Masons and the working classes. No wonder public processions were banned a short time later!

However, spoof and satire soon gave way to a far more dangerous threat – a rival organization. Already by 1723 the Grand Lodge was issuing Warrants to Lodges in the greater London area; and by 1732 there were 102 Lodges listed as being under its authority. Remember however that English Lodges have never been large, like their American counterparts: the average membership is around 30, with a Lodge of larger size splitting into two, in order to allow the new members to go through the Master's Chair, which it is assumed all Masons will do. As Freemasonry grew in strength, the exposés gave rise to a new problem: it was becoming easy for any non-Mason to gain admission to a Masonic meeting, since he now knew the tokens of entrance. In order to try to suppress this problem, in 1739 the passwords of the first two Degrees were transposed. This appears to have been the final straw for a number of Masons, who were becoming increasingly concerned by the apparent relaxation of standards under the stewardship of the Grand Lodge. Eventually, in 1751, possibly the result of years of planning, a rival Grand Lodge was launched, The Grand Lodge of the Most Ancient and Honourable Fraternity of Free and Accepted Masons, and in 1753 it selected its first Grand Master: Robert Turner. What brought about this rival to the authority of what would in time be called the Premier Grand Lodge? Sadly, since part of the marketing campaign of this new Grand Lodge was to call itself the 'Antient' Grand Lodge as opposed to the 'Modern' Grand Lodge, which is disparagingly called the one founded in 1717, it could hardly draw attention to its 'newness' by listing the reasons it had seceded from the Premier Grand Lodge. Therefore, we can to some extent only surmise what caused this rift.

The transposition of modes of recognition was obviously one, but, like the schism of the Catholic and Orthodox Churches in 1054, clearly the difference ran far deeper than two dimensional icons and the filioque clause! Some theories have pointed at such concerns as the admission of non-Christians, neglecting the Feast-days of St. John, removing the esoteric ritual part of the Master's Installation, and most definitely a sense that Lodges were becoming lax in their practices, preferring the social and festive side to ritual and education – a problem which has never gone away, I might add. There were other, ritualistic differences, which may in part point to earlier practices, since it would seem absurd that the Antients would claim to go back to the roots of Masonry yet invent brand new Offices and rituals. Some examples include the fact that the 'Antients' had Deacons, while the 'Moderns' did not. Previously their functions had been taken by Stewards under the Grand Lodge of 1717. Now this may come from Ireland, since Lawrence Dermott, the second Grand Secretary of the Antients and composer of the famous Ahiman Rezon (1761), the Constitutions of the Antient Grand Lodge, had been initiated in Ireland in 1740, where Deacons were used. Indeed, as we shall see later, the very issue of Irishness may have been another big contributing factor to the schism with the Moderns. Other differences included the fact that that they had different passwords for the Third Degree (which is why we now give both in the Third Degree in many States, as a nod to the later United Grand Lodge which adopted both, notwithstanding the fact that the earliest Grand Lodges in the United States self-chartered after secession from England long before the Act of Union in 1813; and the seating of the Wardens and the placing of the Three Great Lights.

Unlike Rome and Constantinople, however, these rival Grand Lodges did not control separate jurisdictions, but rather claimed authority over England and Wales concurrently. This uncomfortable situation lasted for 62 years, despite a number of attempts at reconciliation, and it was only when two brothers of the royal blood sat as

Grand Masters of each in 1813, the Duke of Sussex presiding over the 'Moderns', and the Duke of Kent over the 'Antients'. In this same year the 21 Articles of Union were signed and sealed, and ratified by the two Grand Lodges. The schism was over.

However, this means little to us in the United States, for the Act of Union of 1813 took place long after the colonies had parted company with the United Kingdom. Perhaps the main reason we care about this English spat is because it means our individual Lodges, and later some Provincial Grand Lodges, received their Charters from the different bodies. Did this really matter in the colonies? Some authors have attempted to say 'yes'. But in reality it had next to no effect. Even in England, despite occasion mutual anathemas issued by the rival Grand Lodges, telling their members not to attend the meetings of Lodges under the rival authority, most Masons either didn't understand or didn't care. Indeed, this laissez-faire attitude existed at the very top: in the 1760s William Dickey, Grand Secretary of the Antients was made a 'Modern' Mason without in any way lessening his allegiance to the Antients – indeed he became its Deputy Grand Master in 1777!

Again, it is important to emphasize the fact that the Antients covered a jurisdiction perfectly concurrent with that of the Moderns, and indeed most of their Lodges were in London. That didn't stop either Grand Lodge from issuing Charters overseas, however. Initially, the Antient Grand Lodge tended to favor regiments, and this is the source of the many stories of English Regimental Lodges bringing in members in the colonies. However, this clearly couldn't begin until the formal existence of the Antient Grand Lodge in 1751, and then it could hardly focus on overseas until it had established itself as a viable alternative in England, which would have taken a number of years. Therefore, all the oldest Provincial Grand Lodges established in America – Coxe's Provincial Grand Lodge around 1730, Price's Provincial Grand Lodge of New England in 1733, the Provincial Grand Lodge of South Carolina in 1736, and the Provincial Grand Lodge of New York in 1738 were all under 'Modern' Charters. Naturally any Lodge Charters issued during this time were also 'Modern'. For example, St. John's Lodge No. 1 in New York City was established in December 1757, and appears on the rolls of the Premier Grand Lodge of England (now in the records of the United Grand

Lodge of England) until later that Century, when it was struck from the rolls for non-payment of capitation fees for several years. On the other hand, the Provincial Grand Lodge of Pennsylvania received its Charter for the Ancients in 1761, 10 years after the founding of their Grand Lodge, and New York exchanged its Charter for one from the Antients in 1781. To demonstrate the confusion or perhaps the laissez-faire attitude that existed, on the one hand St. John's Lodge had to be 'healed' into the new Provincial Grand Lodge; while the first Grand Master of the Ancient Provincial Grand Lodge of New York, Robert R. Livingston, was a 'Modern'! These Charters issued by the Antients were often called 'Athol' Charters, since the Third Duke of Athol was installed as Grand Master in 1771, but died in 1774, being succeeded by his son (who was incidentally Initiated, Passed, Raised, Installed as Master and elected Grand Master in four days – and at the age of 19!). He ruled as Grand Master from 1774 until 1813 when union was achieved, and so the Dukes of Athol presided as Grand Masters for the majority of the existence of the Antient Grand Lodge.

I would like to clear up one all too frequent misconception here. It is a fairly common belief in this country that the terms 'Athol', 'Antient' and 'York' are synonymous. This is not the case. However, it is easy to see why this came about. We call our Blue Ritual the 'York Rite', and we all have some knowledge that many American Lodges and as we have seen, at least a couple of what would become major Grand Lodges, were founded by the Antients. Indeed, even in the earliest days, when St. John's Lodge No. 1 of New York came under the umbrella of the Athol Provincial Grand Lodge of New York, it was given the unique privilege of having the epithet 'A.Y.M.' or 'Ancient York Masons' added to its name, an addition it proudly bears to this day. And yet this was a Modern Lodge, brought into the Antients. There was no connection with York whatsoever! Now, there was a Grand Lodge at York, calling itself the Grand Lodge of All England. This had first appeared in the late 1730s, and was even acknowledged in Dr. Andersen's Constitutions of 1738; but at that time it didn't seek to charter Lodges other than declare itself outside the jurisdiction of the new Grand Lodge, something the Grand Lodge in London didn't press, owing to its time immemorial claim to sovereignty from the alleged Assembly of Masons by Prince Edwin. It promptly went dormant until 1761 when, no doubt inspired by the schism of the Antients, it spluttered into momentary existence when the Premier Grand Lodge chartered a Lodge in its perceived sphere of influence. It eventually fell asleep in the early 1790s, having never chartered more than 15 Lodges, and those all local at that.

However, the siren call of York has never been forgotten, and perhaps New York, which bears on its crest the Latin name Novum Eboracum after the Roman name for York (Eboracum), is partly to blame for this arrogation of the name 'York'. After all, Thomas Smith Webb did some of his finest work on the York Rite in Albany. So despite the fact that the account of the first Assembly of Masons under Prince Edwin is quite likely apocryphal, this romantic notion has endured on this side of the Atlantic. As Dr. Brent Morris says in his introductory book on Freemasonry (on page 92): "The York Rite doesn't come from York, England; it is an American creation. Most of the individual pieces come from England, but the Rite was assembled in America."

And now England went its own way. At the start of the Revolutionary War it was still divided between Antients and Moderns, and two other Grand Lodges of little consequence – the Grand Lodge at York and the Grand Lodge South of the River Trent, which coughed and spluttered across the pages of history. But in America the War of Independence was now being fought, and the future of Freemasonry in England was now of little concern to Patriot Masons.

5. Freemasonry Arrives on American Shores

But now we need to rewind a few years.

The period of European influence upon that would become American Freemasonry is relatively short in time. If we remember that, while there may possibly have been Masons – and even Freemasons – in this country prior to 1717, both a lack of evidence and simple logic have to bring us to the conclusion that, prior to this time it either didn't exist, or if it did, its influence was minimal from a social or political standpoint.

From shortly after 1717 until 1753, the only game in town was the Premier Grand Lodge, so any Charters issued to individual Lodges or Provincial Grand Masters would have to come from this source. It is only after 1751, that there was an Antient Grand Lodge to issue Charters. Now, although its first Provincial Grand Lodge in the colonies was Pennsylvania in 1761, there would have been nothing to prevent it from issuing Charters to regiments from 1751 onwards. The American Revolutionary War began in 1775 and lasted until 1783. Consider the fact that New York had barely changed allegiance and changed its 1738 Modern Charter for an Antient one in 1782, before it dropped that one and self-Chartered in 1787, less than two years before the Inauguration of President Washington. The period that the Antients could have influenced this country was slim indeed, perhaps 30 years at the most, 10 of which the country was at war. I think the stories of setting up of Lodges during that period were the exception rather than the rule. Indeed, in New York most Lodges removed themselves from New York and moved up the Hudson Valley (St. John's Lodge being the exception), so there was very little Masonic activity in New York City during the war, for example. Interestingly, the composition of the Lodge meetings must have varied over time, with a steady membership of both Loyalists and Patriots who lived in the city; and visiting Brethren from whichever army was occupying New York at the time.

One point to bear in mind was that the origin of the Antients' Grand Lodge has been traced back to a strong Irish influence. We have seen earlier that Laurence Dermott, Grand Secretary of the Antients and author of Ahiman Rezon, was initiated in Ireland, which had its own traditions, such as Deacons, which we find in the Antient Grand Lodge Rituals. It has been strongly suggested that the nine Lodges represented in the Grand Committee of 1752, representing 'all the Antient Masons in and adjacent to London' included a large number of Irishmen, whose members were mainly mechanics or shopkeepers, according to Pick and Knight. Is it not possible, then, that some of the Landmarks they complained were missing in the Moderns rituals were in fact Irish in origin? Now anyone who knows anything about the historical tensions between the English and their neighbors the Irish and Scots will understand why the newly formed Grand Lodges of Ireland (est. 1725) and, later, Scotland (est. 1736) did not hesitate to recognize the legitimacy of the Antient Grand

Lodge of England over its rival, the Premier Grand Lodge. No doubt that tension carried over into the colonies.

Another distinction between the Antients and Moderns in the colonies was that, according to Professor Steven Bullock, the Moderns tended to be wealthier property owners, while the Antient tended to be artisans and shopkeepers. This would make sense, since the earlier immigrants would have had time to become established, when only the Premier Grand Lodge was in existence; so they could only join Lodges under that Grand Lodge's control.

I will leave later speakers to go into the fascinating subject of how the early Masons in America organized themselves, their trials and tribulation, and their coming together into Grand Lodges which started the great march westward into new territories. However, I would like to end by returning to an observation I made at the beginning of this talk, and illustrate it with just one rather extraordinary story which comes from the pages of my Lodge's own history, and which I feel illustrates the triumph of Masonic thought over individual politics; and also an idea of a shared destiny which so influenced the Founding Fathers of this great nation.

Firstly, I said that, while the stories about Freemasons being actively instrumental in causing the unrest which led to the Revolutionary War, both in signing the Declaration and in actively leading the resistance to the Crown are, in the famous words of Mark Twain about the premature announcements of his death: "greatly exaggerated", nevertheless we are really looking in the wrong place. Freemasonry did indeed have a profound effect. The historian I quoted earlier was really summarizing Professor Steven Bullock's book Revolutionary Brotherhood when she said that after church and politics, Freemasonry was really the 'only game in town'. I commend this book, already recommended by your Grand Historian, to you all. It explains how prevalent – I would use the word insidious if it didn't have a negative connotation – Freemasonry was in society. Being the 'only game in town', it was the Society every man aspired to join. Early in his book Professor Bullock makes the telling point: "Masonry's first century spans the period when equality became a central and explicit national value. The fraternity served as a focal point for this transformation from a hierarchical society of superiors and inferiors to a republican society of independent citizens. Colonial

Freemasonry offered the urban elite an important symbol of gentility and honor. In the years surrounding the Revolution, aspiring urban artists like Paul Revere found their way into Lodges, claiming a fraternal standing that paralleled their new political position."

To me it is this very manifestation of Freemasonry as a group to which all men may aspire which made it so powerful. Having joined, the new member was exposed both to the politics and information formerly available only to the ruling class; and also to the code of morality and honor which would serve as his moral compass during the dark times, and keep him from descending into cruelty or depression.

In my Lodge history there is a wonderful story which, for me, summarizes this beautifully, and I would like to end by quoting from it:

"An incident occurred in 1779, which showed that Masonic principles has a great influence in controlling human actions, and that brotherly love was superior to party spirit or military discipline.

"The record is that Captain Daniel Shays, who headed Shay's Rebellion, recommended a candidate for initiation in a letter addressed to Bro. John Austin, as follows:

"BRO: Our friend Joseph Burnham, has for a considerable time manifested a desire of being initiated in the (friendly and charitable) Society of Free and Accepted Masons, at Fishkill. We do therefore recommend him, from personal acquaintance, to be such a person as, when admitted, will do honor to the Craft, and for that purpose beg your assistance and influence.

"(Signed) Daniel Shays, Captain; Oliver Owen (Lieutenant), Ivory Holland (Lieutenant)

"Soldiers Fortune, April 26, 1776.

"In 1779 the Lodge met at the Green Bay-Tree Tavern, in Fair Street, now Fulton. In that year the said Joseph Burnham was taken prisoner by the British, then in possession of New York. The incident referred to is told in the following quaint language:

"It so happened that Joseph Burnham, a prisoner of war, who was brought to New York, and of course confined in prison, made his escape; but not knowing where to fly, fortunately found his way to the Green Bay-Tree Tavern, in Fair Street, where St. Johns Lodge was held, and, indeed the only one held in this city at that time, where he was kindly received, and brotherly protection afforded him by Brother Hopkins, the Keeper of the house; Brother Hopkins soon prepared a habitation of safety from the pursuers of the afflicted prisoner, by securing him in his garret. One evening, after the Lodge had convened, the prisoner, to pass the night, laid himself down to rest on some planks that formed the ceiling of a closet that opened directly to the center of the Lodge room. The boards being un-nailed, naturally slipped from their places, and the whole gave way; the door too being only fastened by a wood button, flew open and gave the Lodge an unexpected visitor, for the poor prisoner stood aghast in the middle of the room. The brethren, chiefly British officers, enveloped in surprise, called in Brother Hopkins, who explained all, and acknowledged what he had done. They gave him credit for his charitable behavior to a Brother, and made a generous contribution, with their advice, which was, that Brother Hopkins should transport him as secretly and as expeditiously as possible to the Jersey Shore."

I hope that picture draws a suitable pause in the tale of the history of Freemasonry from the English shores to the Eastern seaboard, and that next year you will hear the tale resumed as Freemasonry takes hold in the colonies, and becomes an integral part of the society which will rise up and take control of its own destiny just a few short years later.

'THE JOURNEY' IN ESOTERIC SOCIETIES

 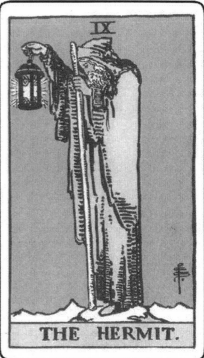

Fig. 1 – The Fool & The Hermit. Reproduced from an original 1910 Rider Waiter Tarot deck by permission of Dr. William S. Burkle.

A few weeks ago when I was in Oxford I took the opportunity to visit Keble College to see Holman Hunt's masterpiece, *The Light of the World*.

Perhaps it is odd that, while I was up at Oxford, I never went to Keble to see it. I guess my mind was focused on other activities. In any case, there was a standing joke at the time which ran as follows: join the Keble College Appreciation Society, admission one brick. Keble, you see, was a Victorian College, much newer than the others, and built out of bricks instead of the beautiful honey-colored Cotswold Stone.

Fig. 2 – Keble College Chapel

As an undergraduate at the second oldest college in Oxford, I suppose this reflected our arrogance. So it was that, early one morning, I made my way to Keble College and into the chapel. It was absolutely beautiful, but it lacked one thing, Holman Hunt's picture. Eventually, I realized that it was housed in a side chapel, and after scaring a nun who was in deep meditation half to death, I finally had the opportunity to gaze upon this magnificent picture. The image is truly breathtaking.

For those of you less familiar with this picture, it portrays Jesus as prophet, priest and king, bearing a lantern, and standing before a closed wooden door upon which he knocks. The door is old, and overgrown with vine and weeds. To me it has always represented the ninth card of the Major Arcana, The Hermit. The man, the avatar, our higher self, perhaps our psychopomp, stands at the threshold between two places, two worlds, represented by the forest and the building. While the Hermit is usually depicted standing in an open doorway, inviting us to enter, in this image the door is closed, firmly bolted, and it is the psychopomp who must persuade us to open it, and allow him in, or us out.

On a stand before the picture is a card giving a detailed description, not only of the content of the picture, but also its symbolic meaning.

While the description certainly helps, given that the picture is very dark and it is hard to make out the details, the explanation of the picture is considerably less helpful. I cannot say for certain, but I hope it was not written by Holman Hunt himself. The task of the painter is to present us with symbols, and allow our own minds to interpret them. For me at least, the moment an individual tries to provide a definitive explanation of the symbols within the picture, that picture dies.

Figure 3 - The Light of the World, W. Holman Hunt (1827 - 1910)

With or without the attempt to explain away the picture, I found myself before it, staring in awe at its beauty and its power, finding it easy to fall into the picture and to become a part of it, experiencing the emotions of its hero as he sought to awaken that spark of life which would embolden the person within to "quit the material and seek the spiritual."

"'Is there anybody there?' said the traveller, knocking on the moonlit door; and his horse in the silence champed the grasses of the forest's ferny floor." Walter de la Mare's famous poem, *The Listeners*, similarly captures this interface, this liminality between two worlds. In this instance, the listeners are phantoms who hear the human's voice, but are powerless both to respond, or open the door to him.

What intrigues me about this picture and this poem, while being in two different artistic media, is the fact that, while the image is static, both strongly imply movement. Jesus, or the psychopomp, must have journeyed to the door; while the man on horseback must have similarly journeyed through his forest in order to arrive at the castle gate. In both cases the hero encounters an obstacle. In Holman Hunt's case, we may want to believe that Jesus was let in through the door. However, in Walter de la Mare's case, the phantoms were unable to comply, and the horseman turns away.

What point am I trying to make?

It seems that all esoteric or spiritual progress requires a journey. Now this journey is not necessarily physical, for it can be made in the mind's eye, and certainly in the two examples I gave the artists use their colorful imaginations to paint canvas and word. Two common examples of this would be meditation and Pathworking. Through meditation we can embark on journeys in our mind's eye. Similarly, through Pathworking we accomplish a focused journey with the purpose of gaining insights or new information. And yet it can be a physical journey, too. Perhaps the two greatest examples are the pilgrimage to the Holy Land under the protection of the Knights Templar (and even now visiting Israel and standing in the places where Jesus was believed to have trod provokes an almost visceral response); and the great pilgrimage to Santiago de Compostela, a pilgrimage still undertaken now, both by devout Christians, and those wanting to experience that spiritual journey in the context of seeking their inner selves, and using the opportunity to distance themselves for a few days at least from the accoutrements of modern life – TVs, iPhones and email – to contemplate, to think, and to be alone.

Let us consider this idea for a moment in the context of Christianity. Anyone who has attended church of almost any denomination is familiar with the concept of secular and sacred space.

Fig. 4 – Secular and Sacred Space in a Church

The narthex is secular. The sacristy is secular. The body of the church is consecrated and therefore holy. But it is the sanctuary, the eastern part, which is especially set aside to the priesthood. And so, at the start of any service, we see the priest and servers formally process from the secular part, through the space set aside for the faithful, to the Holy of Holies or the Sanctuary where they will perform the mysteries, invoke Angels, perform the miracle of transubstantiation (or at the very least perform a memorial act), on behalf of the people.

In his book *Beneath the Shadow of the Cathedrals*, Robert Ambelain suggested that the layout of the cathedral or church was based upon the earlier belief that clearings and groves was sacred to local deities.

Thus, the sanctuary represented the sacred clearing where the Druids or priests perform their rituals, while the body of the church represented the woods where the faithful watched, the soaring columns representing the trees of the forest.

Fig. 5 – Sacred space from Forest Clearings…

Of course caves and caverns were equally popular as a means of separating a cult from day-to-day life, as we see in the Eleusinian and Bacchanalian mysteries, for example. As man learned to build, he recreated these natural environments out of mud, stone, and brick. It is noticeable that all such custom-built places for worship or spiritual enlightenment are but dimly lit. Only the crassest glass cathedrals, with their extensive PA systems and Learjet-owning pastors in their brightly lit edifices, seem to have lost touch with the origins of man's mystical relationship with God. To enter Notre Dame Cathedral in Paris is to step into another world, simultaneously going back a thousand years, while sensing the egregore built up by the prayers of innumerable faithful. What is done in secret is seen by God in secret, and rewarded in secret. As Jesus said of those who wallow in the limelight on earth: truly they have their reward.

It is interesting to note that the journey becomes longer the closer we come to Adeptship. As a perhaps facetious example in Christianity, in the Church of England many refer to "hatch, match and dispatch." This refers to birth (or baptism), marriage and death, the only three times most Brits are seen in church.

But consider the journeys. Now, those of you who are Freemasons know that the journey taken by a Master Mason is longer than that taken by an Entered Apprentice by a factor of three. The journey of the infant is merely from outside the church to the font, which is normally located at the West of the church. Marriage requires the bride to walk the length of the church, and ends in the East, in the sanctuary with the groom. The funeral requires the coffin to make a similar journey, but now leaving the East and traveling West – a route familiar to Masons – but in this case out of the church to the Potter's Field. And this last journey for the faithful leads to a second birth and a second life. Each journey is longer than the last – and we truly hope this represents an increase in knowledge of the person who is about to make the final journey, to knock at that door in the hope that it will be opened to them.

I have identified a number of prerequisites for a journey to be more than simply that, a means of getting from one place to another. I will spend more time on some of these steps than others, since I have covered those at length on other talks. However, to clarify my ideas, these are the essential attributes:

- The person must have a desire to leave the comfortable surroundings of friends and an easy life. In esoteric terms he must 'wake up' from his spiritual slumber and see that there is more to life than rising each morning, going to work, eating, watching TV and sleeping. He must gain that sense of 'is there more to life than this…?' And by the way, I will use the masculine throughout, while of course this all refers to women equally, if not more so.

- He must pass a threshold or *limen*, to use the Latin term. This is what separates this particular journey from, say, a two-week stint on a beach in Florida. This journey requires a passage into another world, a hinterland, a sacred space. It matters not whether this journey is undertaken physically or in the mind's eye, for human beings have an extraordinary capacity to make both identical in terms of personal experience. Without this wonderful capacity we would never have been able to raise ourselves up beyond the human kingdom, having already spent an epoch ascending through the mineral, vegetable and animal kingdoms, which was wonderfully described by Bro. Tommy Westlund, the Grand Archivist of the Swedish Rite, in a recent talk; then rediscovering the divine spark within, which drives this traveling imperative for reunion with our source, the divinity from which we came. Even if this involves an earthly journey, such as the pilgrimage to Santiago,

I doubt you will find any of the pilgrims are doing the walk merely to get some sun and enjoy the Northern Spanish cuisine: there is a far deeper imperative which drives them.

- The journey must be arduous. This is not because we *want* to make it difficult. But, like joining a society which charges only a dollar to join, to paraphrase J. K Kennedy, we value things because they are hard; not because they are easy. This also serves a secondary role of weeding out the thrill-seekers or the idly curious. To prove commitment, one must show just how much one is prepared to invest in this journey. The old saying; "To will, to dare, to keep silent" sums up the very qualities which the Watchers on your journey need to observe in you before they will divulge their treasures. An act of irreversible commitment, a dedication in the face of adversity, and equally important, the ability to be stoic and silent in the face of suffering will show that the seeker is made of stern stuff, that they will be circumspect with the knowledge they gain, and not shout it from the rooftops. Again, as Jesus said of those who fasted yet stood on street corners rending their clothes, covering their heads with ashes and proclaiming "Woe is me!": truly they already have their reward. Now we realize this saying of the Great Adept was in fact one of the secret teachings: "God who sees in secret will reward in secret." To a seeker or an adept, those words ring true.

- There is both descent and ascent. A good friend used to give an extraordinary talk comparing the Monomyth, or Hero's Journey – made famous by Joseph Campbell in his book *The Hero With A Thousand Faces* (1949) – to the path in Freemasonry, while drawing on the symbolism of Star Wars to make his points. The talk was both very entertaining and most educational – a trick many of us envy! The seeker needs to have everything he believes in knocked down; and then from the Slough of Despond he raises himself up to seek the higher goal.

- Finally, having proven himself, the new Adept is welcomed into the new Brotherhood, or acknowledged by the Secret Chiefs, or absorbed into the Godhead, and becomes one with the new community. He will have to return to his earthly abode, but for a moment he can enjoy the successful completion of his journey (for many will never make it), and reflect of the journey and the new knowledge he has gained, both during the journey and now at its completion, before reinserting himself into the profane and mundane world, forever changed. But on his return, he has a duty. He must become a teacher, a guide: The Hermit of the Tarot. It is not his job to simply divulge what he has learned and provide a 'Cliff Notes' version of the journey for others to read in the comfort of their armchairs. His duty is to inspire others to take that journey of self-discovery, and learn the lessons for themselves. For we may be part of one great organism, but it is for each of us to have that personal experience which allows us to grow as individuals.

In sum, the journey requires separation, passage into a new dimension of being, a dangerous journey of descent and then ascent beset with trial and tribulation, before finally uniting with like-minded or higher beings and the exchange of knowledge.

Have you noticed that in many journeys, both religious and esoteric, a psychopomp is required? Someone to speak for us, for we have not the words ourselves? At baptism our Godparent speaks for us and carries us. At marriage the father escorts and presents the bride. And at death, it is the priest who intercedes for us. There is a guide. Dante has his Virgil, while Luke Skywalker, to continue the earlier theme, has his Han Solo.

It is the same in esoteric rituals. In Freemasonry, the Junior or Senior Deacon, depending on jurisdiction, speaks for the candidate. As another example, in the Hermetic Order of the Golden Dawn, daughter of the Masonic Rosicrucians, the Hegemon speaks on behalf of the Candidate. The message is clear. We are not necessarily expected to know the signs and words of admission ourselves, but we must have a sponsor in the higher worlds who is prepared to speak on our behalf.

However, not every hero has a guide: both Bunyan's Christian and Andreæ's Rosenkreutz had to fend for themselves. As an aside, it is interesting to note the Egyptian Books of the Dead suggest that it was necessary for the dead to know the formulae themselves, for they presented themselves alone to give the negative confession before Osiris in the Halls of the Underworld, as they had their heart weighed against a feather in the scale of Ma'at, while Thoth recorded the result

Fig. 6 – Virgil guides Dante through Hell

and the Great Devourer waited impatiently for those who failed this test.

This journey we undertake is not easy. Whether symbolic or real it is full of danger, true or imagined. From Dante's Inferno, though Rosenkreutz' choice of paths at the edge of the forest, to Bunyan's Pilgrim progressing through the terrain, the slightest mistake can end in disaster. This is not an easy road. Even in ritual the journey seems to the candidate to be full of peril. While we know few details about the Graeco-Roman cults, we do know the majority of ceremonies were conducted underground in dark passages, with the candidates probably drugged or at least starved and disorientated being subjected to terrifying visions and special effects. In more modern times we have substituted the blindfold for darkness, but the challenges remain, whether they be menacing guards who bar the candidate's right to proceed; trials by the ancient elements – particularly by water and fire; the sensation of apparently being stabbed, or having blood drawn in order to sign a testament, or even organs removed; or the ultimate sacrifice to the cult, a symbolic death, in order to rise again as a new being, perhaps with a new name. Being deprived of the sovereign sense of sight practically guarantees that these threats will be perceived as very real to the candidate.

If we take this to the next level, we can travel in our mind's eye. There are three common methods in the Western Mystery Tradition for accomplishing this: Pathworking, Scrying, and Traveling in the Astral.

Fig. 7 – Judgement in the Egyptian Book of the Dead

Pathworking is the 'safety wheels on' version. It is actually a guided journey in the mind's eye, led by a person who describes what you should be seeing while you follow along with your eyes closed. It can be a very powerful method of awakening an adult's atrophied power of imagination or visualization. It is also extremely safe – so long as the leader doesn't take the group to dangerous scenes, where somebody with an overactive imagination could find themselves in physical trouble, in terms of hyperventilation or even a stroke. I would not recommend visualizing falling over a cliff, for example! But so long as the guide takes them on a gentler journey, the experience can be very pleasant. Common themes for Pathworkings are not dissimilar to popular role-playing games, and could involve taking walks through forests and encountering fantasy animals; or wandering through a castle meeting interesting characters. In a more advanced mode they can be used to explore esoteric landscapes which the participants may revisit individually later on. Examples of this which I have come across include: traveling along the paths connecting the Sephiroth on the Tree of Life; and joining a gathering of Druids in a clearing.

One area which could use Pathworking to advantage, but has not really explored this avenue to my knowledge, is Freemasonry. I have led one or two in Lodges. I will offer two obvious contenders – and in this instance I am not giving anything about the ritual away which is not freely available on the internet. Firstly, the candidate's journey through the Entered Apprentice Degree can be relived in dramatic form by conducting the experience as a guided journey, taking him along the path which leads to the guards, and then to the sacred space where he will kneel in fear and dread, while King Solomon himself comes down from his throne under the beating heat of the noonday sun to enter the Temple in order to administer the binding oath. Another example is reliving the Journey to the Middle Chamber, incorporating a journey around King Solomon's Temple, very much in the form of the Art of Memory, in which such a tour around a castle or great edifice was used as an aid to memorizing lengthy speeches or ordering logical thought. Both take on a more powerful dimension when practiced using the technique of Pathworking.

Scrying, or the art of seeing, is the next level of commitment. This is usually conducted by a single person, though there are many instances of a person using a second with more ability who performs act of seeing or scrying itself, while the inquisitor writes down his observations. For the classicists, the often quoted example is the Elizabethan, Dr. John Dee and his assistant Edward Kelley's attempts to communicate with the angelic powers to learn the Enochian language. This makes use of a window to the astral world, often a smoked glass, a container of water or other liquid such as mercury, a mirror or a crystal ball. The seer never leaves the present world, but instead peers through this interface, this veil where the two worlds come together, in order to gain insight or knowledge. While it is necessary to know some protective techniques in case some 'uninvited guests' show up to the party, this is again a relatively safe process. The main danger here is obsession, when success with the technique leads the seer to shut himself away from normal society to spend a disproportionately large amount of time in this practice.

Finally, **Traveling in the Astral** is a full commitment from the seeker to roam abroad in these alien worlds. Now fully separated from his earthly realm, he wanders alone in unfamiliar territory, with all the dangers that this may bring. But unless he is extremely foolish, he is not unarmed. By this I do not refer to common weapons, which would have no effect in a parallel universe. Rather, he is armed with the signs, words of command, and knowledge which will serve to protect him, and to help him identify friend from foe. He knows how to compel a creature to give its true name, to bind the bad and to coax the good. He similarly knows how to prove himself a friend to those who might guide him or give him valuable information.

We see the process of descent well-described in Bunyan's Slough of Despond, in Dante's Circle of Hell, and chillingly in Christian Rosenkeutz' dream of the dungeon; as well as physically in the caves and grottoes of the Mystery Schools. Whether the journeys described by Chaucer, Dante, Bunyan, Rosenkreutz were symbolic, physical, or spiritual inner journeys is not in fact important. We have already noted man's capacity to perceive imaginary events as if they were real. If our level of cynicism was too developed to allow this, we would never be able to become so involved in a movie, a television program or a play, since our Higher Self would be constantly telling us that it was not real, and we would not feel that emotion involvement which makes the viewing so immersive and believable. Could you watch an episode of *Law and Order* if your Higher Self endlessly reminded you that all the compelling characters were only actors, that the blood was tomato sauce, that the people being shot were simply activating small controlled explosions in bags of carmine dye; and the grieving widow was being paid tens of thousands of dollars to pretend to cry? Would you care if Lady Macbeth incited her husband to murder if all you could see was the actors playing Macbeth, Duncan and Banquo buying each other pints in the local bar after the performance?

Similarly, following this descent, there comes an ascent into a higher plane. Even though it is quite possible that all these worlds exist contiguously – in other words, we may live in the heaven or the hell of our own making here on earth – it is commonly said that to enter into one of the parallel worlds, in particular the Astral world of Yesod, we need to raise our vibration, and the phrase 'rising up on the planes' is commonly used in esoteric language.

This recalls the concept of travelling in a circle.

Early tribes used to commune with their gods by moving in circles at increasing speed, producing a dizzying effect, like the whirling dervishes who use a similar activity to achieve closeness with God. Many fraternities, from Freemasonry to the Golden Dawn, use circumambulation, or walking in circles, to achieve a raising of the energies. Indeed, while not practiced in the Unites States, in most countries the Fellowcraft Degree is accompanied by a series of spiral steps, reflecting in the Second Degree Tracing Board as the means of arriving at the Middle Chamber to receive the rewards of one's labor. And in the Rosicrucian Tradition the journey to union with God required traveling up Mount Abiegnus, again a vertical ascent. Indeed, the Holy Scriptures also tell us that the Great Exemplar, the Son of Man descended into Hell while his physical body remained in a crypt, before being lifted bodily to a higher plane forty days later.

Fig. 8 – Whorls, circles and spirals…

The image above reflects the commonality of circumambulation in many of our religions and customs. Clockwise from the left we see the devout circling the Ka'aba during the Hajj; hooded penitents in Holy Week in Andalucía, Spain; the winding staircase of Solomon's Temple; Whirling Dervishes; a fractal spiral; Hopi Indians; English Maypole dancing; Druids at Stonehenge; and members circumambulating at a Golden Dawn Temple meeting.

Our Holy Scriptures also tell us that, to commune more closely with God, one was required to offer sacrifice on high mountains and places. Moses talked and walked with God on Mount Sinai. So it appears that it is not only travel, but vertical motion which is required to achieve a higher stage of integration with one's object of desire. As with Moses, the places where man communed with the higher forces was invariably where the space between heaven and earth was considered most transparent, the *omphalos* or navel of the ancient Greeks. They spoke with Apollo at Delphi, and the High Priest communed with Yahweh on Mount Moriah, as did the Cathar Perfecti on Montségur in the Languedoc, and the Lakota Indians on Devil's Tower in Wyoming.

Whether the journey is mental or physical, however, the transformation required to achieve the heights, to commune with saints and angels and receive one's reward, perhaps even to achieve reintegration into one's original or primitive state, is of course internal and not external. The object of the journey is not to amass wealth or trinkets, to accrue fine robes or aprons, to grow six inches or learn a new trade. The transformation must be from within. In Louis-Claude de Saint-Martin's words, the Man of the Stream must learn to become a Man of Desire – *the Zeal of Thy House hath eaten me up* is a popular Rosicrucian quotation from Psalm 69 – and through endeavor this Man of Desire strives to become a New Man, a Man Reborn who is worthy to rejoin with his Maker.

To achieve this, he must learn, in Masonic terminology, to subdue his passions, to work upon himself, to knock of the superfluous knobs and excrescences which prevent the perfect white stone which is within from shining through. For what use is this inner or outer journey if he does not use it to learn and grow, so the talent he has been given by his Master is not used to make two talents, instead of burying it in the ground?

And this, as I am sure you have realized, is simply a euphemism for Spiritual Alchemy, that process of inner transformation. In this paper we have considered the journey. But another paper will consider the inward processes which take place during that journey, which will transform the man who sets out upon this amazing journey, and who will replace his corporeal body with the Glorious Body as he arrives at his final destination.

A MASONIC BESTIARY

NOTE: *This whimsical piece was written for a meeting of the Scottish Rite. I gave this and another paper on an invented alternative Rite which I claimed had nearly beaten the AASR out of New York State. I claimed it had 33 Degrees as well, but only a handful were worked: The Degree of Ho-Bo-Ken, the St. Christopher Degree, then the 9th, 14th, 23rd and 33rd Degrees. In fact, these are simply the stops on the Port Authority Trans Hudson rail system. However, I quickly learned the power of delivering nonsense in an English accent when a crowd of people came up to me afterwards asking for copies of the Rite, and asking for the sources of this piece of nonsense below!*

It is not well known that the well-known Historical Lecture of the Third Degree is actually based on an early North African manuscript, the *"Compendium Animalae Masonici"*, believed to be based on an early version by Aesop, and reworked by Martianus de Cappella, renowned author of "The Marriage of Mercury and Philology". While this document did not catch the attention of the early Christian educationalists, as did his more famous work on the Seven Liberal Arts and Sciences, it nevertheless survived the tragedy of the Alexandrian Library. The document passed into the great library of Cordova, was protected from the anti-Muslim and anti-Jewish pogroms initiated by Ferdinand and Isabella following the re-conquest of Spain which were implemented by the Inquisition, by educated Jews. This document was rediscovered by Thomas Vaughan, who suffered it to be preserved in a private limited printing run, which he passed to close friends. From there it was read by Elias Ashmole and others instrumental in creating the rich lectoral additions to early Masonic ritual.

While the teachings were considered profound by these eminent early Freemasons, they realized that allegories based upon animals never seen by northern Europeans would be less effective in transmitting moral teachings than implements used in daily work. Thus the animals were substituted by the common building implements we know and use in our teachings today.

For the interest of the readers, I have included below the original Working Animals lecture from the Third Degree, rendered into modern English for ease of reading.

142

"The three working animals of the Third Degree are the Aardvark, the Warthog and the Giraffe. The Operative uses the Aardvark, which is a rough and horny animal with a long proboscis, for the purpose of clearing huts of ants, cowans and eavesdroppers. The Warthog, from its ugliness, is used to scare off evil spirits and visitors from rival jurisdictions, and its sharp tusks serve to impale rude and unpleasant widows and orphans. The Giraffe, from its unusual height and tiny brain, is attached to a pencil and used to delineate the boundaries of those early Lodges held in lonely hills and mountaintops. They are also used to replace lightbulbs, and to spit at suspended or expelled members.

"But we, are Free and Speculative Masons, apply these beasts to the more noble task of improving the quality of life, thus: the excrement of the Aardvark provides a powerful fertilizer to encourage the most difficult vegetable into growth. The Warthog's head, mounted on a plaque and hung on the wall, increases a man's stature in his tribe as a "killer of difficult but pointless things to kill." The giraffe can be turned into a most acceptable rug, covering the knobs and rough excrescences of a badly-cut ashlar, so making it a useful occasional table.

"Thus through the horniness of the Aardvark, the countenance of the Warthog and the intellectual vacuum of the Giraffe we learn that even the most rough, ugly and stupid person may serve a truly noble purpose."

COMPLETING THE CIRCLE

*A TALK FOR THE 14° DEGREE OF THE ANCIENT &
ACCEPTED SCOTTISH RITE*

The Mason who takes the 14° Degree of the Scottish Rite completes a circle. Actually, it is more like a spiral, because he ends up in the same place he started when he first knocked on the door of the Lodge seeking Light; but at a higher level. The symbol of this Degree, the ring, is therefore an appropriate emblem, for it is a circle of gold, a ring of eternity. In this paper I want to touch on a couple of the many symbols used in the 14° Degree, which also have parallels in the York Rite, particularly the Holy Royal Arch. These are the ring and the cubic stone or altar stone, upon which are discovered certain signs and symbols, representing the sigil and the Ineffable Name of God.

Masonry is a journey – every Degree we pass though involves a journey, a movement forward along the perfect path which leads us to grater knowledge and understanding. It is a Pilgrim's Progress. As we progress we make our daily advancement in Masonic knowledge, and grow in our understanding of ourselves and our relationship to our fellow man. For in the greater scheme of things the first fourteen Degrees are about self-knowledge; which is a critical prerequisite to our understanding of God. To know God, we must first know ourselves.

To understand this journey, we must first arm ourselves with some knowledge. This is the language of symbols, by which we can look beneath the surface which is presented to us, and perceive the hidden meaning beneath.

Fig. 1 - Thoth

But first, let me introduce my little friend (I had a little statue with me). Do you know who he is? His name is Thoth, and the Greeks knew him by the name Hermes Trismegistus, or Thrice Great Hermes. He was the Egyptian God of learning. Many books are attributed to him. One in particular, a picture book which claims to contain all human knowledge, we will look at later. I like to think of Thoth as the 'little god' of Masonry. He is the archetype of learning and wisdom, those very attributes for which we strive.

Given that all of the symbolism is based upon the Old Testament, the first book I would recommend anyone seeking further light in Masonry to read is the Old Testament. This is not merely an exhortation to be godly. It is an important step to understanding the Degrees themselves, since all of them are based on stories from the Holy Bible. When the Degrees were written everyone had a good working knowledge of the biblical stories, so the symbolism and meaning behind the ritual allegories would have been immediately grasped by the Brethren present. Sadly, this is not the case nowadays, and for many, the rituals recall no memories of Old Testament passages.

As well as the Sacred Writings themselves, the Hebrews had a number of commentaries intended to interpret those writings. One such system of philosophy – which focused upon a mystical interpretation particularly of the first five books called the Pentateuch – is called the Kabbalah. The Kabbalah treats of the creation of the Universe, and particularly of Man, in a series of stunning and evocative images. One of the most famous of these is the Tree of Life, a series of ten universal attributes (called Sephiroth) arranged in a particular manner, and which trace the act of creation from God to Man. For a Mason these ten Sephiroth may be arranged upon a diagram of a Temple, which is appropriate.

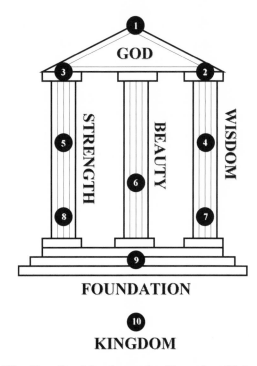

Fig. 2 – The Ten Sephiroth on the Temple of Masonry

Note that the three top Sephiroth form a triangle, which we can call God. God is perfect unity, but in Genesis we are told 'male and female created He them'. Thus God created duality from his perfection. Light and Dark, Peace and War, Male and Female, Master and Servant, Richness and Poverty, White and Black, Good and Evil. Many religions depict God as a trinity: the Hindus, Egyptians, Greeks, Romans, Norse and Christians among others.

The Summit is supported by three columns, familiar to us Masons: Wisdom, Strength, and Beauty. Wisdom is MERCY – remember the story of Solomon and the baby. Strength is SEVERITY – we need to keep our sword hand free while building the Temple with the trowel in our left hand! We should strive to balance these two extremes: for as one ritual puts it, "an excess of severity is but cruelty, while an excess of mercy is but weakness. Seek thou the Middle Path". It is our Masonic goal to attain the Middle way, the Middle Pillar, the straight and narrow road, which leads straight to God.

When we first joined a Lodge we were prepared in darkness – in our case a 'convenient room adjoining the Lodge'. In some forms of Masonry this is taken to an extreme, and the Candidate is placed in a "Chamber of Reflection", a small claustrophobic cabinet painted in black with emblems of mortality contained therein, and the light of a single candle. This represents the womb, from which the Candidate will be born into Masonic Light. As a Candidate, symbolically naked and blind, with a cable tow (an umbilical cord which linked you to your former existence…) you then knocked on the door of the Lodge. You were admitted and placed between the two pillars of J and B, which are Mercy and Severity. Here, unconsciously and blindfolded, you stood at the very place it will take all your Masonic career to return to. For that first fleeting moment you <u>are</u> the Middle Pillar, the Pillar of Beauty. From now on all the learning, all the work on smoothing the rough ashlar to make of yourself the perfect cube, the smooth ashlar the holy altar worthy of God, at this time unveiled and without a blindfold: armed with the knowledge we have learned in our long journey to the 14° Degree. It is no coincidence that one of the titles of the 14° Degree is Perfect Elect Mason. Finally understanding self, having made of himself the perfect ashlar, man may once more stand between these two pillars, this time fully conscious and without veil or blindfold. He has made of himself the Middle Pillar, the Middle Way, the straight way to God. He has returned to his original station, but at an exalted, perfected level.

So we make our journey and at the end of our long journey we arrive at (complete) the perfect cube, which is now worthy to bear the imprint of God. This imprint is a curious device – a circle containing a triangle containing a dot. What does it mean?

Well, the dot is not a dot at all. It is a 'Yod' ('). Yod is the ninth letter of the Hebrew Alphabet. This alphabet was said to be the language of the Angels, and written in fire.

All the letters of this Fire Language, this Angelic language are created out of Yods. The penultimate letter, "Shin", for example, is made of three elongated Yods upon a base (ש).

The Yod looks like a flame. It also looks like a seed, or sperm. And indeed it is, for it gives rise to all the letters in the Hebrew alphabet.

This seed, or thought of God, gave birth to the entire universe, which is often depicted as a full circle, or a serpent biting its tail.

ALPHA & OMEGA

Fig. 3 – The Hebrew Letter 'Yod'

The Yod begins the world through the Word of God, the Logos. And the universe shall end with fire. Thus, the Yod in the circle is the Alpha and the Omega of us all.

The Yod is emanated from God, who was represented by a triangle in many, many religions and philosophies. The triangle represented God in Egypt, the Sacred Delta of Pythagoras was the earthly representation of God to the Greeks. Many religions see God as having three natures, Omnipotent, Omniscient, Omnipresent, or again as three being in one: the Ineffable and the male and female, or Strong and Wise attributes. The triangle is in eternal contention, it is a dynamic diagram, two contending sides constantly united by the third.

Yod is also the first letter of the name of God, in Yod-Heh-Vav-Heh, known to us as Jehovah, or Yahweh. So the ring is an appropriate reflection of the ineffable name of God. The ring itself is the circle, and the triangle of God contains both the initial of His name and the seed of Creation and all Potentiality.

By the way, isn't it interesting that God has a sigil! For that is what it is. Magical traditions tell us that all angels (or demons) may be summoned if one has three things: their true name, their seal or sigil, and a triangle of manifestation, for the triangle represents another plane of existence into which they can manifest. God gave Moses his true name, and there is a theory that Moses only received the laws later – that the stones upon which God wrote with His finger on both sides was in fact his seal. Finally, here we have the triangle into which God could manifest, when summoned by the High Priest once a year.

Yod – Heh – Vav - Heh

Jehovah

Fig. 4 – The Tetragrammaton

As an aside, let us return to Thoth. The picture book attributed to him is? The Tarot, or Book 'T' as the Rosicrucians named it. Now, Yod is the ninth letter of the Hebrew alphabet, and to some people corresponds with the ninth card of the picture cards in the Tarot deck. This is the Hermit*.

The Hermit is an appropriate emblem for Yod. He is the seeker after wisdom (as we all are). He holds the lamp of truth (remember that the name of the ring is Zerubbabel, of Truth). I chose this particular version of the card as it shows much of what we have been looking at. Note the age of the man, an Ancient, in fact. He carries the lamp aloft, and the light of Truth is…a Yod! He stands within a circle formed of the Ourobouros, or serpent biting its tail. He is within infinity, within the universe, and he bears the lamp of wisdom to guide other seekers. Beyond is darkness. We must return to the crypt – as we shall see shortly.

THE HERMIT

Fig 5 - Reproduced with kind permission from the New Golden Dawn Ritual Tarot by Sandra Tabatha Cicero, Llewellyn Pub.

Finally, the Cubic Stone upon which the Ineffable name and sigil of God rests. It has served its purpose. The Mason has indeed turned the rough ashlar into the cubic stone. We now know that the cubic stone carries the name of God. In a way, the 1st to the 14th Degrees in Scottish Rite masonry represent sub-degrees of one greater Degree, and now the Perfect Mason is elected to rise up to the next level. Finally balanced between the Pillars, himself forming the Middle Pillar (in which position he stood hoodwinked and unaware on his first entry into a Lodge), he leaves the Temple realm and comes full circle. The seed returns to the womb. The Man enters the crypt. In his next incarnation he will have no further use for a physical Temple, for he has learned that it is within him.

Now at the next level the cubic stone, which only permitted man to view its exterior in prior degrees, will open to reveal its inner nature.

Let us open the cube, and catch a glimpse of what lies within. This symbolism we find in the 18th Degree, the pivotal Degree of the

Scottish Rite System. The symbolism of that Degree is, of course, a whole other paper!

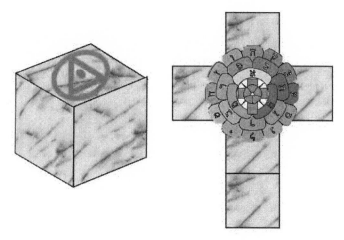

Fig 6 – From the 14th to the 18th, from the Cube to the Cross

So wear your 14° ring with pride, for its simple device contains all the secrets of the Universe!

FREEMASONRY & THE MARITIME WORLD

NOTE: *This short talk was delivered on the occasion of Mariner's Lodge No. 67 conferring a Degree on the high seas in the presence of the Grand Master, M.W. William J. Thomas, who had given special permission for this to be done on a cruise to Bermuda from New York. It seemed appropriate to call for a few papers with a nautical theme to honor the occasion.*

In the minutes of St. John's Lodge No. 1, A.Y.M., dated January 2, 1802, we read: "The Worshipful Master *pro tem* gave information to the Lodge that they were called together upon a particular emergency in the case of a seafaring gentleman who being about to leave the city before our next regular meeting, he had obtained a dispensation from the Deputy Grand Master, for conferring the Masonic Degrees without the usual forms, but several of the members conceiving it to be an irregular proceeding, and not in accordance to the Constitution of the Grand Lodge, a discussion of the subject took place, which terminated in a resolve to confer the aforesaid degrees upon him immediately."

It is clear that Captain William Hull, the 'seafaring gentleman' was not known to the members of St. John's Lodge, nor were they likely to see him again. Similarly, he was neither to receive all the enlightenment of the full rituals nor any mentorship, education or other privileges associated with membership. Yet he was prepared to pay a fee of twenty pounds to become a Freemason, and apparently felt he had to become a Master Mason immediately prior to setting sail.

Why would he want to do this?

To answer this question, we will look at the link between Freemasonry and the Maritime at two levels. We will start with the benefits to the individual sailor. Then we will look at the broader picture of the network of sailing routes and how Freemasonry played a significant role in the spread of empire and ideas.

Firstly, we must remember that, historically, all civilizations were based by the sea. This was an absolute necessity for trading with other countries. Think of London, New York, Athens, Rome, Alexandria, Ashdod. Indeed, one would be hard-pressed to name a major city in those times which was not either on a major river or on the ocean. Maritime life was intimately interwoven with the business and political worlds. This was how countries communicated, where ambassadors disembarked, goods from other countries were processed, fish were landed, and ships equipped themselves against enemy nations and corsairs. It was only after the industrial revolution, and the consequent invention of steam engines and the need for coal, that cities began to spring up inland. In New York we have only to think of "Clinton's Ditch" to be reminded that the cheapest and most efficient way of transporting goods and people to the Northern Central States was via the Hudson and Mohawk canals.

Yet sailing was a very uncertain and dangerous career. Ships could easily get lost or overtaken in storms; the threat of starvation was ever present, and an illness could rapidly become an epidemic in those cramped and unsanitary quarters; the threat of war or pirates was ever present; mutinies were not uncommon, given that many of the sailors were press-ganged into service and therefore not willing shipmates. The daily routine was dangerous in an environment where even a minor scratch could result in major infection, for there were no antibiotics or nurses. All this contributed to a very high likelihood of major injury or death.

Being a Freemason provided a measure of security to the sailor's loved ones left behind in an uncertain New World. Masonry's first purpose was as a Friendly Society, where Masons would especially look after the widows and orphans of their Brothers, an obligation enshrined even now in the rituals. While these phrases might seem a little anachronistic to us in the present day, they were of deadly importance two hundred years ago.

The melting pot of sea ports also allowed networking to take place – both horizontally and vertically. Horizontally one could rely on shipmates who belonged to the same 'club'; and on shore one could find out about imminent sailings which required seamen. Links to associated arts and crafts would put Masons in touch with shipwrights, financiers, chandlers, sail-makers and all the professions associated directly and indirectly with the sea. Vertically one could associate with men who were politicians and financiers, and learn the important news as it happened. And this was not only with people in the town or city: this networking occurred between sailors from other towns and countries as they passed freely through the ports. This is in direct contrast with normal village life, where a man might not move more than twenty miles in a lifetime from where he was born. In a conference held in Greenwich University, London in 2008, Prof. Andrew Prescott informed the delegates that Masonic Lodges in Liverpool at that time could have members from as far afield as America, Russia, Sweden and Germany!

It is worth noting also, that since Masonry was described as being the "Handmaiden of religion", it must have had a particularly salutary effect on the Merchant and Royal navies. Sailors are notoriously superstitious, and a manifestation of this is often the repetition of an action perceived to ward off danger. The rituals of Freemasonry, with their religious overtones, would surely have been an ideal vehicle for those 'in peril on the sea', so often without a priest on board, to satisfy their need both for a watchful and caring Deity and the familiarity of the repeated activities of ritual.

In sum, then, becoming a Mason if one was in a nautical profession guaranteed a group of men on board who would defend you in the face of trouble; a useful set of contacts in your profession and its allied trades; immediate contacts in a foreign port; and if the worst came to the worst, the knowledge that your loved ones would be taken care of. This may well have been the motivations behind Captain William Hull being so determined to become a Master Mason prior to sailing off to ports unknown.

While this may have been the personal motivation which incentivized sailors to seek out Freemasonry, the Craft also functioned, nay thrived and expanded, as its members took Masonry around the world.

The sea was a natural – if not the only – way for Masonry to spread through countries separated by water. Given that "Britannia Ruled the Waves" at that time, and the burgeoning Empire was expanding year by year, it took those very people from England, Scotland and Ireland who practiced the Craft to ports all around the world.

In her excellent paper on how the spread of Masonic Lodges across the British Empire helped to cement a universal "imperialist" identity common across the Empire, Jessica Harland-Jacobs emphasized this aspect of Freemasonry, lamenting the fact that it had so long been ignored by historians. Several historians had studied the movement of people across the Atlantic Ocean, and later the world, during this period, and the accompanying exchange of cultures, the establishment of travel and communication networks. She points out that by shifting the focus from land masses to the transatlantic networks, a whole new vista of research and focus has been opened up. But she feels the scholars, in sidestepping Freemasonry, have ignored a key input to the establishment of what she calls "supranational identities", as nation states and empires stabilized during this time, and says categorically that, by: "creating a global network that had both practical functions and ideological dimensions, Freemasonry played a critical role in building, consolidating, and perpetuating the empire."

To Harland-Jacobs, the Masons who traveled to America, and later around the world, found solace in their Masonic rituals, which linked them in both a ritual and historic-sentimental sense to England, their Motherland. After all, she points out, "early Freemasons drew both on their well-rooted traditions and the contemporary Enlightenment milieu of which they were a part." The English were then a regimented and moral people, or at least tried to be, and Masonry spoke to these character traits. It is no surprise that a society which both celebrated the glorious history of the English and placed them firmly at the forefront of contemporary scientific thinking would be eagerly embraced.

It also led them in most instances to respect other religions and cultures, too, since Masonry only requires belief in a Supreme Being and adherence to a set of ethical codes; and this also permitted men of other religions and cultures to join, further assisting in the assimilation of the local people into the 'English' way of thinking. While Lodges had until then been a purely European phenomenon, the issuing of traveling Lodge Charters, initially by the Grand Lodge of Ireland, and later by Scotland and England, encouraged the spread of Masonry across the Atlantic and elsewhere. Reciprocally, when a colonial returned to the Homeland, he was assured of a warm welcome and an instant set of friends in Lodge.

Harland-Jacobs traces the spread of Freemasonry as being due to three principal agents:

1. Geographical flexibility (due to the spread of merchants, soldiers and sailors carrying Charters);

2. Colonists bringing their home traditions with them; and

3. The appointment of Provincial Grand Masters to oversee the local growth of the Fraternity, much as a colonial Governor or Viceroy would represent the Crown abroad.

Notwithstanding America's later independence from the Empire, the values of cooperation, and the ability of Freemasonry to meet the emotional, intellectual, social and material needs of members still held true, and this is probably why Masonry was not rejected in the newly-liberated colonies as being a manifestation of the detested overlords. Indeed, the colonies embraced the Craft and made it their own. As well as meeting the spiritual side, it also satisfied the social needs of the men in the community, bringing them together on a regular basis, both in a formal and festive setting, linking intellectual pursuit with eating and drinking, and creating a harmonious atmosphere in which men could bond and stand together against an often hostile world.

So Freemasonry has much to be proud of, both as a haven for men in uncertain times, providing familiarity, solace and the opportunity to network locally and globally, as well as the comfort of knowing one's loved ones would be taken care of in the event of a disaster; and as a key vehicle in the spread of a set of morals and attitudes which ended up spanning the globe.

As a final point, we note that there is a rather unusual character in one of our rituals: the seafaring man, whose purpose is to guard the harbor and admit none to the boats without the pass, in this case a physical passport from the King. Perhaps this, too, is a vestige of the close association Masonry used to have with the sea, and shows the seafaring man in such a favorable light. I will end with a poem written by Donald Weisse, Sr., who went to the Grand Lodge above in 2001.

The Sea Captain

I've sailed my ship for many a day
Across the stormy sea;
Many a ruffian I have carried
and never refused but three.

They met me on a summer day
And saw my gallant ship,
And sought a passage to the other side
Upon a hurried trip,

They offered all the dough they had,
Mixed with a little sass;
Which made me kind of hesitate
And I asked them for a pass.

They deemed a pass unnecessary
For men of their degree,
And insisted that I take my ship
And sail it out to sea.

An old man who was standing by
Noted what they said,
Saw them kick me in the ribs
And strike me on the head.

He heard them say they'd steal the boat
And put it out to sea,
And sail away to the other side
To some strange country.

But now the coward of the bunch
The one you'd think was brave
Suggested that they turn again
And hide in a mountain cave.

And as the day went slowly by
I heard the truth in time,
I found that they were murderers
And guilty of a crime.

So, as I sail my sturdy ship
Until my life has ceased,
I know not who my friends may be
Unless they've traveled East.

AN EXEGESIS ON THE MOST EXCELLENT MASTER DEGREE

NOTE: This paper, while it covers parts of the ritual contained in the Most Excellent Master Degree, includes nothing which cannot be found by doing a simple Google search on the internet. However, I used this Degree as a teaching tool to try to get behind the words and to get a glimpse of the people who put it together, and what message they were trying to convey. This led me to title the paper 'An exegesis' since, like biblical study, scholars are taught to use what they have in order to peer behind the veil to better understand the 'why' behind the 'what'.

This paper might make some of you uncomfortable. It is intended to! When I moved to the States some 20 years ago, I used to discuss the importance of perceiving the messages behind the symbolism used in our beautiful rituals. Believe me, this fell on completely deaf ears. The point of ritual to most was to learn it by heart and recite it perfectly from memory, preferably with a member of the Ritual Police – otherwise known as the Assistant Grand Lecturer – to pace round the room and bark out corrections when a nervous Brother left a 'the' or an 'a' out of the recital. What was the point of thinking about it, discussing it, or analyzing it? It just 'was'; and we performed it to the best of our ability. My attempts to suggest that there was more to the ritual than memory exercises was met with ridicule…

How times have changed! Now we find many young men knocking at our doors in search of light and spiritual growth. They come already more expert than many of our members, thanks to the internet and the vast amount of information readily available. They come well-versed in the books of Dan Brown and other authors, sometimes academically inspired, sometimes worryingly inaccurate. Now, when we tell them there are 'no secrets in Masonry' we are met with uncomprehending stares, and the question: "but how can you profess to be a Brother of this organization when you don't understand any of your own teachings?"

My Companions, we are being held to a different set of standards now. If we wish to engage and retain the many young men who knock at our door, we need to offer them more than clam bakes, rubber chicken dinners, calls for charity and poorly memorized and executed rituals. They are coming in search of education and personal growth. Our Craft – and our rituals – are perfect vehicles to satisfy this hunger for purpose in a mundane world. But to be able to teach we need to understand the lessons ourselves.

This paper is offered as an example of what one can learn from a ritual if one takes the time to read and reread it, preferably with a few good reference books to hand. Our rituals are not only exquisite poetry; they contain maxims and epithets to live by; they contain glimpses of history and religion; they contain symbols and analogies worthy of meditation; and they ultimately contain profound truths and a unique perspective on life for those willing to make the effort to uncover them. And yes, they contain secrets which, like the *prima materia* of the alchemists, is right under our noses if only we look, and capable of being transformed into spiritual gold.

The thoughts and analogies I draw using the Most Excellent Master degree are largely universal. However, some interpretations are my own, and I encourage you to seek *your* own. The beauty of a symbol is that it allows each person to see it through the prism of their own personal life experience: the general substance may be the same to all but the accidents will differ for each person who views it. So here is a new – and perhaps scary for some of you – way to look at ritual, using the Most Excellent Master degree.

When you read a ritual, you can often determine how it was created. Some rituals clearly come from a single person's ideas; some appear created by committee; some show the impression of many years' development; and a few reflect inspiration from a higher source. The degree of Most Excellent Master is one of the latter. Traditional history tells us that it was penned by Thomas Smith Webb and mention is made of it in Middletown, Connecticut in 1783. However, there were a number of degrees with similar names being conferred in the United Kingdom, including a Most Excellent Master degree in Scotland, which F. G. Spiedel claims to be the basis of Webb's degree in his book 'A History and Handbook, the York Rite of Freemasonry'.

The degree is based on the completion of King Solomon's Temple, and reflects a strong familiarity with biblical teachings and especially the Psalms. This is not surprising from an age where the first book any family would possess would be a bible, which would not sit in a bookshelf but would be studied by the family every day. What is surprising is how the degree seeks to draw a parallel between God's creation of the world and his creation of Man, and Man's creation of the Temple, which is often said to be a microcosmic representation of creation.

For Masons, the analogy may be even deeper.

Kabbalistic tradition informs us that God created man first, before the rest of creation, and He did this to know what he looked like. In a way the first man, Adam Kadmon, was a reflection of God, His mirror image. In a similar manner our tradition tells us that the physical Temple of Solomon was – and is – a symbol of man, with its outer courts containing representations of parts of the physical body, while in the center, the Holy of Holies represented the spiritual core of man, where God dwelled. Was the Temple also seen as a living entity? Whether the original celebrations at the dedication of the Temple at Jerusalem reflected this we will probably never know. However, the Masonic ceremony we have before us clearly points in this direction.

Perambulations – or circumambulations – in the form of a circle have long been believed to raise energy, most commonly at the center of the circle being described. You only have to watch the Disney cartoon 'Fantasia' to see the magician drawing three quick circles with his wand before thrusting it forward and see the magic 'bolt' shoot out of the end of the rod! In a similar vein, recreating past events linked them to the present – a technique seen in just about every culture in the world, where the storyteller has the power to cross time by evoking images and tales of former times.

With this in mind, let us examine the first part of the Most Excellent Master Degree.

In six days God created the heavens and the earth. This is the 6th Degree in the York Rite system. If the Degree refers to Adam Kadmon, or the perfect man before his fall, then we would expect to find evidence of this in Hebrew teaching. The tradition of Kabbalah is based on the Tree of Life, which is composed of ten Sephiroth, or emanations from God. The 6th emanation is Tiphereth, which is the direct reflection of God. It is referred to the Sun, and also to perfect balance; and in Christian mysticism to Christ. As Adam Kadmon, it is the reflection of the Spiritual Temple in its primitive glory and perfection.

God created the world in six days. It is interesting to note that, in the first part of our ritual we circumambulate the Lodge six times, and each time we pass the East we give a sign to indicate we are now at a higher grade – or level – than before. We move from East to West, following the 'morning and evening of the first' and subsequent days. Finally, after the sixth circumambulation we remove our aprons. We rest.

This is analogous to common times of prayer practiced in most traditions of The Book. For example, the Jews prayed at 9:00am and called this hour of prayer "Shacharit". At 3:00pm they held the second hour of prayer, called "Minchah" or "Gift-offering" from the offerings made in the Temple; and "Arvit" was the evening prayer, added after the destruction of the Temple in C.E. 70. For Roman Catholics, monastic time followed this tradition, counting from dawn, which was fixed at 6:00am. "Terce" (or Third Hour) took place at 9:00am; "Sext" (Sixth Hour) at noon, and "None" (Ninth Hour) at 3:00pm. It should be easy to see why the Master is associated with 9am or Terce; the Junior Warden with Sext; and the Senior Warden with None, when Craftsmen would have their work inspected before the light failed. I will leave the analogies in the Passion to your imagination, but recall at least that the three key times in the Passion were the crucifixion at Terce – the Master's time, the fall of darkness over the realm of light at Sext – the Junior Warden's time, and the death of the Teacher at None – the Senior Wardens' Time; and throughout this story are numerous references to the Temple and its destruction.

So we have just reenacted the creation of the world. In a way it is a kind of Mystery Play, in which we play the creating forces. Can we find any analogy between what is described in Genesis and the grades or levels we have just passed through? I will make a suggestion, but it is only my thoughts on the subject:

• On the 1st Day God created light. We bring the Light of wisdom to the Entered Apprentice. Light is traditionally provided by candles, representing Fire.

162

- On the 2nd Day the waters above were divided from the waters below. We teach the lesson of duality to the Fellowcraft, in the two pillars of the Temple. The element referred to is Water.
- On the 3rd Day dry land and vegetation appears. It is noteworthy that the Third Degree has as two of its most potent symbols the images of soil, burial and the acacia. Here we are immersed in Earth.
- On the 4th Day the sun, moon and stars are created to govern the day and night, which divide and mark the divisions of time. Air is the focus of these actions.
- On the 5th Day sea creatures, animals and birds appear. The force of life is bestowed upon the earth and all is fruitful and multiplies.
- On the 6th Day God creates man, or places him on earth (many traditions have God creating man first, then placing him in the spot He has made for him considerably later). This introduces the Soul, or Spirit into the vivified Elements of Fire, Water, Earth and Air noted above, and introduces the spark of the divine in this unique creation, placing Man above all other animals.

Purification by the Elements is a requirement of many religions and rituals, in order to render one worthy to receive the spirit. Anyone who has seen the Entered Apprentice Degree worked by Garibaldi Lodge in New York City will know this!

As the Candidate is brought in, Psalm 24 is recited. According to the United States Conference of Catholic Bishops: "the Psalm apparently accompanied a ceremony of the entry of God (invisibly enthroned upon the ark), followed by the people, into the temple. The temple commemorated the creation of the world." The Candidate participates in this activity of invoking life and power into the ceremony. He functions on two levels: in one he represents the living temple; and in the other he represents the 'spirit' which is about to bring the temple to life. He is prepared for this symbolic role through the Obligation.

At the Obligation, the Brothers are instructed to stand around the Candidate and altar in the form of a circle. The Candidate is made to be the 'point within a circle', which itself is often considered to be the perfect shape, even a representation of God. The ritual of Emulation includes the beautiful words: "and the circle is the emblem of the creative mind by which the perfect circle is made manifest." In the Obligation the Candidate swears to dispense (Masonic) light, and as the point within the circle in his state of perfection, Adam Kadmon is the prism of God's light. There is another odd phrase in the Obligation, too, where the Candidate promises not to "derogate from the character I am about to assume..." The words 'about to assume' tell us that the Candidate is indeed about to become something different. The word 'derogate' means to stray, or prevaricate; and we all know that, just as Adam broke his vow not to eat of the Tree of Knowledge in Genesis, so the next Degree in the York Rite will show us the Temple broken and destroyed, because the people of Israel, who represent the body of Adam Kadmon, broke their vow to God.

But at this moment all is perfect; the Temple is completed; and man before the Fall is the true reflection of God.

So the Degree of Most Excellent Master is both a retelling of the story of Creation in Genesis, while giving a more direct focus on the creation and duties of man; and also a shining example of the sublime heights to which ritual can rise when it is truly inspired.

At the end of the first section of the degree the postulant is given the name of Rabbonai or Rabboni. It is explained that this signifies "My Great Master" or "Most Excellent Master". It is interesting that this term is not used in the Old Testament, but twice in the New Testament. Here the word is generally accepted to be Aramaic, meaning "My Master". In Mark 10:51 Jesus asks a blind man what he wants of him, and the man replies: "Rabboni, I want to regain my sight!" In John 20:16, when Mary Magdalene recognizes the resuscitated Jesus outside the tomb, Jesus said to her, "Mary!" She turned and said to Him in Hebrew, "Rabboni!" (which means, Teacher).

In both cases the point of the story can be summarized by the phrase "I was blind but now I see." This was the phrase used by the blind man healed by Jesus when challenged by the Pharisees; and a phrase which has often been used in Rosicrucian ceremonies, too. The phrase is used to excellent effect in both cases: in the first as a physical miracle, and in the second to emphasize the fact that Mary Magdalene is the first person to recognize the resurrected Master or Teacher. The message again is more important than the medium. Regardless of the religion, this tells us of that instant when the scales fall from our eyes, and we see things as they truly are. Recognizing the true message that God dwells within us was introduced in the first section of the Most Excellent Master degree as we relived the days of creation, and took a solemn obligation as an image of purification prior to being admitted to the mysteries of the Temple.

Now as we begin the second section we see in our rubric that "the Kings and Marshal do not wear Aprons". To a regular Mason working through the degrees of the York Rite, and therefore unfamiliar with the Chivalric Rites, which move beyond the use of aprons, this first sight in their Masonic careers of the leaders of the Lodge not wearing what they have been taught is an essential part of Lodge regalia, must engender either a sense of liberation or a feeling that this group is somehow 'mad, bad and dangerous to know'!

Now we see the procession carrying the Keystone into the Lodge, and its 'proper' placement at the top of the Arch. The Temple is completed, and worthy to receive God. The body is perfected and worthy to receive the spirit. But if the body is perfected through a long career of Masonic introspection and the removal of the surplus excrescences of profane life, then man must have – at least symbolically – retrieved his primitive state of innocence to merit this union of earth and spirit, body and Godhead.

Here the verse of the Dedication Ode tells us that there is no longer a need for Level or Plumb Line, Trowel or Gavel, Compass or Square. In other words, we have just jettisoned all the implements we have relied on in our Masonic journey. We are perfected. There is no further need for work. Now, before we get ahead of ourselves, we must remember that these are Mystery Plays. We are not really 'perfect': we are enacting mythologies which help us to understand the true lessons of Masonry.

Now comes the really amazing moment of this degree, the one which for me indicates the true genius of Webb.

We are told: "It is no longer necessary that we should wear craftsman's clothes. Let the aprons be taken off and laid aside."

Wow!

As we saw earlier, we find ourselves transported back to Genesis once more. Remember that when man fell, according to one world view, he tried to emulate God by carrying out an act of creation himself, but only ended up becoming stuck or enmired in the earth – his human body. Now interestingly, Genesis 3:7 says: "Then the eyes of both were opened, and they knew that they were naked; and they sewed fig leaves together and made themselves aprons." Aprons! When we were given our white apron in the Entered Apprentice Degree it was compared to the Golden Fleece and the Roman Eagle in grandeur. We also knew it was a symbol of probation. We now learn that it was the outward emblem of our nakedness, or possibly sin – but surely more certainly the fact that our eyes were being opened to knowledge and we were beginners on the road to enlightenment. Wasn't that the function of the serpent in the first place, to lead us away from blissful ignorance and into the real world of free choice? We cannot exercise free will without knowledge, and yet we are told we were created without free will: that an external agent was needed to give us this faculty. Perhaps Masonry does contain Gnostic secrets, after all. That phrase alone should guarantee a particularly high pile of brushwood around my stake from the Fundamentalists!

Now we find our colleagues symbolically removing this sign of apprenticeship, of sin, or Gnosis. We have been declared Perfect Masters. We are no longer Apprentices, Fellow Craft, Masters, Mark Masters or Past Masters. We are Perfect Masters, Perfecti. We are symbolically perfect vehicles for the spirit. Like butterflies we emerge from the chrysalis and are formally received by King Solomon and King Hiram in our new incarnation. The two pillars of Boaz and Jachin, now represented by living beings, accept us as the Keystone: the answer.

We are perfected, no longer bound by earthly ties, formally acknowledged in our new role, and a worthy vessel for the spirit, just as the physical Temple was the worthy vessel of the abode of God. Just as a passing observation, the Kings are not content with congratulating the Postulants. They have to touch each one. Notice how they shake hands with the Candidates. This takes us into a whole new realm of the fact that we live on the earthly Plane, and how the only way we can communicate with each other and with other realms is through the element of Earth. This is why we transmit lines, traditions, successions, initiations, filiations by the laying on of hands, or even, as in Masonry, concealed in something as simple as a grip...

And here we come to the Dedication of the Temple. When we think about it, Dedication is a process rather than a singular event.

One might say 'I dedicate myself to healing the sick', but this is a commitment to a lifestyle change, not a momentary activity. Similarly, the dedication of an object implies it will be henceforth set aside to that use and that use alone. This is precisely the explicit commitment required for the mystical union, or mystical wedding, to take place. We have seen the close connection of the narration of the building of King Solomon's Temple to the story of Creation in Genesis. What was the purpose of the Dedication? To set aside the Temple for God's use. What was the result? The decent of the Shekinah, which turned a lifeless form made of stone, precious metal and wood into a living organism, an intimate uniting of the material and spiritual worlds.

We can see the similarity to the creation of Adam, when the vessel created out of the materials of the earth was dedicated to the service of God, and the wind of life was breathed into the form to make a living being, an admixture of the material and spiritual. Neither took place until the vehicle was both finished and explicitly dedicated.

There is one moment in the Masonic telling of the Dedication which departs from the biblical story, and which in a way seems to be telling its own story. There was no sorrow at the dedication of the Temple in the Holy Scriptures. However, in our dedication the following words are put in the mouth of Hiram, King of Tyre: "I recall with profound sorrow the death of one long associated with us in the building of the Temple and deeply deplore his absence from an occasion that must present to every beholder astonishing evidence of the magnificence and excellence of his handwork." In our version, the planners are present but the actual builder is not. Is there the slightest hint here of the several apocryphal and Kabbalistic traditions that there were intermediaries in the creation story, that God used agents to create the universe? Even in Proverbs, Sirah and the Book of Wisdom, Wisdom or Sophia is described as God's agent an assistant in creation.

Returning to the events before us, 2 Chronicles tells us that 'the building of the Lord's temple was filled with a cloud. The priests could not continue to minister because of the cloud, since the Lord's glory filled the house of God. Then Solomon said: "The Lord intends to dwell in the dark cloud."' The 'dark cloud' is also mentioned in 1

Kings. Now King Solomon gives his somewhat long prayer, followed by which the Shekinah descends. Now in our ritual the Shekinah hovers around for quite a while. It appears before King Solomon's prayer, apparently waits until the three-page speech (in the Red Book) is ended, then descends.

I puzzled over this for some time, but drew my conclusion from Ockham's razor, that the simplest answer is usually the best. It was probably easier – and more impressive to Candidates for the Degree – to see a fire hovering over their heads, which suddenly flew down to light the brazier, than to fill the room with a dark cloud, which no doubt would have had the cast and candidates running, coughing, from the room, and also ensured a timely visit by the fire brigade! No mystery here, then.

It seems wholly appropriate that the descent of the Shekinah is followed by the antiphonal recital of Psalm 122, also known as 'A song of Ascents', or 'A Song of Degrees, by David'. The antiphonal recitation by the two Kings is interesting, and may reflect the belief that, from the way the psalms are laid out, with each verse usually having two parts, the second a response to the first, these were meant to be read by two people. This stands apart from the rest of the ritual, where either the Chaplain sings or recites the psalms, or the entire group sings the Odes, or the parts are given to the protagonist (e.g. King Solomon's prayer) with the Chaplain as narrator. However, at this point, the two Kings speak antiphonally. For me this reflects the idea of speaking in tongues: the divine fire has descended and as a result the voice now speaks as though from two sources. According to Socrates of Constantinople, antiphonal singing was introduced into Christian worship by Ignatius of Antioch, who claimed to have seen the angels singing in alternate choirs.

Now the main part of the ritual is complete and the educational part, in the form of an Address, takes place. The speech is a masterpiece of teaching and profundity, and gives a compelling summary of the purpose of the Degree system, and it is best to reread this excellent speech for oneself. However, there is one point which is worth noting. The Address begins with a foretaste of the Degree to come, the Holy Royal Arch, and ends with one of the most powerful statements by the Worshipful Master at the close of the Entered Apprentice Degree – surely no coincidence. To begin with the end, which is itself the beginning, the final words "...for that far-distant country from whence we shall never return" is reminiscent of "that undiscovered country" referenced in the Blue Lodge. And finally, the Address begins with the communication of the final sign, the Sign of Admiration, again both reflective of a sign once given during the Inner Working of the Worshipful Master's Installation, and more pertinently, a foretaste of the sign to be communicated in the next Degree. Perhaps it is worth quoting a part of the Address here, for then the link becomes more obvious: "The multitude on beholding it were struck with bewildering amazement, and raised their hands in admiration and astonishment at its wondrous magnificence, and well as to protect their eyes from the effects of its exceeding brilliancy." And so the beauty of the original will be once again be reflected in the eyes of those sent to seek it out in the next Degree.

The theme of future destruction is continued in in the Address following the description of the duties in each Degree: "And although we know of a certainty that all earthly things are transient, and that in process of time, even at the best, the decay of ages will crumble our magnificent temple into dust..." However, it is clear that the temple being referred to is not that of King Solomon, for the most casual reader of the bible knows that that edifice did not decay over time but was pulled brick from brick and razed to the ground in a single act of vandalism.

This was the result of man's deviation from the will of God. And just as Adam and Eve turned away from God's law in Eden, and were cast out, so the Jewish people, the collective Adam turned from God and were cast out of Israel. Yet, just as Adam's body may be bruised and broken, still the spirit lived within, although in a trancelike state; so did the Temple lie in ruins, but the elements of its salvation remained buried deep and hidden from casual inspection, until the wisdom of future generations discovered and brought them to light.

But for the moment, while the storm clouds of history and ignominy gather on the distant horizon, we allow ourselves a moment to contemplate the glory of the temple in its original state, a reflection of primitive Man in his initial state of perfection, the reflection of God, and clothed in a glorious body, which dazzled with "the effects of its exceeding brilliancy."

I hope you have found some things in what I have said of interest, and perhaps even inspired you to do further research. The point I have been trying to make to you is this: if a new Mason or a prospective member comes up to you and asks you to talk about the purpose of Ritual in general, or a Degree in particular, which answer is more likely to induce him to join and become a lifelong devotee of our gentle Craft: "I dunno, we just learn them by rote, do them to the best of our ability, and then go for a drink", or: "that's an interesting question. Ritual is a means to hold a mirror up to ourselves, to try to better understand why we are here, how we relate to the Creator, and how to make ourselves more serviceable to mankind, by studying the mysteries contains within them"?

ROSICRUCIAN HISTORY, & THEMES IN THE ROSICRUCIAN DEGREES

Before we can begin this talk our first question naturally has to be: 'What is Rosicrucianism?' The 17th and 18th Degrees of the Ancient Accepted Scottish Rite meet in a Chapter of Rose Croix, which is French for Rosy Cross (hence 'Rosicrucian').

Whatever its original intent, nowadays it has become a bucket definition which seem to contain just about anything you want it to. All we can really be certain of is that is utilizes mystical Christian symbolism, particularly its signature one of a red rose in the center of a golden cross, and that it claims links with alchemy and the Kabbalah. Perhaps its very vagueness is the reason it has survived as an idea – or ideal – according to Christopher McIntosh, the noted authority of Rosicrucianism. Initially against the Catholic Church, it allowed itself and its symbols to be used by that body; and by the Freemasons the Church so violently reacted against, when their Enlightenment ideas threatened their control of the minds of the people. It is used by bodies which charge for paper pamphlets to be delivered in the mail; and by esoteric bodies who give the teachings freely in an imagined adherence to the original manifestos. As we saw at the beginning, even the symbol of the Red Rose and Cross of Gold as a symbol of Christ on the Cross have been challenged by those who see instead, further alchemical symbols, for in French 'ros' means 'dew' and the cross as alchemical shorthand for the crucible.

To understand its origins and what the original movement, which has gained such a broad interpretation in the 21st Century, we need to review some European history.

The period of several hundred years following the fall of the Roman Empire was a sad time for Europe. Known as the Dark Ages, the continent was divided up into a large series of small fiefdoms. The vast majority of the inhabitants were little more than slaves, working for Lords of the Manor over whom there may or may not be a monarch, and whose pitiful tenements could be subject to being overrun and destroyed by neighboring Lords at any moment. Education was non-existent, and what libraries which had survived successive incursions from foreign powers were locked away in the monasteries. It was even forbidden to read the Bible, and by saying the Mass in Latin, the vast majority of the people didn't even know anything much about their religion other than what the priests wished them to know. What they didn't owe to their Lord in taxes they owed to the Church in tithes, and if the Lord had total power over life and death, the Church had total power over what happened afterwards. This state of complete ignorance suited both the ruling powers and the Church. The environment of complete enslavement for ninety-nine percent of the population led to immense corruption, of course. A manifestation of this which was eventually to prove a major tipping point was the sale of 'Indulgences'.

For those who don't know the term, let me explain. In the Catholic Catechism there were two types of sin: mortal and venial. A mortal sin led to an eternal consequence; a venial or lesser one to a temporal consequence. However, a sin may be atoned either in this life or after death in a transitional place called Purgatory. This place involves pain and suffering. Clearly it is better to resolve one's potential for a time in Purgatory while still alive! The Church possessed what it called – and calls, surprisingly – a 'Treasury' composed of the 'Superabundant Merits of Jesus Christ and the Saints'. Effectively this means in layman's terms that the Saints accrued more 'celestial brownie points' during their lives than they needed (of course Jesus was purely a depositor in this 'Treasury', since he had no sins, and since his satisfaction is infinite, the purpose of roping the Saints into this exercise is puzzling). The Church quickly saw a profit in this potential trade, and soon as selling Indulgences (actual documents) to people, promising remission of time in Purgatory in exchange for money. Indeed, much of St. Peter's in Rome was paid for this way. Of course it wasn't as flagrant as this. An Indulgence was granted, and by pure coincidence the relived sinner would make a generous donation to the Church. There were even tables listing the numbers of days, months or years one got off Purgatory depending on the Indulgence issued (and no doubt the amount paid)!

This cozy arrangement was to end with the coming of the Renaissance.

The Renaissance was a broad movement spanning nearly 300 years, from the 14th to the 17th Centuries. It was a period which saw great advances in literature, art, philosophy, diplomacy, music, science and religion. It brought a number of important aspects into play. Firstly, the rediscovery of books by the Roman and Greek authors, and the migration of Greek scholars after the fall of Constantinople in 1453. Private libraries were built up and translations of these works into Latin and the vernacular began. The invention of the printing press in Europe by Gutenberg in 1450 allowed the spread of philosophy. The introduction of humanism through such authors as Pico della Mirandola's text *Oration on the Dignity of Man*, and the increasing availability of the Bible (one has to remember up till this time almost all libraries were housed in monasteries and access strictly controlled by monks). This movement, beginning in Italy and spearing rapidly across Europe, took the church by surprise. Initially supportive, patrons of the new form or realistic art (Michelangelo, Da Vinci, Botticelli, Caravaggio, etc.) and the development of music into polyphony from plainchant, it was the challenges to the Church's view on science and dogma which began to turn it again the movement. The earth was flat, the sun revolved around the world, dissection was illegal, alchemy – the precursor to chemistry – was alternately praised and proscribed.

This tension between the Catholic Church, particularly in the increasing accusations of corruption, and the increasing availability of information to the masses, invariably led to challenges to its authority.

Perhaps the greatest of these was the challenge to Roman supremacy of Rome by Martin Luther in 1517 with his Ninety-Five Theses. Protestantism spread through Europe both through belief and political scheming. He was excommunicated by Pope Leo X, the very man who was reconstructing St. Peter's Basilica using money from Indulgences. No conflict of interests there... Excommunications were common – but meant little to the Protestants who often saw expulsion from a corrupt Church as a badge of honor.

However, broadly speaking, towards the latter part of the 16th Century an accommodation had largely been secured, with Catholics and Protestants living side by side. In 1555 the Peace of Augsburg, signed by Charles V, Holy Roman Emperor, ended the war between Lutherans and Catholics, establishing the right of ruler to determine the religion of their country. However, the Peace was tenuous, and the rise of Calvinism, which had played no part in the Peace agreement, introduced a new destabilizing force, and wards of succession further rocked the Peace.

Nevertheless, it was a Golden Age of tolerance during this time under Rudolph II, the Holy Roman Emperor. In 1583 he moved from Vienna to Prague, where he encouraged alchemists, astronomers (Tycho Brahé and Johannes Kepler both attended his court), astrologers and all manner of esoteric thinkers to come and join him. His early upbringing in Spain had made him wary of his royal Spanish relatives and their intolerance of Protestants, and he also supported the Jewish community in Prague, and sought their advice on the Kabbalah and philosophy. It was this tolerant environment which attracted both John Dee and his assistant, Edward Kelley to sojourn there. Even Nostradamus prepared a horoscope for him.

The problem was, his successor. Dying without marrying, and therefore with no heir, he was briefly succeeded by an elderly relative who also left no heir. The natural successor Ferdinand I of Austria, was far more Catholic and intolerant than the Bohemians of Prague wished for, and eventually they favored Frederick V, the Elector of Palatine and his wife, Princess Elizabeth Stuart, daughter of King James I of England. He was crowned in 1620. Naturally they assumed that James would protect them again any Catholic attacks, since his daughter sat upon the throne. They were wrong. Ferdinand I called on his uncle, Philip IV of Spain, for help. After only one year, the so-called 'Winter King' (because he ruled such a short time) was defeated and expelled, and in revenge the Catholics repealed the tolerant Decrees issued by Rudolph II, persecuted the Jews and attacked the Protestants.

Of course the determination of the Catholic Church – and their supporters across Europe – to seize the opportunity to overtake Europe once more ultimately to lead to the Thirty Years' War, which completely changed the political face of the continent, and left several countries worse than decimated (decimated literally means the death on one man in ten, but in parts of Germany, for example, up to forty percent of the common people perished, and some cities took one hundred years to reach their former populations).

England and much of France were relatively unscathed, due to King James I's shameful lack of support for his daughter, which went against the wishes of most of the people and especially Parliament, which was certainly one of the factors which started to turn the tide against the monarchy, ending with the regicide of Charles I. But its neutrality made it a perfect place for the Rosicrucian movement to take hold.

What is particularly tragic in all this is that the Rosicrucian Manifestos appeared just before this time: the *Fama Fraternitatis* in 1614 and the *Confessio Fraternitatis* in 1615. I will not go into their content – they are freely available and very short. But their length belied their impact. Basically they announced the existence of a secret Order devoted to healing, and the study of alchemy and Kabbalah, and source information from the East and West, which had been gathered by a mysterious leader, Christian Rosenkreutz, or Rosy Cross. He had founded an Order which professed several articles, the most important being:

- To heal the sick and that gratis;
- To dress according to the customs of the country in which they traveled;
- To meet once a year at the Domus Sancti Spiritus, the 'Invisible College';
- To find a worthy successor;
- To use the mark of 'CR'.

One of the most important points of the Manifestos was that they were vehemently anti-papist and pro-Protestantism.

From this very short and tenuous introduction, so much has been assumed! However, the frenzy it caused, both for and against, was extraordinary. The great thinkers of the Age positively lined up to join, and since the only way they could be asked was to make their intentions know publicly, they did so.

Why did it catch the Spirit of the Age, the *zeitgeist*, so completely?

Firstly, the timing couldn't have been better. The Thirty Years War had not yet begun. The Golden Age of Rudolph II showed the thinkers and Protestant monarchs how a court could be a glory of the Age. This was the first glimmer of Enlightenment (with a capital 'E'), when the theories and philosophy of the Renaissance were now moving towards action, and man was taking his first bold steps away from the control of the Church and realizing man's capacity for independent thought and study. Man was seen as a composite being, joining the divine with the temporal, and not necessarily evil from birth, capable of achieving his own salvation. And in these last days before the War, the Protestants in particular warmed to a message which seemed to predict the demise of Catholic hegemony. It also provided an opportunity to syncretize the esoteric currents of the time into one field of study, drawing spirituality, alchemy, astrology, medicine and Kabbalah under one roof.

Even when the Thirty Year War laid waste the heart of Europe, Rosicrucianism had a fertile ground in which to grow and prosper: England. The very fact that James I stayed out of the mainland War permitted these ideas to develop and grow. There are many theories of how its current led to the establishment of the Royal Society, Freemasonry and so forth. Whether Rosicrucians founded Freemasonry or Freemasonry drew from a number of Rosicrucian teachings is probably irrelevant, for many streams ended up in Masonry, and once the war was over, Rosicrucian thinkers in Germany and France most certainly made up for lost time.

In Germany, for example, the 'Golden and Rosy Cross' was a loose alchemical Brotherhood which transformed over time into a Masonic organization. It is notable that one of its more famous members was Frederick-William II of Prussia, who joined in 1781. He was the nephew of Frederick the Great, who was the sovereign whom the Southern Masonic Jurisdiction of the AASR claimed had drawn up the Constitutions of the Scottish Rite. By now the tenets of Rosicrucianism had far outgrown the vague and tantalizing hints of the original Manifestos, and it had become a mix of spiritual Christianity, alchemy and Christian Kabbalah, which had led to the establishment of 9 or 10 Grades based upon the Tree of Life, each Grade replete with its own esoteric teachings.

That alchemy, or at least its symbolism, persisted in the development of later Masonic Rites can be easily seen. Following on from the Golden and Rosy Cross, Baron von Hund's 'Rite of Strict Observance' saw an offshoot created by Johann Augustus Starck, called the 'Clerici Ordinis Templariorum', which were given over to the study of alchemy, Kabbalah and, for that matter, necromancy!

At the reconstitution of the Strict Observance into the 'Scottish Rectified Rite', whose rituals were written by Jean-Baptiste Willermoz, a prominent Lyon Mason, and who was credited by A. C. F. Jackson in his seminal history of the Rose Croix Degree with writing our 18th Degree. We must also remember that he was fascinated by Alchemy, and indeed his younger brother went to Marseilles to study both Chemistry and, in his spare time, alchemy. Many of Willermoz' rituals are heavily base upon alchemical symbolism, most strongly, perhaps, his 'Aigle Noire Rose-Croix', or Order of the 'Black Eagle Rose Croix'. Willermoz was also a member of a mysterious Masonic group called the 'Elus Cohen', founded by Martinez de Pasqually, which professed a gnostic form of Christianity, and actively practiced magic operations.

So it is perhaps a bit of a disappointment that our present version contains so little alchemy!

However, we should remember that, while alchemists were bent over furnaces while their students manned the bellows which kept the retorts and athanors warm, their search was as must about the alchemical transformation of the soul. For their actions were firmly rooted in the axiom of the Emerald Tablet, 'As Above So Below', and that what they perceived in Nature, or the macrocosm (the Universe, and the planet Earth) was also reflected in their person, the microcosm.

Thus, while we may not find the answer to making gold out of lead in a physical sense we will begin to discern some of the purer teachings of the *Fama* and *Confessio* within our beloved Degree, and also find clear alchemical pointers to how we should take the destroyed Temple of our pitiful state, and transform it into the cubic stone, foundation of the restored Temple, which means our reintegration into our primitive or original state of perfect union with God.

My talk has primarily been to give you a framework of the history behind the development of the Rosicrucian current. However, I will not leave you in suspense! I intend to give you a few pointers about what to look for in our own precious Degrees.

However, there is a caveat: the Degrees are not simply given out to anyone who asks. You have to work to receive them. In other words, if you volunteer to help in the Scottish Rite Degrees, then you will receive copies of the rituals on which you are working. So if you wish to study these great rituals, you will have to put some effort into the Valley yourselves. I will not deny there are dark, dangerous corners of the internet where you may find some of the Rituals. But think of your karma!

The first point to notice is that the 17th and 18th Degrees (actually the 15th through the 18th) tell the story of Christian Rosenkreutz. In his story we learn that he traveled the Shores of the Dead Sea and to Damcar or possibly Damascus in search of enlightenment, continuing to Egypt and finally Fez before returning to the West, bringing his knowledge with him. I am sure you will recall the 17th Degree, being a Knight of the East and West, in which you traveled on all shores of the Mediterranean in search of Light. Finally, in the 18th Degree you received enlightenment, and were asked to become teachers, just as Christian Rosenkreutz founded his College.

In alchemy the *prima materia* or common material from which gold may be spun is black, but passes through successive purifications in which it first becomes white, and finally red, the Philosopher's Stone. This red stone has only to touch a person to heal them. Also, it can touch base metal and turn it into gold. Is it any wonder that the device of the Order is a red rose upon a golden cross, for the very presence of the red catalyst has turned the base wooden cross into gold? Many esoteric traditions hold that Adam, the First Man, was created from red clay. Again, is it any wonder that Christ, the Second Man, would be represented as a red stone, or red rose? As we saw at the beginning of this talk, some even suggested that the term 'Rosicrucian' comes not from the Rosy Cross, but from the two Latin words 'ros', meaning 'dew', and 'crucis' for the cross, which was a common alchemical shorthand for a crucible.

I have no doubt there will be future lecture from someone on Practical Alchemy. In the meantime, remember that the Hermetic Axiom, As Above So Below: meant that these seekers performed alchemical experiments to help them identify what they observe within themselves. For they were working upon their own perfection through Spiritual Alchemy, burning off the dross of the excrescence of daily mundane life to find perfection within, that spark of life we Freemasons refer to as the cubic stone. This is why the Cubic Stone poured forth blood and sweat: the sacrifice on the cross had to burn off his humanity so that nothing but the god remained. Wow! Bring on the pitchforks! Jesus as Avatar, showing us that any of us can re-integrate with God, without any intermediary, any dogma. We all have the divine spark in us. Perhaps the early Freemasons simply substituted the analogy and symbolism of alchemy for building?

Neo-Platonists reminded their Renaissance antecedents that there were four Elements, and four forces ruling them: Earthy, Air, Water and Fire. The Gnomes ruled the earth. Common to German and Scandinavian myth in particular – to say nothing of J.R.R. Tolkien – these hard-working souls labored underground to find precious stones and metals. The Emerald Tablet tells us to descend into the earth for a great treasure. Again, if we understand Christ as an exemplar: we find a Great Secret: a man who was placed in the earth, like an Athanor, for three days, and was reborn, like the lessons of the alchemist. This is a great secret which belongs not only to the Christians, but the Gnostics and any religion which understands that man has the divine spark within him. Why do I say 'Gnostic'? They were but a loose collection of proto-Christians who lost out against the organized religion of Rome. But they understood one message the Catholics needed to stamp out at all costs, and probably with the complicity of Emperor Constantine, who had an Empire to run. This was the message of the Gospel of Thomas: "Lift up a stone and there you will find me. Split a piece of wood and I am there also." (Sayings 33 + 77b). In other words, you do not need a church: you have all that is necessary within yourself.

The Rosicrucian movement had its own 'patron Saint' as it were, a mysterious character called Elie Artista. Elias the Artist was first mentioned in Paracelsus as the Master of Alchemy, a Messianic figure whose return, when all that was hidden and occult would be revealed, was hoped for. He wrote: "This Elias Artista shall restore the true spagyric medicine of the old Egyptian Philosophy which was lost over a thousand years. He shall bring it with him and show it to the world." In the American ritual we have the rather prosaic Master of Ceremonies leading the candidate around. Not so in the English version! Here the conductor is given a name: Raphael. This 'secret' conductor is not named until the final scene, where he is revealed as Raphael. The rubric to this is fascinating: the Conductor is instructed to teach the Candidate to say the four responses on his own. In other words, when the Most Wise Master asks him: "Who was your Conductor?", the Candidate replies unprompted: "Raphael". Another "Wow!" moment!

Up till now, as normal in Masonic ceremonies, the Senior Deacon, Conductor or Leader speaks for the Candidate. In most ceremonies this is simply a matter of expedience: the Candidate doesn't know what to say. But in Rosicrucian circles the matter is entirely different. One of the great goals of Spiritual Alchemy is gaining knowledge of one's Holy Guardian Angel. This force can be seen as one's Higher Self, as one's Inner Voice, or even as an external Being charged with leading one into the Light. However, one wishes to rationalize it, gaining this conscious knowledge is an integral part of spiritual progress. Here, naming the High Being means the Candidate or Neophyte had finally become an Adept in this mystical circle of Adepts, and can name his Higher Self, or Guardian Angel. "Wow", again!

And finally, think on the words learned during the Degree. You learned the Three Virtues which would unlock the Key during your circumambulations, or raising of magical power. And finally you discovered and brought to light the True Word, which in this case was four letters indicating a profound alchemical truth. It has meant many things through the Ages, but here in our alchemical context it states (as you will read on Mark Koltko-Rivera's blog!): "Igne Natura Renovatur Integra", or "the Whole of Nature (our Nature) renewed by Fire". And by three and four steps we arrive at the summit of Jacob's Ladder. We have learned all there is needed to know to achieve union with God – if only we can understand what we have learned.

And all this from a Degree!

THE DARK SIDE OF GOD

NOTE: This paper was written for a meeting of the Red Cross of Constantine, as a deliberately provocative means of getting a robust debate going at what is often a rather torpid meal. Little did I realize that the event was going to be attended by an archbishop! What to do? I had nothing else prepared, so with an apology to 'his Grace', I launched into my paper. The clergy are nothing if not gracious, and after the event he came up to me said told me that, while he didn't necessarily agree with everything I had to say, it was a most interesting evening!

If God is all good, why does he do so many nasty things?

In Hebrew mythos, in Bereshit (Genesis) darkness was upon the face of the deep before God called forth the Logos. If God is all then he was also the darkness.

In one tradition, it is said that God created Adam Kadmon (explain) so he could gaze upon his own image and learn what he looked like. Kadmon was therefore the image of God, and after the fall Adam fractured into millions of tiny sparks which we contain, as we reassemble ourselves into Kadmon, before being reabsorbed by God.

This tension of duality exists in all religions and in all philosophy. Our own pillars of B and J are similar but not identical, and represent opposites which we strive to reconcile. But not until the Holy Royal Arch Degree do we reconcile them with the Arch or Ark or Bridge, which contains the Keystone, the White Stone, the Stone of the Philosophers, the Christ, who now becomes the original Pontifex or bridge between the worlds of darkness and light, earth and heaven, as symbolized by the columns of earthly and divine wisdom.

A prevailing Gnostic idea was that, since the God of the Old Testament seemed to be so keen on fire and brimstone and punishment, while the God of the New Testament was all about love, they must be two different identities. A duality of Godhead. They saw the God of the Old Testament as a demiurge (one theory even has the entity residing on Mount Sinai as a local 'god' or djinn which persuaded the Israelites to carry it away from the locus to which is was bound, and which needed a constant stream of blood offerings for food. But behind this demiurge is the 'true' God, who is rather like an indifferent

Victorian parent to the Gnostics. Finally, this distant father saw what was going on in His creation, and reluctantly decided to intervene, and restored balance by sending an avatar or pattern for us to follow if we wished to break away from the vicious cycle in which mankind found itself trapped. This, of course, was Jesus, the good God's emissary – therefore we are all Christs. Indeed, one of the Gnostic texts even has a scene in which Jesus is seated on a hill looking down at the crucified man and laughing at the stupidity of it all.

In the teachings of Pasqually, God emanated spirits who prevaricated. Now, if God is omniscient he would know they would prevaricate, yet he did nothing about it. Is God weaker than evil? Or does God have a dark side? Most early religions seem to allow God to have a dark side, and it is predominantly the newer religions, including Christianity, who have a problem with this and seek to externalize the darkness into a separate entity – in our case Lucifer or the Devil (who was a largely Medieval invention, drawing on stereotypes of existing, competing Gods)

In the New Testament Jesus is tempted but not explicitly by the Devil. If the Gnostics believed the Christos inhabited Jesus, a man, then equally the dark force may have inhabited another man, as beautifully portrayed in Pasolini's Gospel According to (St.) Matthew

This is an archetypal battle, like the legends of old and even the Star Trek episode – two fighting for the freedom of all, a reduction of war to the chess board

Under these interpretations, the Rosicrucian axiom "*sub alarum tuarum, Jehovah*" or 'beneath the shadow of your wings, Jehovah' takes on a sinister meaning.

VITRIOL – Visita Interiorem Terrae Rectificando Invenies Occultum Lapidem – is the great secret of spiritual alchemy. We have to go into ourselves and face the darkness to find the white stone! The spiritual temple, not built with human hands, is not erected easily: in the archetype of Zerubbabel on must built it with a trowel in one hand and a sword in the other, to keep our darker nature in check.

Note that we always refer to buried treasure! Wagner's Ring Cycle reminds us that treasure belongs to the earth, that it must be freed and refined just as Marie Curie freed and refined radium from pitchblend, as our Hero descends to the realm of the gnomes to liberate the gold. The Alchemists tell us that the raw material for making (spiritual) gold is common, and all around us. It is often protected by a sleeping dragon, and I cannot help but be reminded of the serpent kundalini, curled around the spine. Perhaps this is why wealth is seen as such an aphrodisiac, which turns bald, pot-bellied, ugly little men into sexual gods in the eyes of young girls, hungry for designer clothes and all the trappings of Malkuth...

Now, this brings me to my central point. Again, to go to Star Trek, Kirk's good and bad sides are separated during a 'beam me up, Scottie' moment, and the moral of the story is: neither can exist without the other. For each comprises part of the Tree of Life. As the Golden Dawn says: "an excess of severity is but cruelty, and an excess of mercy is but weakness...seek ye the Middle Path".

So here is my radical theory: when God decided he wished to contemplate himself as if in a mirror, and exteriorized himself as Adam Kadmon, thus beginning creation, did he diminish himself in a way, become less than complete? Is that why fractured Adam – mankind – has free will? No so much because God willed it as God couldn't prevent it, as Adam was part of him? Now if Adam fractures and each of us contains a spark of God, does God seek to reintegrate with us as desperately as we seek to reintegrate with him, to collect the microcosms that we are and bring them back into the macrocosm?

For me, this gets even more interesting when we contemplate the nature of the split. The split was not of opposing natures – God was not intending to divorce himself from his dark side. Rather he was endeavoring to gaze upon his features. Therefore, the split was not into good and evil, light and dark, but into two entities containing both light and darkness, good and evil.

Did Christ, as the reconciler between two opposing forces, who was, to use the beautiful phrase "unfolded into the light", then suffer to reconcile not man and God but the two natures of God himself as well as man?

Karl Jung suggested one interesting way to explain the apparent conundrum of a God who seems as dark as light, in his book Answer to Job. Man is wayward and prone to evil, tempted by Satan or God's darker side. At length, in his most daring challenge, Satan tells God that the most faithful man on earth, Job, is only faithful because life is easy for him. Make life difficult and he would soon lose faith. God allows Satan to do what he will with Job, who endures the systematic destruction of all he holds dear with equanimity, until, being afflicted from head to foot with boils, his resolution cracks and he asks God "Why?" God answers by thundering at Job about his own omnipotence, and that he can do as he pleases. This is not a God anyone could love; only fear. This is a despot, a megalomaniac, drunk with power. Possibly as bad a Satan – the side he allows to tempt him in the first place. Jung suggests that God becomes aware of this dilemma: "Could a suspicion have grown in God that man possesses an infinitely small yet more concentrated light than he, Yahweh, possesses?"

So God himself learns, changes, begins to emphasize his kinder nature. His experience with Job was the lowest point of his development, for God develops and learns as man develops and learns. Now Wisdom appears as a feminine balance, Sophia, to counter masculine severity. Wisdom is hailed in Solomon and eulogized in Proverbs. Ultimately God wishes to transform himself by becoming human. At the moment of greatest despair in the agony of the cross, Jesus cries out "My God, My God, why hast thou forsaken me?" At that very instant God identifies with Job and the suffering he so callously caused him. Man learns from God and God learns from man. Both grow and develop through time. Therefore, God is subject to time – but that would be a whole other paper!

I do not suggest I have the answer. I am merely suggesting the way to a new way of looking at creation. For me the conclusion is so beautiful I almost cannot think about it without crying for joy. For I know that God is not sitting on some high throne waiting for us sinners to find our way back to him. I know he does not wait for us to work out the path and try to drag ourselves up to his plane of existence. I know God is working as hard as we to reconcile with us, that there is not one step we take towards him without his running a mile to draw closer to us. And from that I take great comfort, for I know one of the greatest arcane secrets: the road I take leads to the same goal as God, and he walks beside me for we are both traveling he same path towards the same destination, where we will be reconciled forever.

THE ILLUSTRIOUS ORDER OF THE RED CROSS

Fig 1 – Babylonian 'Rosetta Stone' describing Cyrus' conquest of Babylon

1. Introduction

In the movie "Indiana Jones and the Last Crusade", Indiana has to select the Holy Grail from a table covered with goblets. Finally, eschewing the gold, silver and bejeweled chalices he reaches for a simple little pottery cup at the back of the table. From among the sea of 'empty vessels' he has selected the simplest, the least impressive of those on offer: and he has chosen the most important treasure of all, the Holy Grail.

In a similar vein, we often search for meaning among the better known Degrees and Orders in our beloved Craft, yet sometimes the greatest treasure lies in a place we least expect. The *Illustrious Order of the Red Cross* is often seen as a curiosity, a mildly interesting piece of whimsy which we put on before the 'important' Orders of Malta and Temple. This quaint little play in three Acts about a man being sent to the court of a king, crossing a bridge only to be arrested, and then restored to his former estate seems to teach us little. And the strange debate within the Order, about Wine, Kings and Women seems almost out of place in a Masonic ceremony.

185

Yet this little Order is one of the oldest of all Masonic degrees, and so venerated that it occurs in the Allied Masonic Degrees in England under the title of "Red Cross of Babylon", is strongly alluded to in the Royal Order of Scotland, and even features in the Order of Knight Masons, the *ne plus ultra* of Irish Freemasonry. Further afield, in continental Masonry it is the 16th Degree of many Scottish Rite systems, and is the only Order surviving intact from the mysterious rite of the *Elect Cohens of the Universe* of Martinez de Pasqually.

Why would such an apparently innocuous Order be thought worthy of such preservation, especially in such exalted bodies as the Royal Order of Scotland and the Knight Masons of Ireland? Even stranger: why would it be considered a pivotal degree in early magical systems, this Order which talks of a journey and an apparently frivolous debate?

In this paper we will have a brief look at the Order known history. We will then examine three of the symbols used in this sublime Order: the journey, the bridge, and the debate (incidentally I will also explain the meaning of the two mysterious passwords which to my knowledge are not explained in the United States!). I hope that, by the end of this paper, the listener will have developed a far greater respect for this jewel of an Order, and will promote it to its rightful place in the pantheon of York Rite Degrees[7] and Orders.

2. History of the Order

According to the Old Testament the meeting between Zerubbabel and Darius never took place: it was Tatnai and Sethar-bosnai, local governors[8], who reported the rebuilding of the Temple to Darius in a letter. Darius, after locating Cyrus' original decree, endorses it and

---

[7] In order to allow this paper to be circulated, I have not written anything which is not freely available on the World Wide Web (regrettably that extends to a site I have found which lists the entire text of almost all the Degrees, including passwords and signs), in books or in catalogues.

[8] Strictly speaking, only Tatnai is identified as a governor: "...Tatnai, governor on this side of the river, and Shethar-boznai, and their companions..." *Ezra V, 3.* In a later verse the 'and' is dropped: "Tatnai, governor beyond the river, Shether-boznai, and your companions..." *Ezra VI, 6.* In this latter case it could be argued that Shethar-boznai is the river's name.

tells them to lend what aid they can to the enterprise. There is no indication of any communication between Zerubbabel and Darius, although the Historical Lecture suggests that the Order is based upon a story by Josephus and the debate from the Apocryphal Book of *I Esdras, 4*, where we learn of the debate, but not the identity of any of the debaters, other than the fact that they were his three bodyguards (note that *II Esdras* goes on to predict the destruction of the "Great Harlot", Babylon). The prize requested is permission to continue to rebuild the temple and city at Jerusalem without let or hindrance.

If the Order is not based on sound biblical reference, but rather on apocryphal writings, why was it written, and what lesson is it trying to teach us?

There is very little information about the history of this Order. Indeed, *Spiedel* refers to it briefly as a preparatory Order to those of Malta and Temple and makes no further mention of its symbolism, devoting the rest of his booklet to a detailed description of the history, rites and charities of Knight Templary.

We do know that it is "of considerable antiquity" (*Preface to Red Cross of Babylon Ritual*). In one form it was certainly being conferred in France in the 1760s. In his *"Encyclopædia of Freemasonry"* A. E. Waite mentions that this Order (under the form of *Prince Mason*) was the 33rd degree in the Early Grand Rite, and an older recension of the Red Cross of Babylon. He goes on to say that "it conveys nothing and marks no stage in the Emblematic Art". This statement is so incredible, coming from a man who was prominent in his membership of such mystical and magical bodies as the '*Hermetic Order of the Golden Dawn*', the '*Fellowship of the Rosy Cross*', the '*Chevaliers Bienfaisant de la Cité Santé*' and the '*Societas Rosicruciana In Anglia*', that I can only conclude that it was a blind to draw the reader's attention away from the immense significance of the "Emblematic Art" contained in this Order!

There is a claim that Passing the Bridge – the central section of the Order – was worked in an 'Antient' Lodge in Sunderland, England, as early as 1755. The old title of the Order was "*Knight of the Eagle*", and members were known as "*Knights of the Sword*" and as "*Knights of the Red Cross of Palestine*". In the Baldwyn Rite of Bristol, England it is worked as the "*Knight of the East, Sword and Eagle*".

Apart from these basic references there is little more to unearth. Now the question arises, if this Order is as 'slight' as the historians and mystics would have us believe, then why has it been preserved in almost every significant system of European Masonry, usually at the highest levels, and why has it been used as a vehicle to transmit some of the most arcane allegories in all of the Craft?

3. The Journey

The Order is usually split into three Acts. In Act I the Jewish Sanhedrin lament the fact that their efforts to rebuild the City and Temple at Jerusalem are constantly thwarted, either by aggressive enemies or by indifferent edicts. They elect to send an ambassador to the Court of Darius to plead their case: Zerubbabel offers to go, as he is known to the King at Babylon. In Act II, Zerubbabel attempts to cross a river by means of a bridge, but is arrested by guards and imprisoned. In Act III he is brought before the King, and his commitment to Truth and to his vows result in his being released and exalted, and, following the famous debate, he is allowed to return to his native land bearing gifts, with the promise of a free pass for him and his fellows.

Although the journey is sandwiched between what appear to be two more impressive sections, do not let this distract you. The journey is in fact the most important part of all!

Now, many Masonic Degrees explicitly talk of a journey: the Second Degree, the Third Degree, the Most Excellent Master Degree, the Mark Degree, the Most Excellent Master Degree, the Holy Royal Arch, the Royal Master Degree, the Select Master Degree and the Super-Excellent Master Degree all contain journeys, and if one accepts that all circumambulations are a symbolic journey, then all Masonic Degrees contain such a journey. We find the symbolic use of a journey in many important books, not least Chaucer's "Canterbury Tales", Bunyan's "Pilgrim's Progress" and Dante's "Inferno". Of all the Masonic systems of Degrees, the journey undertaken by Zerubbabel in the '*Illustrious Order of the Red Cross*' is perhaps the most strange of all.

In the Holy Royal Arch, we learn that the name Zerubbabel signifies *"Truth"*; Zerubbabel, like the "Pilgrim" of Bunyan, is therefore the embodiment of this quality. It is *'Truth'*, therefore, which undertakes this extraordinary journey, traveling, it might be noted, from West, or Jerusalem to East, or Babylon, in a surprising reversal of the usual journeying which leads to the Holy City. In this case enlightenment is sought not in the Holy Land but beyond its shores, perhaps an echo of the Knight of the East or Knight of the East & West Degrees, where enlightenment is sought abroad among both Eastern and Western Schools of Philosophy. What, then, does Babylon represent, this city usually associated by fundamentalist Christians with the *'Whore of Babylon'* of Revelations, and the City of Sin *par excellence*?

What is most important about this particular journey is that it is two-way. The immense significance of this will become apparent when we consider the fact that the journey involves crossing a bridge.

4. The Bridge

It is truly tragic that in our time the bridge has become so little understood, we do not even bother to have a floorcloth to represent one of the most potent symbols of all. The United States ritual actually calls for "a practical bridge", but I have yet to see one used (though following the first delivery of this paper we built one for our Commandery!). A physical bridge is also used in the highest grades of the Antient & Accepted Scottish Rite.

It is unlikely to be the river Jordan, as Darius is unlikely to have had that river closely guarded, as he already has governors in the region. It is also unlikely (although this was suggested by A. E. Waite) to be the Euphrates, for Babylon straddled this river. Where or what, then, is this mysterious river over which Zerubbabel must cross? An indication of the answer, surprisingly, lies in the Preface to the "Red Cross of Babylon Degree", published in England, which is worth quoting at length:

"In the great religions of the world – for example Christianity, Judaism, Islam, Zoroastrianism, Confucianism, Shintoism – there is a tradition that the soul has to cross the river of death, usually over a bridge, but sometimes by ferry as in Greek mythology, or by dividing

the waters as Elijah did before his translation…In all the Rites Crossing the Bridge is a symbolical representation of Death, while the subsequent experience of the candidate is emblematical of the judgment of the soul."

In this sense the bridge is also like Jacob's ladder in the First Degree – it is a means of crossing a divide or chasm which separates two places. Much is made in the Book of Ezra about being 'over the river', 'this side of the river' and 'beyond the river' so using the idea of the river as a key delimiter between two lands or empires. So what is the nature of these two worlds, this river and this bridge?

The river has often been used as a symbol for the veil of forgetfulness or death, and its waters wash both cares and remembrances from the transitioning soul. The two lands represent the conscious and subconscious worlds. In Jewish Kabbalistic thought, the earthly, material plane is called *Malkuth* and the plane of Dreams is called *Yesod, which* is also associated with the moon, night and sleep. There is a veil which separates these two worlds, and this can only be pierced by means of traversing a Path or Bridge. As the plane of *Yesod* or Dreams is also known as the plane of images and the plane of deception, it is necessary to hold firm to what is true and what is false in order successfully to cross this bridge. The bridge is sometimes seen as that watery symbol which God placed in the heavens following the inundation of the earth – *Qesheth*, or the Bow. And so Truth crosses the bridge into that world which for mystics and Kabbalists is the world of Dreams, Images, Archetypes, and Angels.

As an aside, in the 16th Century Henry Cornelius Agrippa created a magical alphabet – not unlike the Masonic alphabet introduced in the Holy Ryoal Arch Degree – which he based on the Hebrew alphabet, called 'Passing The River'.

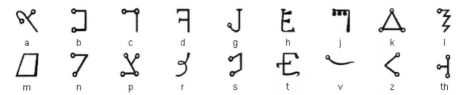

Figure 2: Passing The River Alphabet of Agrippa

Incidentally, this river is sometimes given the name of *Starbuznai*, an interesting corruption which is very close to the name of the possible river, Shethar-Boznai (*see Footnote 8, above*). For the keen student I have transcribed this as (שתאר בזני) whose numerical value would then be 970, making the name similar through Gematria to *Tharsis*, ruler of water, or *etz*, a tree, both of which seem appropriate! If anyone reading this paper has other theories on the meaning of the word, I would be most interested to hear them.

Truth, then, crosses the bridge between the earthly world and the celestial plane, there to be detected as an intruder (naturally, for he is both conscious and living); yet he was chosen for this task because in the legend – from the Red Cross of Babylon – "Zerubbabel … was formerly well-known to the King, (and) now offers his services to undertake the hazardous enterprise of traversing the Persian dominions, and seeking admission to the presence of our Sovereign." So it appears that *Truth* was accustomed to crossing this bridge in the past in order to communicate with this mysterious 'King', but may have forgotten how to do it, which is why he is stopped, recognized as not belonging to that second world, and apprehended. In Kabbalistic work it is important to know the names of the guardians and the necessary passwords, in order to gain admittance to higher realms, and imprisonment or banishment is often the price of forgetfulness.

However, on receiving an audience with the mysterious 'King' he is recognized and a final test is put to him. This test is one of determining that he understands the importance of silence or secrecy.

Truth demonstrates his understanding of the importance of keeping silent on secret matters, and the 'King' now welcomes him as a friend. The mortal is accepted in the land of the dead, or the subconscious world. But has his mysterious bridge been 'burned', and will he be allowed to return to the material plane with the gifts he will learn on this journey?

As a final aside in this section, I hope you now understand why taking the time to create even the most rudimentary representation of the bridge is crucial to the transmission of the purpose of this Order, and I commend its construction, either in physical form or even as a drawing on a piece of cloth, to any Degree team wishing to put on this Order. Indeed, in some versions of this ritual the bridge is even decorated with signs of mortality, including human skulls and bones, thereby making the symbolic allusion of this bridge even more explicit.

5. The Debate

Now we come to the most perplexing part of the story – the Immemorial Discussion, in which three arbiters argue the supremacy of wine, the power of the king, women, and truth. At first glance this debate seems almost out of place in the scheme of things. Why would this be a central part of the ritual? If accepted at face value, it has little to teach us, but we have learned by now that the debate itself is a symbol of something else, something higher.

To better understand the debate, we must first identify who is talking. In the previous section I explained that this part of the drama takes place in a Court ruled over by a mysterious 'King', surrounded by his courtiers. In Kabbalistic tradition we are now in the realm of dreams, the plane of *Yesod*. Traditionally this plane is populated by the angelic host. Moreover, it is within this level that, metaphysically speaking, we find the 'archetypes' of all that exists on earth. Philosophers from Plato forward have argued that everything on earth has a 'perfect' counterpart, or 'archetype', in a higher plane of existence. If we accept this belief, held by these philosophers, metaphysicians and mystics, we may conclude that *Truth* now finds himself, like Pilgrim and Dante before him, in the mystical realm of the angels, ruled over by a chief. Who better to recognize Zerubbabel as a 'friend of my youth' than his own guardian angel, perhaps, with whom Zerubbabel is once again joined in spiritual communion?

The discussion which *Truth* hears, and in which he takes part, is a rehearsal of the 'archetypes'; in this case rehearsed for his benefit – for he is here to learn, after all. If he can learn what he needs to know he will have the information needed to build that spiritual temple which has lain untended and unbuilt for several years, perhaps due to his preoccupation with material goals and temptations. And so the debate of archetypes is tailored especially for him, as his angel gently leads him towards understanding.

The topic, not surprisingly, is about strength. Can the goals of Zerubbabel be achieved through physical, material or temporal objects, such as wine, women or kingly power (and remember that Christ himself was tempted with bread and kingly power)? Even though Zerubbabel is given the task of arguing the strength of women, he comes to realize that only *Truth* can set him free. That is to say, that the strength which he seeks to build his personal Temple lies *within himself*. Well pleased with this result, the 'King' asks him what he needs, and he replies the ability to return as needed, in order to learn more. This is granted (in the symbolism of passports). And this is no casual gift, for *Truth* now has the ability to pass between the two planes of existence without further let or hindrance. Furthermore, he is lavished with more gifts and talents to take back with him to the material plane.

And finally, in a supreme gesture, the King/angel gives him words of power and a sigil to enable him to make the transition in future. In knowing that the power to transform and to build the Temple within lies inside himself, he now has the power to move between life and death itself. Death no longer holds any terrors for our hero.

The circle is complete, and the lesson has been learned. The message which was take away from this Order is the importance of Truth: that we *are* Truth, and that Truth lives within us. Yet now comes the most difficult part of all – as Pontius Pilate said; "What is Truth?" Meditating on this question, my Companions, is the work we must do ourselves.

6. The Sash & Jewel

The passwords given in this Order do not hold any particular significance. Indeed, the two which are not explained in the American ritual have been adequately explained above for those who know where to look.

Of far greater interest is the sash and jewel.

In Masonry the predominant colors are usually white, black, red and purple. Uniquely in this Order we find the color green. This alone would suggest an antiquity to this Order. It is worth pointing out that several other Masonic orders which contain at least a germ of this ritual use red and green regalia, including the Knight Masons, the Royal Order of Scotland and the Scottish Rectified Rite. The color red, explained at length in the Holy Royal Arch Order, represents zeal. But what of green?

Green is the color of initiation, a profound and spiritual initiation into the High Mysteries of Life and God. We see the color in the popular concept of the Holy Grail as a cup carved from an emerald, or from the Emerald Tablet, which contains the classic hermetic axiom "As above, so below". Green is also associated with Venus – both planet and goddess – and in alchemy with the metal copper (so chosen for Venus and Initiation as the metal is both malleable yet sound, and through the action of air oxidizes to the color green, or verdigris). And so red and green signify a zealous spirit, and initiation into the *Arcanum Arcanorum*. On the Tree of Life of the Kabbalists, it is associated with the Sephiroth of *Netzach*, whose attributes include the color Green, an attribution to the planet Venus, and also to the philosophical element of Fire. Just as Fire is Red and Zealous, so its complement, Green, is the most passive color, and are fitly joined together. One final point: *Netzach*, our green Sephiroth, is the Seventh Sephira. Now, the jewel associated with the Red Cross *and* the Knight Masons *and* the Scottish Rite are all seven-pointed stars!

Fig. 3 - Apron of Elect of Zerubbabel (Elu Cohen Rite).

Note the Sword and Trowel, the Chains and the Bridge.

What are we to conclude from this? Truth, having "carried away the victory" (by the way, *Netzach* means "*Victory*"!), is rewarded with the celestial equivalent of a multiple entry pass to the Celestial world to commune and learn at leisure. His pass is a seven-pointed star, bearing the green color of high initiation and the bright blood-red color of zeal and enthusiasm, containing both the most passive and active of colors. Armed with this sigil, and the names of the guardian of this plane (our 'governor') and of the abyss (our 'river') he can now pass back across the bridge to the material plane, carrying the receptacles of knowledge he has learned from the Strange Land he has just visited.

Fig 4 - Royal Order of Scotland Jewel.

Incidentally, for the keen student, the penalty may also be found in Ezra VI, 11.

7. In Conclusion

This paper has not been intended to be an exhaustive summary of all the symbolism contained in the illustrious Order of the Red Cross. It is intended, however, to demonstrate that there are many, many levels to the symbols used which, of course, is the purpose symbolism in the first place.

Lest the reader think that all this is merely wishful thinking, let him remember that the people who wrote these Degrees and Orders were firstly scholars who, in their time, would have been well-versed in Latin, Greek; and the fruits of the Renaissance, which created an environment in which astrology and astronomy, alchemy and chemistry, science and religion were appreciated side by side (Sir Isaac Newton has already been mentioned several times in previous papers as an exemplar of this breadth of study). In addition, they were involved in the exciting religious and politic turmoil which was the revolutionary age of the 18th and 19th Centuries. Finally, the great resurgence in mystical knowledge, the fascination with chivalric Orders (and the secrets they concealed), and the first contact with socio-religious systems of Eastern Asia and other parts of the world, including Egypt, alongside a diminishing of Rome's autocracy and supremacy in matters religious, were leading to a remarkable upsurge of interest in the occult.

For all these reasons, we can be certain that the many levels on which this ritual can be read is not due to some happy coincidence. The writers knew exactly what they were doing, and by applying ourselves we can enjoy the multilayered symbolism, and profit from the profound messages they contain.

In ending, I hope I have encouraged you to see this Order in a new light, and a new atmosphere of respect.

THE TETRACTYS

According to "A Bridge To Light" by Ill∴ Rex Hutchens, 33°, "Pike intended that candidates have a thorough understanding of the Tetractys of Pythagoras before they receive the instruction of the Council and Consistory degrees" – indeed, in Morals and Dogma he even recommends that this symbol be *restored* to the pantheon of Third Degree symbols as being one of the most important of all, even though there is no indication that the Tetractys was ever included – he recommended a lecture be given on the subject after the Eighteenth Degree of the Ancient Accepted Scottish Rite, before the Brethren were allowed to continue on their Masonic journey through the Nineteenth to the Thirty-Second Degree. Hutchens continues: "Pike recommend that candidates receive this lecture as soon as possible after the conferral of the 18th Degree". Several of us have tried to find a copy of this lecture, so far without success. This brief talk, therefore, is offered as an introduction to the symbol of the Tetractys, considered so important by Pike, until such time as "the original may be discovered and brought to light"!

It is a fact that many religions have visualized their Gods in groups of three, or possessing three attributes. Many ancient pantheons contained triple Gods, including Isis, Osiris and Horus of the Egyptians; Shiva, Brahma and Vishnu; Kether, Binah and Chokmah; and the Father, Son and Holy Ghost. With regard to the attributes of Deity, these can be seen in the 'trible voice' of the Royal Arch, where the Three Principles invoke Omnipresent, Omniscient, Omnipotent God, words which closely reflect the attributes of Beauty, Wisdom and Strength respectively. Another example might be the three attributes of Cybele or Hecate – Virgin, Mother and Crone. Similarly, it appears to be more than a coincidence that a large majority of languages have given their deity a name consisting of four letters. To cite some example, Amun of the Egyptians, Ζεύς of the Greeks, Dieu of the French, Gott of the Germans, Odin of the Scandinavians, and YHVH of the Hebrews. This is an important fact, since again many religions hold that the world was created by God, and that this required an action, normally represented by a sound, and more particularly by God uttering his secret and ineffable name. Remember that in Genesis, God gives Adam or original man the power to name the animals, and by naming them they become subservient to him. This power of naming can also be seen in the medieval Grimoires, in which an angel or demon was conjured up then named in order to put that entity under the power of the magician. Names can be important!

Thus we have two important themes which appear to be common to many religious beliefs. Firstly, that attributes of God may be represented by the number '3', which in geometry can be viewed as a triangle. Also, that the manifestation of God in His creative act can be seen in the number '4'. Examples of this would include the 4 ancient elements of Earth, Air, Water and Fire which together represented the totality of creation.

Pythagoras is believed to have been born somewhere between the 7th and 8th Century B.C.E. He was by all accounts an extraordinary man. We do not have time to review all the accomplishments of this great philosopher. We will, however, focus upon one particular aspect. He founded a philosophical system in which respect for deity, represented by the 'Sacred Delta' or triangle, was required. His followers would take their most solemn and binding oaths upon this 'Sacred Delta' – a custom which persists in the Scottish Rite today, for between our Square and Compasses, and upon the Volume of the Sacred Law, rests a metal plate in the form of an equilateral triangle. This symbol represents the triune nature of God, while in the still center, in some representations, may be found the *oculus dei*, the Eye of God so familiar from our banknotes. The triangle is an interesting device to use to represent God, for it is eternally restless and moving. As a ritual in the Hermetic Order of the Golden Dawn puts it: "Two contending forces and one which unites them eternally. Two basal angles of the triangle and one which forms the apex. Such is the origin of Creation – it is the triad of Life." So the triangle can almost be seen as a constant tension between two side, while the third holds them together, just as the two pillars of Wisdom and Strength are united in the Middle Pillar of Beauty on the Kabbalistic Tree of Life.

Within this equilateral triangle are arranged a series of dots or periods, one on the top row, two on the next, three on the next and four on the bottom row:

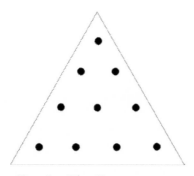

Fig. 1 – The Tetractys

We can see that the dots each result in the number four; and that the sum of the dots is the number ten: $1 + 2 + 3 + 4 = 10$. For Pythagoras and his followers, all numbers could be reduced to a number between 1 and 9, using a process called Theosophical reduction. For example, if we take the number 1923, by adding the number together we get $1 + 9 + 2 + 3 = 15$. Adding these together we get $1 + 5 = 6$. For Pythagoras, therefore, the nature of the number 1923 could be explained by studying the number 6, which he considered to be the 'root' of the former. If all numbers can be reduced to $1 - 9$ (remember that the concept of '0' was a relatively recent invention of Arabic mathematics), then these numbers must be intimately involved in the creation of all things. The Triangle can be seen as God emanating his Name to create the heaven and the earth. Indeed, to the Pythagoreans this idea was fundamental to their beliefs. Now most of us know that music is a mathematical progression, that harmony and vibration and volume are all based on numerical progressions. This was discovered by Pythagoras, and he was the first philosopher to postulate that beautiful idea of the 'Harmony of the Spheres', an idea still echoed in one of our Degrees, which evokes a God who sings, and the vibrations of which still echo through the corners of the universe, which angels thrill to hear and under whose spell the Planetary Intelligences move. This simple diagram contains all the secrets of the Universe if one knows how to find them. This is why Pike believed an understanding of this diagram was so important in the education of Scottish Rite Masons.

If God is represented by the number '1', creation was effected by the creation of duality, or 'God' and 'Not God'. This gave rise to opposites, which we recognize in male and female, good and evil, night and day, black and white...Boaz and Jachin. So God acts upon the two contending forces and unites them, and our impression of God is therefore of a Force manifesting in ternary form. The Triune God sings His Name, and the universe comes into existence. The elements appear and all created things take their appointed place. Finally, God creates Man, represented by the number '5', or the four elements into which He has breathed the 'Ruach' or spirit of life, the essence of God. Thus, if we look at the Tetractys, we see that, whatever side we begin with, the fifth dot is always in the center, ruling the four base dots on all sides. And yet this tells us a sad story as well, for the spirit of man, represented by the middle dot, is also surrounded and ensnared by those very elements he was sent to rule. Man's role is to break through the elements and reach God once more, as represented by the triangle surrounding creation.

The Hebrews had been exposed to Greek philosophical thought, and the Kabbalists in particular took to the Tetractys, seeing in it a representation of their own theories of the Ineffable Name of God and the Divine Emanations of the Sephiroth which resulted in Creation. Thus, they replaced the dots with the letters of God's Name:

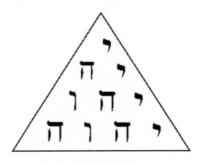

Fig. 2 – Tetractys with Hebrew Name of God

This approach was copied by the Rosicrucians many centuries later, when they redrew the Tetractys to use their New Testament version of the Tetragrammaton:

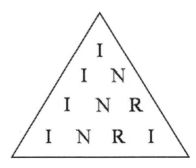

Fig. 3 – Tetractys with Rosicrucian Motto

While the Tetractys of the Greeks demonstrated their love of logic and mathematics, it is a cold thing compared to the use to which the Jewish Kabbalists put it. By substituting the dots for letters, they imbued the Tetractys with life. As I mentioned in my previous talk on the 14th Degree, a Hebrew letter carries a number of attributes, as did the language of the ancient Egyptians: for all letters carried a hieroglyphic, or pictorial value; a hieratic, or sacred value; a numerical value; and a phonetic value. This subject is too complex to go into here, but all Masons are encouraged to make a study of the teachings of the Kabbalah, since so much of our symbolism derives from it: it is a source of imagery and symbolism which has been deeply drawn upon by Masons through the centuries.

The Tetractys can be used to generate any number of objects familiar to Scottish Rite Masons. I will not bore you with lengthy explanations. You have sworn to make a daily advance in Masonic knowledge, and I challenge you to do this. I will just point out a few of the symbols which can be generated from the Tetractys:

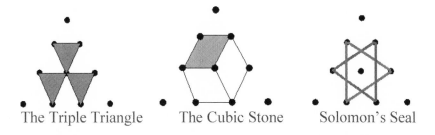

The Triple Triangle   The Cubic Stone   Solomon's Seal

Note also that each shape is surrounded by the three points of the Delta.

In conclusion, as a symbol of God and His creation, the Tetractys is a very powerful symbol indeed. It is fitting that this symbol plays so important a role in the Scottish Rite, and that Pike should have insisted on its importance being explained to all new members of our beloved Rite.

ALCHEMY IN FREEMASONRY

Fig. 1 – Photo taken by the author of a statue of Baby Buddha in Kathmandu by the author. Note the seven lotus flowers behind where he took his seven steps, and the fingers pointing in characteristic 'as above, so below' posture. © Piers A. Vaughan

1. Introduction

The subject of this talk is Alchemy, and what we can discern of its influence on Masonry. Now that would be a huge topic, and if I went into the Scottish Rite for one, we would be here for weeks! So I will limit myself to the Blue Lodge, and evidence of alchemical signatures in its rituals.

This is a call to all you Adepts of the sacred arts – may you never be 'Puffers'! This term, coming from the French term 'Souffleurs' referred both to the tyros who were tasked with keeping the Alchemist's furnace, or athanor, constantly heated by operating the bellows, or equally to those boastful and empty pretenders who claimed, without proof, to have produced gold from base metal. It was the failure of the many 'Puffers' which gave alchemy such a bad press – those vain people who wished to boast of their success in creating gold from base metal, and by the seventeenth century, when the Age of Reason began to take hold, the Alchemist was often portrayed as an impoverished idiot, seeking to make money out of common material, like the story of Rumpelstiltskin, who worked against the new Master – Empirical Science – and had to pay accordingly for his folly.

A famous poem found in *Theatrum Chemicum Britannicum*, by Elias Ashmole, and published in 1652, describes alchemists thus:

> Their clothes be bawdy and work thread-bare,
> Men may smell them for multipliers where they go;
> To file their fingers with corrosives they do not spare
> Their eyes be bleryd, and their cheeks both lean and blue…
> They search for the stone in soot, dung, urine, wine, blood, eggs.
> To see their houses it is a noble sport,
> What furnaces, what glasses there be of divers shape;
> What salts, what powders, what oils, and waters fort,
> How eloquently, de material prima, they clape
> And yet to find the truth they have no hap.

There is no doubt they received a bad press! But let us turn to the purpose of their labors. This can be found in a very famous poem:

> 1. 'Tis true without lying, certain & most true.

204

2. That which is below is like that which is above & that which is above is like that which is below to do the miracles of one only thing.

3. And as all things have been & arose from one by the meditation of one: so all things have their birth from this one thing by adaptation.

4. The Sun is its father, the moon its mother,

5. The wind hath carried it in its belly, the earth its nurse.

6. The father of all perfection in the whole world is here.

7. Its force or power is entire if it be converted into earth.

7a. Separate thou the earth from the fire, the subtle from the gross sweetly with great industry.

8. It ascends from the earth to the heaven & again it descends to the earth and receives the force of things superior & inferior.

9. By this means you shall have the glory of the whole world & thereby all obscurity shall fly from you.

10. Its force is above all force, for it vanquishes every subtle thing & penetrates every solid thing.

11a. So was the world created.

12. From this are & do come admirable adaptations where of the means (or process) is here in this.

13. Hence I am called Hermes Trismegist, having the three parts of the philosophy of the whole world.

14. That which I have said of the operation of the Sun is accomplished & ended.

For those probably few people who do not recognize it, or a version of it, this is 'The Emerald Tablet', reputedly written by Hermes Trismegistus in ancient Egypt, after whom the Hermetic Sciences are named. But the translator of this unique version may surprise you. It is Sir Isaac Newton, and was found among his alchemical papers.

Now we are all taught in school that Sir Isaac Newton discovered gravity and was a famous scientist in England in the late 17th Century, living until ten years of the foundation of the UGLE, writing many learned volumes on astronomy, physics and chemistry. What the schoolteachers don't mention was that he wrote even more books about astrology, alchemy and esoteric philosophy. As President of the Royal Society, which many scholars see as being much involved in the bringing to birth of the present incarnation of the Freemasons, he was almost certain to have encouraged the esoteric studies which they initially pursued.

2.   Alchemy in Blue Lodge Rituals

But why would Masonry be linked to Alchemy? What is Alchemy anyway? Why would we care if there were any mentions or hints of alchemy in our rituals?

I intend to limit myself specifically to the three Blue Lodge degrees. There is an important reason for this, other than the issue of time: while it is interesting to chart the influence of alchemical thought in the so-called 'Higher Degrees', this to me is little more than listing the symbols deliberately introduced by their authors, who were creating rituals out of thin air in some cases, and were therefore at liberty to draw from any source which interested them. In his book *In the Shadow of the Cathedrals*, Robert Ambelain says: "This offensive reputation, that the Rose+Croix shared this province with the Freemasons themselves, was made more to enhance the mystery of the fictional brotherhood than anything else. It is a fable and nothing more. As for the Masonic Grades with nowadays bear this name (8th in the Rite Français and 18th in the Scottish Rite), these are similarly of no philosophical importance. Masonically speaking, only the three Degrees called "St. John" can claim true initiatory esotericism."

Now, if we can find instances of alchemical thought in Blue Lodge rituals we are right back at the beginning of Freemasonry, and maybe, just maybe, we will be seeing links with a past much older than the Grand Lodge of England! I am not alone in this thought. In a rare comment by Fulcanelli in his seminal book *The Mystery of the Cathedrals* – of which more later, we read: "Our great cathedrals, built by medieval Freemasons in order to ensure the transmission of hermetic symbols and doctrine, have from the time of their appearance exercised a marked influence on numerous more modest examples of civil or religious architecture." Given the fact that his entire book is a masterpiece of circumspection, subtlety and understatement, it is indeed surprising to read this sentence – the word

'Freemasons' is even italicized – written in such an open an unequiv-
ocal manner. We are clearly meant to spot it. But is it to be taken
literally, or symbolically, like the rest of Fulcanelli's words?

3. Setting the Scene: The Alchemical Symbols of the Opera-
tive Masons

To begin our search, we will take a fresh look at our operative
forebears. Then we will consider some basic aspects of alchemy, and
try to see if any of these basic principles can be detected in our Blue
Lodge rituals. If we can, then our question must be: does this prove a
direct link between our operative ancestors, and did they indeed have
arcane knowledge beyond cryptic commentaries and secret grips and
passwords to pass onto their successors? Is Freemasonry unconsciously the deposit of something much larger than rubber chicken
dinners, oversized seats, charitable donations and a predilection to
talk about famous men who happened to be Masons?

This is not a place to go back into the old theories about our ancestors. If we were descended from the builders of King Solomon's
Temple, from the Egyptian or Greek Mystery schools, from the
Knights Templar, that is a subject for other papers. However, most
scholars agree we were connected with the operative stonemasons of
Medieval Europe. This group of builders were responsible for the
building of the great Gothic Cathedrals in Europe, and for many
stately castles and homes. They banded into guilds, protected their
arts through a complex set of passwords, grips and rituals, and were
responsible for many of the Mystery Plays, enacted throughout Europe at those times, when they celebrated their Patron Saint's Day by
enacting biblical stories. For the Masons the most popular were, of
course, the stories of King Solomon's Temple and Noah's Ark, both
of which have found their way into many Masonic rituals which we
still practice.

However, one aspect of our predecessors has remained relatively
obscure until this century – thought no doubt apparent to the Adepts
of the ages in between. Now, we have to remember that our Medieval
European counterparts remained close to the earth religions, even
while they embraced Christianity. Eternal salvation was an attractive
prospect, but one still had to live off the land, and the vast majority of

Europe at the time was untamed forest, full of dangerous beasts, such as wolves and bears, and many of the early religions based their belief systems around harvest and fertility.

Fig. 2 – The Green Man – a carving found in many medieval churches across Europe. Several may be seen in Rosslyn Chapel

In much of Europe the 'Green Man' was an incarnation of these fundamental archetypal forces, often depicted as a Man with foliage growing out of his mouth and nostrils. Herne the Magical Hunter held sway in the forests of Robin Hood in Nottingham, and the sacred hind, the stag with antlers between which blazed the Cross of Christ was a common image of the absorption of Christianity into the older cults. Even while the forest was being cut down to provide the wood for the scaffolding of the mighty Gothic cathedrals, the builders, in deference to their desecration of the groves to build the houses built with hands, the vegetable creating the mineral, recreated the trunks of the forest trees in the columns and the flying buttresses. Above these mighty oaks of stone, they often placed gargoyles, and the frequency of the Green Man makes one wonder if they were carved there to appease the ancient gods for the desecration of their forests. Ambelain says in his book *In the Shadow of the Cathedrals*: "If the interior of the cathedral, with its marvelous perspectives, its play of light and shadows, shafts soaring upwards from its columns, is intended by its ensemble to recall the old Celtic forest, in the heart of which initiatory or magical rites took place (the Normandy forest bore the name of Green Forest…), … the choir is the sacred clearing, the exact spot for magical operations. After the darkness of the forest, the traps, the fatigue, the monsters to vanquish, the clearing is the image of the final goal, of liberation, of return to the divine light."

However, it was not until Fulcanelli's book *The Mystery of the Cathedrals*, and later Robert Ambelain's book *In the Shadow of the Cathedrals*, that the full mystery of the carvings of the great Gothic cathedrals was made known to 20th Century mankind. Apparently our clever predecessors had spent an enormous amount of time and energy carving alchemical symbols into the stonework of the great European cathedrals! Now ponder the significance of this. The majority of churchgoers in those days were illiterate. And given the fact that the services were rendered in Latin and not the vernacular, the walls, the stained glass windows, the screens and pews were carved to depict the lives of the saints and Old and New Testaments stories, to make up for the total alienation of the average churchgoer, and to teach them the stories of the bible through symbols and depiction, and while the congregation sat literally in what Saint-Martin called the 'forest of errors', only the priest and his kind stood in the symbolic clearing at the center of the forest, offering no guidance to his flock about how to join him there, but only mumbled faintly in a language unknown to the people still sitting in the 'forest'.

Another interesting fact: modern scholars have shown that the Cathedrals and churches were painted in an almost gaudy manner, using strong primary colors to adorn the statuary. Fulcanelli states in a footnote that: "In the cathedrals everything was gilded and painted in vivid colors. As proof of this we have the words of Martyrius, the fifteenth century Armenian bishop and traveler. This author says that the porch of Notre-Dame of Paris was as resplendent as the gates of Paradise. Purple, rose, azure, silver and gold were to be seen there (p 40)." To anyone who wants to get a taste of what a church or cathedral might have looked like in Medieval times, I only need to refer them to pictures of the church in Rennes-le-Château, that gloriously painted Gnostic affront to orthodox Catholicism! Fulcanelli goes on to tell us: "The alchemists of the fourteenth century used to meet there once a week on the day of Saturn…Denys Zachaire tells us that this custom was followed until the year 1539 'on Sundays and feast days'. Noel de Fail says that 'the great place for those academy meetings was Notre-Dame of Paris'. There, amid a dazzling array of painted and gilded arches, of string-courses and copings, of tympana with multi-colored figures, each philosopher would show the result of his labors and work out the next sequence of his researches. It was there that they assessed the probabilities and discussed possibilities and studied on the spot the allegory of the Great Book. Not the least animated part of these gatherings was the abstruse explanation of the mysterious symbols all around them."

Fig. 3 – Asmodeus (of Book of Tobit fame – see the paper on Raphal) bearing the stoup in Rennes-le-Château Chapel

Interestingly, it was usually the external, rather than internal walls which were coated with alchemical symbolism. But the two books by Fulcanelli and Ambelain are filled with these descriptions, and it is hard to absorb the fact that every entrance to Notre Dame in Paris, for example, has no portal which allows you to pass into the Cathedral without passing through a veritable initiation into the alchemical arts! And how clever they were, our operative ancestors, for nobody noticed! Now, I do not mean to suggest that the church authorities were ignorant of these carvings – far from it. Indeed, alchemy, by couching its operations and language in terms both Christian and obscure, appears to have avoided the branding of heresy, and there are few cases indeed of alchemists running afoul of the Catholic Church, unless like John Dee their travels were seen to have political, as well as alchemical, purpose. Indeed, in this case the danger came from greedy rulers, who were not above torturing or murdering the poor alchemist if he did not give up the secret of trans-mutation. Among the menu of punishments were to be hanged from gilded gallows, have one's bones slowly broken, starvation, branding and worse. Sethon, on being summoned to the court of Christian II, the Elector of Saxony, refused to divulge the secret of the Philoso-pher's Stone, and was daily scalded with molten lead, beaten with rods and punctured with needles.

It was as if the church was a sacred space, set apart from the pro-fane world, in which rich tapestries and vestments and jewel-encrusted gilded reliquaries and crosses were set before the common people, while their nostrils were, for once, filled with sweet incense rather than the pungent odor of decay and unwashed bodies, and their ears delighted to the ethereal, floating melodies of plainchant, as though the ceremony desired to give the peasants a foretaste of the Heaven they would inherit if they obeyed the church without ques-tion.

And in order to enter this sacred space they have to pass a thresh-old which linked the profane with the sublime worlds, using alchemy to signify the spiritual quest by which those who could understand the lessons could discover the spark of true gold within themselves and reunite – or reintegrate – with the Source of All.

It is interesting to note that the famous Old Man of the Mountain allegedly employed a similar technique to create fanatical warriors out of the young men who were drugged and kidnapped, then awoke in a place they truly thought was Paradise, before being drugged again and trained to become fearless warriors – the Hashishim – who believed in laying down their life in battle they would instantly be transported back to the artificial 'Paradise' they had tasted.

4. Linking the Past to the Origin of the Premier Grand Lodge of England

Alchemy, for those who know little about it, was the science of turning base metal into gold. For the 'Puffers' this was the only goal. But those with any with about them understood that a far greater truth lay behind this pursuit. And this is the point of the Emerald Tablet, which proclaimed the basic Hermetic creed: "as above, so below". This secret was so powerful to our ancient Brethren they had to hide it behind obscure symbols and obtuse language. While the first two degrees confine their implements to those of building, the third degree, for those who have passed through it, expand these to many other symbols which have often played their part in alchemy. For alchemy has been keen to use symbols which were employed by the Church, to conceal their real purpose: to unite heaven and earth. In a way alchemy could be said to predate the Gnostic gospels by centuries, for in their teachings on "as above, so below", they preached a religious philosophy which had no need for priests, for churches, for cathedrals. As we read in the Gospel of St. Thomas (Saying 77): "split a piece of wood: I am there. Lift a stone and you will find me there", meaning that God is omnipresent, and not housed or confined in churches or monasteries, unlike the God of the Old Testament, which appeared to need a building built to his specification in which he could live, and apparently found it impossible to travel from Sinai to Jerusalem without transportation. But that is the subject of a whole other paper!

In a recent book entitled *Isaac Newton's Freemasonry* by Alain Bauer, the author raises the now familiar theory that the Royal Society and Freemasonry were intimately linked, and that Sir Isaac Newton was close friends with two prominent Freemasons, Sir Robert Moray and Rev. John Theophilus Desaguliers, who became, respectively, President and Secretary of the Royal Society, suggested that Freemasonry had little in common with Operative Masonry, and had been largely invented to give educated men a chance to study the Hermetic sciences and alchemy, both subjects of great interest to Newton and his friends. One point he makes is that at the time of the formation of the Grand Lodge of England, modern science was hardly being embraced with both arms by the majority of people: the clergy fulminated against it, Oxford and Cambridge refused to teach the sciences, and even the general public were deeply suspicious of them. Hardly surprising, then, that one place where a speaker from the Royal Society was always welcome was at a meeting of one of the Lodges, and as the 2004 Prestonian Lecturer, W. Bro. Trevor Stewart reminded us in his paper, delivered at St. John's Lodge No. 1, A.Y.M., New York that December, scientific experiments were common at these meetings. In his paper he cites examples of a Lodge witnessing an execution to answer the question: can a person killed by firing squad hear the sound of the bullet which kills him? In one instance the minutes of a Lodge meeting mention the activity of the day was the dissection of a corpse – in the meeting place. May I dare presume that more than one alchemical experiment was viewed and debated as well?

Whichever theory of the origins of Freemasonry one follows, I find it interesting that the Operative Masons appeared to know so much about alchemical symbolism, and whether or not it was this interest which spanned the centuries until the arrival of Speculative Masonry, or whether the injection of alchemical symbolism into Masonry derived from the personal interests of its founders or its 18th Century 're-inventors'.

In order to search for clues in our rituals, however, it will be necessary to understand certain principles of Alchemy. This again could be a lifetime pursuit, and if just one of you is inspired to learn more on this subject following this talk, and take time to explore this field which has occupied people as diverse as Newton and Jung, then I can count this brief talk a success. However, in this paper, I will limit myself to two aspects: the types of alchemy and the major stages of the alchemical process.

5. Some Basic Alchemical Principles

To understand the arguments which follow, one needs to understand a few aspects of alchemy, and not necessarily those facts most people think of when they talk of alchemy.

There are three forms of alchemy, which interestingly enough correspond to the three earthly kingdoms – vegetable, mineral and animal. The alchemy of plants and the making of medicine, ultimately the elixir of life, is the alchemical art of *Spagyrics*, or the *Wet Path*. The rather more dangerous alchemy using metals and minerals is known as Mineral Alchemy, or the Dry Path. The application of the Hermetic axiom 'as above, so below' in seeing lessons within these paths to oneself is called *Spiritual Alchemy*. Both Spagyrics and Mineral Alchemy lead to Spiritual Alchemy, for it is not enough to perform the experiments: one much be in a suitable state of purity for the reactions to take place. The test tube was, in a way, a symbol for the human body. The corpus itself, or physical shell was represented by Salt; the Soul by Sulfur and the Spirit by Mercury. Just as the aim of physical alchemy was to fix the volatile, so within us the aim was to tame the flighty mind (mercury) imprisoned within the body (salt) through the fixing action of the soul (sulfur). The purpose was to break asunder the false ego or fixed shell we have built around us like a carapace, to recapture our original innocence, and thus achieve communion with our inner genius, or true chrysoprase. I'm sure more than one of you here today can quote whole sections of the rituals of the Hermetic Order of the Golden Dawn, and explain in far more detail than I ever could on how the Outer Order uses the Tree of Life and key alchemical concepts to decompose the Neophyte into his or her constituent elements, in order to examine and reassemble themselves, now purified and renewed, having confronted and combusted the dross of the old self, much as Martinism uses the more passive methods of meditation and introspection to negate the self and its reliance on outside influences to fan the flames of the divine spark within all of us.

There are many systems of alchemy, so I will be honest and say it is all too easy to select the series which best fits our noble Craft, and offer it as evidence of the close link between alchemy and Masonry. However, now that I have given this warning I will do just that! The physical purpose of the processes is to take base metal or what is often described as something of no value and all around us but unseen by profane eyes, and, through a series of steps, transmute it into gold. This gold is really spiritual. Jesus the Nazarene said "my Kingdom is not of this world", yet he was misunderstood by the zealots of his time who saw in him a fighting Messiah who would rid them of their Roman masters. This, surely, is a common goal on most Mystery Schools, whose mottoes are really all one and the same, and which has never really been better expressed than that inscribed at the entrance to the Temple of Apollo at Delphi: γνῶθι σεαυτόν (gnothi seauton), or Know Thyself. For by knowing oneself one perceives the divine spark within, the Philosophers Stone. Then one can truly bring about spiritual alchemical change, using this as the catalyst.

The seven steps – there have to be seven, don't there! – are Calcination, Digestion, Putrefaction, Solution, Distillation, Conjunction, Sublimation.

Calcination reduces the raw materials through the action of elemental fire to ash. Digestion is the long, slow process of gently warming the materials in acid or base to allow the result to transmute. Putrefaction ferments the reside and separates it into its constituent parts. Solution uses elemental water to wash away the dross, while the air of Distillation isolates the parts suited for the high purpose. Conjunction reunites and reconciles the opposites – the liquid with the solid, the male with the female, the King of Philosophical Gold with the Queen of Philosophical Silver. Finally, in the last step before the 'achieving of the one thing', Sublimation causes the doubt and suffering, the Long Night of the Soul, sometimes seen in the little death of the King and Queen after coupling, when all is feared lost before the dawning of the new day and the realization of the long sought-after goal: the *summum bonum*. I do not need to tell you that these processes were worked upon the alchemist himself or herself, as well as in the laboratory: from the physical process the alchemist learned lessons to apply to the spiritual process – and vice versa.

Surely we can see the initiatory process in this procession as well in our Lodges. The raw material is the profane candidate, who is stripped of his earthly belongings and placed in a dark Chamber of Reflection to contemplate his mortality, in the stage of Calcination, which represents the death of the profane. On being brought to light he is presented with the tools with which he will symbolically reshape himself; and through Digestion, through guidance and education, he learns to understand the meaning of the experience through which he has just passed (so much for one Day Classes!). As he learns to interpret the symbolism of Masonry, he begins to knock off the knobs and excrescences of his rough exterior in the act of Putrefaction. As we pass to the Second Degree the newly-prepared Fellowcraft is taught to improve himself through learning, and is presented with the seven great subjects taught in all universities at the time of the founding of the Grand Lodge of England – the *trivium* and *quadrivium* of the seven Liberal Arts and Sciences (but the 'Sciences' of Mathematics and Geometry – not Physics and Chemistry!) as he is encouraged to elevate his mind from baser pursuits in this act of purification or spiritual Solution. The second part of the Middle Chamber Lecture takes the symbolism of this activity further, as the enemies of the Hebrew people, the Ephraimites, are driven into the River Jordan.

The Fellowcraft Degree is worthy of closer inspection, for it is in this Degree that the alchemical teachings are seen in the Middle Chamber Lecture at their most transparent. The lecture expounds on the practical steps of alchemy, then describes the state of the practitioner necessary to achieve the desired results. The Fellowcraft Lecture is almost a microcosm of the three Degree system, whose overall purpose is to teaching us our duties towards, God, our fellow man, and ourselves. Although the Second Degree is seen as the least important of the degrees – indeed, even its title, 'Passing', suggests a transitory step between the first and third – within its teachings lie the keys to self-development. Freemasonry lost its way somewhere in time, and the important message taught by all mystery schools, to work on oneself before working on others, has been lost. Now we are taught to be charitable, but the importance of working on oneself first has been lost. Masonry was never meant to be a charitable organization: but its lessons were meant to affect one in such a way that one could not help but be charitable if one internalized its teachings. So charity should be an outcome, a result; not the underlying cause.

If the First Degree prepares the ground, the Second plants the seeds. In the Lecture we move from the material to the spiritual, from matter, through the Liberal Arts, which represent the archetypal powers in human thinking, expressing themselves in human thought, to the Cardinal Virtues, which represent the archetypal patterns in the consciousness of mankind expressing themselves in inner spiritual development.

The seven Liberal Arts have their counterpart in the days of the week, the planets, the musical scale, the angelic orders of heaven, and

216

the ancient metals. It is hardly surprising, then, that the alchemists saw close ties between each of these aspects of the number seven, and believed that each could be an influence on the others. As above, so below. Dante proposed a link between the Seven Liberal Arts and the seven planets, allowing us to create a table of correspondences between them:

#	Art	Planet	Metal	Sign	Day
1	Grammar	Moon	Silver	☽	Monday
2	Rhetoric	Venus	Copper	♀	Friday
3	Logic	Mercury	Quicksilver	☿	Wednesday
4	Arithmetic	Mars	Iron	♂	Tuesday
5	Geometry	Jupiter	Tin	☽	Thursday
6	Music	Sun	Gold	☉	Sunday
7	Astronomy	Saturn	Lead	♄	Saturday

Note the *trivium* – Grammar, Rhetoric and Logic – which awarded a Bachelor of Arts, and the *quadrivium*, which resulted in a Master's Degree, were taught in a specific order, which corresponded to the perceived orbits of the planets. The first was Grammar, thought to be the easiest to learn, and the last Astronomy considered the hardest, as it was related to Saturn, which was the slowest of the seven planets.

If the Seven Liberal Arts corresponded to the alchemical process of transformation, by which the acquisition of education served to mold the individual and perfect them so that they would be ready vessels to aid mankind, this study had to be performed in a particular frame of spiritual purity for the lessons to truly take root and grow. This to my mind is summarized in the second part of the Lecture – the rehearsal of the biblical story of Jephthah and the Ephraimites.

This has long been a fascinating allegory to me, ever since I heard it at my Passing in England in 1980. Permit me a moment of self-indulgent exegesis! A river, as we know, is used as a symbol of a barrier between two states of consciousness or realms in most if not all religious writings, from the Styx to Starbuznai of the Elus Cohen. The bridge allows people to cross from one state to another, or at least communicate between the two, for the title Pontifex, arrogated by the

Bishop of Rome lays claim to this ability to communicate between Heaven and Earth, and transmit to mankind the Law of God from his cathedra or throne. A permit signified one was allowed to cross in both directions, as was given to Zerubbabel in a similar story. This signifies, for example, a journey from Malkuth to Yesod, across the astral barrier – a topic I cover in depth in my paper about the Red Cross Degree. So here we have these forces of Ephraimites crossing the river from the astral and invading the terrestrial plane. Jephtha not only discovers the means to identify these evil forces, but even calls of God to stay the light of day (could this be the 'step into the light, honey' of the movie Poltergeist – a facetious comment, I know, but it's actually a good analogy) to allow this dross, the dark side of man's personality, to pass into the light? In the story, as told in the Old Testament, he separates those who cannot speak – or think – in the same manner as the Chosen People, and thus protects the pure from the impure elements through an act of Distillation or Reduction. The number he 'releases', 42,000, is also interesting. Of course I reached for my trusty Godwin's *Cabalistic Encyclopedia*, and found that 42 (we can normally discount the zeros after numbers) to mean, among other things, חלך (cheled), which means World or our own earth, suggesting in a way the sins of the world were removed from the Chosen Ones. But let us return to the central alchemical process...

Finally, in the Third Degree the Mason reunites the two pillars within himself, but as a final step to achieving the symbolic transformation which he must strive to reflect in his daily life, he must yet endure that Long Dark Night of the Soul, as he identifies with Hiram, for only out of this final test can he be reborn anew as the perfect man, Adam Kadmon, and be reintegrated with his Brothers as Abel reborn.

Ultimately, of course, the key representation of this process in the Lodge is the ashlar, which represents the Mason. Firstly, he is presented with the rough ashlar, the *prima materia* or raw material which he is, and is handed the tools by which he can reshape himself. The raw material, we are told, is common, visible all around us, and considered on no value to man. Of the name of this material in mineral alchemy no one is allowed to speak: but in Spiritual Alchemy it is of course Man. Man is common, all around us, and yet held in no esteem by any but those who possess the understanding of Man's place in the celestial hierarchy and of the divine spark he contains: for those who know this truth Man is more precious than fine gold. As an aside, consider the strongly Martinist teaching of the Mark Degree, in which the workmen labor in the quarries, separating the rough stones which will later be shaped into perfect ashlars from the quarry walls. The quarry represents the 'Man of the Stream' who has no yet awakened into true consciousness, and the act of separation from the bedrock the awakening of the sleeping Man into dim consciousness. Having been separated from the bedrock Masonry now gives him the tools to complete the job, and the Entered Apprentice now passes through the stages of alchemical development until he stands once more before the Sanctum Sanctorum as the finished work, the Stone of the Philosophers, the Perfect Ashlar. While is it obvious why Masons use the perfect ashlar as a symbol of personal perfection through labor, it is interesting that, of all the symbols Alchemy could have used to describe the *summum bonum*, they chose a stone. It seems there is a closer link between Alchemy and Masonry than we may have originally thought…

6. Thoughts and Conclusions

Is this stretching the analogy? It is hard to know. Unless we can discover whether the rituals we use were truly written in a room in London at the turn of the 18th Century, or are adapted from ancient rituals which date back to the time that our operative forebears were fashioning alchemical stories about the portals of the medieval cathedrals, we can only conjecture. However, a very recent article gives me a new direction of study. In the first edition of the quarterly magazine on Hermetic subjects, published by Hermetic Virtues, Bro. Tommy Westlund, Grand Archivist of the Swedish Rite, writes about the Gold und Rosenkreuz Order. In this article he writes: "The initiation rituals were influenced by the Masonic blue degree rituals and very often sought to explain alchemical meanings and symbolism hidden therein." The writings and source materials of this fascinating 18th Century Masonic group may well provide a key to this train of thought, a group which allegedly grew out of an alchemical group referenced by Sincerus Renatus, or Samuel Richter, in 1710.

One ray of hope can be found in Robert Ambelain's fascinating book entitle "Spiritual Alchemy". In it he develops a theme found in a book written by my namesake and, I like to think, my Welsh ancestor, Thomas Vaughan, entitled "An Open Entrance to the Closed Palace of the King". Here he sees the climb to the summit of Mount Abiegnus depicted as a pyramid of four, three, two and one elements. The base is composed of Earth, Water, Air and Fire, which make up man's physical body. Upon these sit Sulfur, Mercury and Salt, to represent our Soul, Spirit and Body. In turn Sulfur and Mercury combine to form alchemical Silver; and Mercury and Salt to form alchemical Gold. At the highest level the Philosophical Silver Queen and Gold King combine to create the Philosopher's Stone, which Ambelain interprets to be Divine Light.

An interesting model. But now he adds something which intrigued me. He equates the four elements as follows: Earth with Prudence, Water with Temperance, Air with Justice, and Fire with Strength – or the four Cardinal Virtues. Upon these Sulfur equates with Faith, Mercury with Hope and Salt with Charity, which are the Theological Virtues. Silver and Gold equate with Wisdom – Chokmah and Understanding – Binah, or the Sublime Virtues; and the Philosopher's Stone is the gift of the Holy Spirit, which we can interpret to be knowledge of our Holy Guardian Angel. The process is so strongly equated with the Cardinal, Theological and Sublime Virtues, that it is hard not to see a connection between the alchemical elements and relationships and the very virtues we profess to practice.

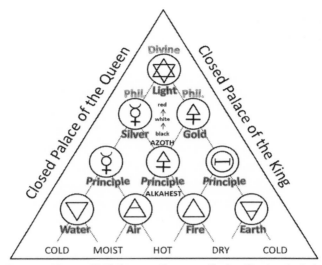

Fig. 4 - From *l'Alchimie Spirituelle* by R. Ambelain

But this is all very theoretical. Why would we bother to do this? I found a most intriguing suggestion in Dennis Hauck's excellent book, *The Emerald Tablet*. On page 388 he says: "Intentionally or not, our founding fathers incorporated the philosophy of the Emerald Tablet into the very foundations of the new commonwealth." Pointing out that the vast majority of the signers of the Declaration of Independence were Freemasons, he quotes Doctor and Gnostic Bishop Stephan Hoeller's book entitled '*Freedom: Alchemy for a Voluntary Society*': "The chief inspirer of the American republic was not Moses or Jesus, and even less St. Augustine or St. Thomas Aquinas, but rather Hermes Trismegistus…The Hermetic principle, more than any other, came to permeate not only American government but the entire history of the United States." Ranged against the Hermetists are the Fundamentalists, whose Old Testament God is unforgiving and vengeful. Dr. Hoeller goes on: "A profound and seemingly irreconcilable conflict still rends the soul of America in two…Only by recalling and supporting the Hermetic qualities of the American vision will the beneficent alchemical operation envisaged by the founders be permitted to do its work."

This theory suggests that the alchemy contained in our rituals was for the express purpose of being understood consciously by Masons and then taken into society at large in order to change it. The opportunity to found a new country on such principles is very rarely given. It was done here in the United States, and it was done to some extent in France. But the process of alchemy requires a gentle heat, not a roaring fire, for the transmutation to take place without the danger of a major accident: the roaring fire of the French Revolution and the bloodiness of the peoples' revenge upon their former masters is a good example of this. Perhaps this is the real calling of Freemasons, the majority of which have sadly even forgotten that there are any lessons to be learned in the Craft. Perhaps we are tasked by our ancestors to work the alchemical process upon ourselves, until we create the Philosopher's Stone within us; then, taking this gift among the people who inhabit our society, we convert everything and everyone we touch to gold...

I will leave you with some homework, as I always do! Try to map the Lodge Officers against the seven ancient planets. I accept this is more difficult in America than it is in jurisdictions which follow the post-Reunification in England, for America was left with six main officers, while England split the role of Junior Deacon into two: the Inner Guard, who guards 'the hither side of the portal', and the Junior Deacon, who conducts candidates for the Entered Apprentice Degree. And voilà! Seven Officers. So bear in mind our Junior Deacon actually incorporates two roles of the seven officers. Now, we are told that the Senior Warden is the Moon and the Master the Sun. Is the Junior Warden Venus, the Morning Star? I ask you also to contemplate the significance of the blazing star, shining forth above the Master's head. This is the star we are bound, like the magi of old, to follow. It leads us to immeasurable realms of discovery.

However, a word of caution: all our studies are vain if they result in nothing more than an increase of knowledge. Masonry, like alchemy, is a practical as well as symbolic or theoretical art. Religion is empty if we sit in the pew on Sunday but do not practice the virtues we are taught within. Similarly, Masonry is nothing more than a hobby unless we practice the lessons derived in our daily lives and strive to 'make a daily advance'. So perhaps it is not enough to practice Spiritual Alchemy in our Lodges. As W. Bro. Trevor exhorted us to do, perhaps we should try to recapture the excitement and learning of the early Lodges and bring the athanors, the bains-maries and the retorts back into the Lodge room?

But what shall we use as the fire to progress our experiments and bring them to fruition? The fire must be gentle but insistent, not the fire brought about with charcoal. The ancient alchemists were most insistent on this point. To Robert Ambelain, the answer was simple: the Philosopher's fire is – Prayer.

To end this brief look at Alchemy in Blue Lodge Masonry, I call therefore upon you to heed the lessons of this talk, and strive to be 'Spiritual Adepts', not 'Puffers'!

EARLY RITUAL OF THE HOLY ROYAL ARCH

Fig. 1 - Early Royal Arch Scarf and Apron
– courtesy of www.phoenixmasonry.org

NOTE*: This paper is the exception to my rule of not including references. It was given at the Thomas Smith Webb Chapter of Research in New York State, and relied heavily on original manuscripts as well as books. I have included the ritual quotations, since these are freely available in any library of research.*

1. BACKGROUND

The origins of the Holy Royal Arch Degree are, like Blue Lodge Masonry, shrouded in mystery. We should remember that in 1717 there were only two degrees, and that the third was added just before 1740, and it is also about this time that we find the first hints of a fourth degree. It was this that caused this degree to become one of the major sticking-points between the Antients and Moderns, with the latter becoming ever more entrenched in their official attitude of non-recognition towards it.

As we are taught, the 'official' founding of the Grand Lodge of England took place in 1717. Many papers have been given suggesting that the earliest rituals may have in fact focused on the legend of the Ark – now preserved in the Royal Ark Mariner's Degree – and in an earlier paper I commented that the word 'Arc' in French can refer both to an Ark as a ship and as an arch, as in 'arc-en-ciel' (rainbow) or the 'Arc de Triomphe' in Paris. Pick & Knight say that "some students believe that the Royal Arch was born in France as one of many degrees created after the spread of Freemasonry to the continent", and idea which we will return to later. It is interesting to speculate whether the translation of the word 'Arch' led to a completely new series of Degrees being focused on a mistranslation! In all cases we see the idea of something which was lost being found, whether it is Hiram's body, the Ark of the Covenant, dry land (in Noah's case), Enoch's pillars of knowledge, or a triangle of gold with a message to mankind inscribed upon it. This has always been a powerful myth for man, as we see in Parsifal, Excalibur, the Holy Grail and other European legends.

However, the first known mention of the Royal Arch, according to Charles Leadbeater and others, is found in the minutes of Youghal in Ireland in 1743, when it is reported that two Excellent Masons carried the Royal Arch; and again in 1744 in Dr. Dassigny's 'Serious and Impartial Enquiry into the cause of the Present Decay of Freemasonry in the Kingdom of Ireland' (and this only 27 years after it was founded!), in which he tells us of the existence of an Assembly of Royal Arch Masons at York.

Various references suggest that part of the Royal Arch may have been found in other early Degrees. For example, a parody from 1726 refers to "the necessity there is for a Master to understand well the Rule of Three." A catechism from the previous year contains the words:

  43. Whence is an Arch deriv'd? From Architecture.

44.   What cloth it resemble? The Rainbow.

Already by the 1750s Laurence Dermott, Grand Secretary of the Antients was calling the Royal Arch Degree the "very root, heart and marrow of Freemasonry." This suggests that the Royal Arch must have been popular enough – at least among the Antients – to have developed into an independent Ritual quite rapidly. Certainly the Royal Arch was worked in Craft Lodges from the inception of the Antients, along with the Mark Degree and the Order of Knights Templar a little later.

At first, its government was exclusively in the hands of the Antients; while the Moderns officially ignored its existence. We find in Dermott's Book of Constitutions, entitled Ahiman Rezon or Help to a Brother, published in 1756, the following comment in Rule II:

"The Master of a particular Lodge has the right and authority of congregating the members of his own Lodge into a Chapter upon any emergency or occurrence."

Despite its labeling as an 'Antient' ritual, there was no shortage of 'Modern' members, and a good deal of fraternizing between both sides outside of London and the eagle eye of Grand Lodge! That the Premier Grand Lodge was not hostile to the idea of the Royal Arch itself can be seen in the fact that, when a Modern Grand Chapter was created in 1766, the Grand Master, Lord Blayley, was also titular Head of the Royal Arch; and when the Grand Lodge moved to Great Queen Street in London in 1775, the Hall Committee:

"Resolved that Bro[ther] Riley be permitted to use this Society's Room for the accommodation of the Society calling themselves Royal Arch Masons."

However, we should remember that, while the Premier Grand Lodge did not proscribe the Grand Chapter, it did not officially recognize its existence. Samuel Spencer, Grand Secretary (1757-1768), wrote to Gogel, the Modern's Provincial Grand Master for the Rhinelands in 1766 to deny that the Royal Arch Degree was recognized by the Grand Lodge – this in reply to a question about how to deal with the newly formed Rite of Strict Observance, which was a chivalric body containing a Royal Arch Degree (as well as Rose Croix and Templar Orders), and asking for advice on how to deal with them.

The next Grand Secretary, James Heseltine (1769-1780), replying to the same Province of Frankfurt-am-Main during a resurgence of problems with the 'Strict Observance', wrote the following fascinating reference to the Royal Arch, which is an excellent summary of the Premier Grand Lodge's position at that time:

"...With respect to the information you have rec[eive]d as to the Grand Lodge of England's having Degrees and Mysteries superior to the three Degrees already communication to you, you may rest assured it had not the least foundation of truth. I now give you my word of honour as a Mason that the Grand Lodge of England has not any other acknowledged Degrees. It is true that many of the Fraternity here belong to a Degree in Masonry say'd to be superior to the other three, call[ed] the Royal Arch. I have the honour to be a member of this Degree and its principles and proceedings are truly praiseworthy - but it is unknown in Grand Lodge, and all Emblems or Badges or distinction in that Degree are prohibited from being worn in GL."

The oldest documents specifically of a Royal Arch meeting (as opposed to indirect references) come from the United States, when, on December 22nd, 1753, three Brethren were "raised to the Degree of Royal Arch Mason" in Fredericksburg, Virginia.

The fact that there was by no means a single Royal Arch Degree is demonstrated by the pithy comment of C. Shirreff to William White in 1789: "I met three R:A: and they all differ'd". Indeed, this paper will focus on the fascinating differences between early rituals available to us.

Around the time of the Act of Union, the debate over whether the Royal Arch should be included in the Degree system raged. A fine example of the Antient's position in the matter can be read in W.H. Dee's eloquent argument for a four Degree system. At the time he was Zerubbabel of the Chapter of Goodwill, Braintree, having been Exalted in 1796, and his argument, from "Royal Arch Ritual & Discourses" is worth quoting here:

"The reasonablenefs and necefsity of progressive Degrees in the pursuit of every Society, Art, and Science both Ancient and modern. no unprejudiced person will deny. The Efsenes among the Jews, who were a kind of Pythgorians, had 4 distinct degrees in their society. The Antient Kings, Philosophers and Rulers of Egypt had every one 3 or 4 Probationary-degrees. The Jewish sect called the Levites had 4 distinct degrees. The Eastern schools about the time of our Saviours Nativity had all of them 4 separate clafses, under the denomination of Disciple, junior, bachur or elect, and graduate. Pythagoras, who flourished about 500 years before Christ, never permitted a pupil to speak in his school, till he had undergone a probation of at last 4 years. Amongst the learned Societies of Almost every Denomination, for instance, in Academic Degrees there are Bachelor, Master, Doctor: in the Church, Deacon, Priest, Bishop, and Arch-Bishop: in the municipal law, those of Student, Barrister and Serjeant: in the Civil law, and physics, Student, Bachelor And Doctor. In each of these Degrees the Disciple or Scholar undergoes proper examinations, and must, or at [least] ought to be found well qualified prior to his Admifsion to a Superior Rank. Hence the Institutors of our Society have with the greatest Wisdom, and prudence adapted sundry Probationary Degrees not to attained but by time, patience, probity and Application."

As an example of the diversity of rituals at the time, we can cite a letter from William Raper of Chichester to William White in 1800, which alludes to "the Ornaments of our late Chapter", and mentions specifically "the Anchor, Cock and Triangle" which cost "upwards of Sixty Guineas". A strange ritual indeed - though I should temper this by suggesting that the items may have been code words for the more familiar Volume of the Sacred Law (Anchor of our Faith), Compasses (Triangle) and Square (Cock which, like the Master, announces the rising sun and the time to commence labor).

In the second Article of the Act of union, it was stated that: "It is declared and pronounced that pure Antient Masonry consists of three degrees and no more, viz those of the Entered Apprentice, the Fellow Craft, and the Master Mason, including the Supreme Order of the Holy Royal Arch." So the degree beloved of the Antients and many Moderns was preserved … but in no particular form.

In 1817, four years after the Act of Union, there is reference to a single Grand Chapter, arising out of the Modems Grand Chapter and that part of the Antients which administered the Royal Arch Degree. However, the first 'official' ritual, the Sussex Ritual named in honor of the Duke of Sussex, was not actually published until the mid-1840s, indicating that there were a large number of individual rituals practiced around the United Kingdom until then; and Chapter regulations continued to be printed as part of the rules for Lodges right up to the 1830s.

What are we to draw from all this? Firstly, that the Royal Arch either grew out of diverse Blue Lodge rituals or possibly came to us from the continent. Secondly, that we have no full published ritual before the 1840s. Before this time we only have ciphers, excerpts and diaries from which we can obtain some idea of what the early rituals might have been like. This also implies that variants were actually accepted and approved by the United Grand Lodge for some thirty years after its creation.

Finally, before we turn to look at the rituals themselves, we may conclude that, far from being a clear-cut progression, the Royal Arch was practiced in many forms across countries, with the Antients predominantly – but not exclusively – favoring the use of veils. In Companion G. Claret's, "The Ceremonies, Etc. of The Holy Royal Arch also Passing the Vails", the first published Royal Arch Ritual in 1845, there is a footnote to "Passing the Vails", which reads: "This Ceremony usually takes place soon after the Obligation. It is not much known or practiced in London. It was always given in the Athol Chapters before the Union in 1813, but not in those under the Prince of Wales. I am aware that it is still practiced in some parts of the Country, as such it may be given or omitted."

On the American side of the pond, we have a book by John Sheville and James L. Gould dated 1867 which, we should remember, was a good 70 years after the separation from England. Their adherence to the Antient Grand Lodge is evinced by their comment in the History of the English Royal Arch that: "the first authentic account of it is the history of the assembly of Masons at York A.D. 926 at which EDWIN presided as Grand Master." This does not exactly inspire us with confidence as to the accuracy of their pronouncements!

By virtue of claiming independence from England before the Act of Union, we have been bequeathed the Antient version of the ritual. We have also missed out on the Domatic version, largely practiced around the world, and because of this our ritual, little altered in 200 years, provides a fascinating link with early Freemasonry.

Now we will examine some of the differences in rituals around the British Isles in the late eighteenth and early nineteenth centuries.

2. EARLY RITUALS

Rather than laboriously recount the several rituals researched, I have included them in an Appendix to this paper, and the interested Companion may peruse them at his leisure at a later time. However, I would like to draw attention to four particular points, which may aid him in his reading. Firstly, I consider some of the different Openings and how they differ. Secondly, we briefly look at a couple of early penalties which remind us that these went through a number of variations before being united in 1845. Thirdly, and probably the most interesting, we find that several stories were used in outlining the ritual, and may perhaps conjecture that as the story of Enoch was apocryphal while the story of Zerubbabel could easily be found in the Bible, this eventually became the model. Finally, I quote in full a particularly beautiful soliloquy on death, which may well have inspired the writing of Hiram's famous soliloquy in the Royal Master Degree of the Cryptic rite. This comes from the Baldwyn Rite of Bristol dated 1878, and is likely an early version of what came to the United States with the Antients. If this is true, it is quite possible that this speech inspired the authors of the Cryptic Rite which, we should remember, was invented in New York and promulgated by Columbian Cryptic Council, the Premier Council of the World.

2.1 OPENINGS

The Virtual Past Master Degree allowed Brothers who had not received the benefit of Installation to be received as Royal Arch Masons. It is interesting to note that, while this custom is continued here, in England the rules were amended. Now only one month's standing as a Master Mason (originally one year) is required to be invited to join a Chapter (the Royal Arch being to all intents and purposes the Fourth Degree). Indeed, in England all Chapters are 'moored' to a Lodge and bear the same name and number. However, even in the Domatic Rite only a Worshipful Master can be installed as one of the three Principal Officers. This leads to an interesting question: how is the Royal Arch formed? In the Domatic rite only the three Principal Officers for the Royal Arch and speak the ineffable name, while the other members watch. Indeed, the Opening (and

Closing) is quite a 'slight' ceremony, the Three Principals approaching their thrones in the East by seven steps, while bowing and pronouncing "Omnipotent", "Omniscient", "Omnipresent", before Zerubbabel offers a brief prayer. They then "meet and agree" to keep the secrets (but there is no mention of "Raising the Royal Arch"), then announce the Chapter duly opened.

Of the texts available to me, I could find no reference to the lengthy, involved and militarized ceremony which is now practiced here in the United States. I was interested to note that in the reconstruction of an Opening based on an early 19th Century ritual in Canajoharie, New York, earlier this decade, that the ritual was broadly as it is now.

In Sir A. Commins opening dated 1795 we find the rituals almost identical to the modern day Domatic, with the addition of the Christianizing: "In the beginning was the word..." also spoken with 'trible voice', that is to say, by breaking the quotation down into three parts, each spoken by one Principal Officer. However, in William Finch's manuscript of circa 1800, and from Bengal or Calcutta, we see the words: "We three do agree the Royal Arch to raise." But this is said with right hand on left breast. The Bristol Rite expands on this still further, also including the briefest indication of duties, and also of interest to us, requiring of the Candidate that he prove himself proficient in the preceding three degrees by signs and words. Here we may detect the elements which went on to be far more developed in the Antient side. It does not take a great leap of faith to surmise that the overall layout of what finally became the seventh degree now largely followed the format of a Blue Lodge Opening, with the addition of proofs form the Candidate, and an increasingly elaborate raising of the Arch. Given that the Domatic rite only requires the three Principals to support the bible with their left hands, and to place their right hands upon it in the form of a triangle, we can also guess that the great elaboration of the raising of the Royal Arch was a later and whimsical addition. However, my review of the documents to this date only allow me to speculate on this. I hope another Companion may be inspired to research how, why and when the Opening went from a short and simple ceremony to the involved ceremony we are now used to. Is it possible that Thomas Smith Webb took the deliberate step of distancing the ritual from the English version by making significant changes?

It is noteworthy that, while in England the First Principal is Zerubbabel the King, in the United States the First Principal is Jeshua or Joshua the High Priest. Popular belief ascribes this to the hatred of monarchy at the time of the rewriting of the rituals in America; but the High Priest ruled in the Temple, where the drama is set, and it is more likely that Thomas Smith Webb, in reworking the rituals, simply deemed it more appropriate that the High Priest should be the First Principal.

2.2 PENALTIES

The modern day penalty of Royal Arch Masons in the United States has always fascinated me. Given all the generous allusions in the biblical stories surrounding Moses as the Candidate makes his way through the veils; or equally thinking of some of the gruesome things which could be done with an unfaithful companion in a subterranean vault, it seems odd that we have ended up with a penalty which, while undeniably bloodthirsty, does not seem directly connected with the story.

Unfortunately, most penalties in the diaries are entirely missing. This is largely because any parts of ritual are in cipher or shorthand, it being not permitted to commit the rituals to writing. However, there are a few instances where the penalty can be discerned or guessed at. The Arundel Chapter Index, for example, gives the penalty as: "may my right arm be withered and changed to a state of Leprosy and my left arm struck by a Serpent and the contaminated matter circulate through every vein of my body that this corrupt frame of mine is totally…[illegible]." This is rather more in keeping with the general story. The Bristol Ritual contains the penalty of: "having the hand struck off with the sword of human justice, and publicly exposed in token of my infamy, or the Royal Arch fall in on me and crush me beneath its ruins".

It would be interesting to conjecture that originally there were as many penalties as variations in ritual. However, how we ended up with a penalty which seems more at home in a Foreign Legion movie than a royal Arch Degree Ceremony surprises me.

2.3 STORIES

One of the most fascinating differences in early rituals is the different settings for the ritual story. While some most certainly focused on the building of the Second Temple, at least one is set in the time of King Solomon, and involves the building of the secret vault and the discovery of the vault of Enoch. We mentioned earlier that the story of the Ark of Noah is one of the oldest of all Masonic devices. The story of Enoch is intimately intertwined with this story, leading us to suspect that the Enochian slant also reflects an early version of the myth.

In the Finch manuscript of circa 1800 we find the most fully developed version of this particular story. Enoch is taken to heaven and shown the triangular plate bearing the name of God; then a vision of an underground vault with nine arches one upon another, within which is a white marble pedestal. God commands him to build this, as well as two pillars of brass and brick, containing all the knowledge of mankind (later seen in the Second Degree lecture, this time pertaining to the pillars at the entrance to the Temple of Solomon). This he does. In this version we are then transported forward to the time of King Solomon, who is commander not only to build a Temple but also an underground corridor, and he is promised that on completing the Temple the true name of God revealed to Moses would be restored. According to the text, next to Mount Moriah was another Mount called Mount Calvary, which the workmen were excavating in order to lay foundations for another building. They come across the ruins of a more ancient building, upon vertical arches. Solomon tells his three principal architects to investigate, which they do, lifting each keystone by its ring, and in the ninth arch they discover the pedestal and the triangular plate.

This story also introduces us to the mysterious names of the three architects or sojourners: Stolkyn, Jacobert and Giblim. This extraordinary development is, perhaps, the strongest hint that the Degree is indeed descended from the French system, as we will see in the conclusion.

Most of the other Rituals studied are rather more familiar, dealing with the rebuilding of the Temple by Zerubbabel, Jeshua and Haggai. The use of three sojourners is common to all, as is the idea of descending into a place of darkness, there finding something bright which in many rituals shines with its own light. In most cases, too, the pedestal is a double cube – more of an altar – which means its surface is square, containing a triangle (of gold) containing a circle: a device familiar to Masons in the more Hermetic degrees. Sometimes the language is quite fun. For example, in the Bristol rite the sojourners angrily reply to Zerubbabel's taunt that they may be "of the lineage of that set of traitors who fell away during the siege and went over to the enemy", that: "we are not, Most Excellent, of that timorous race of parasites who…fell away and deserted their trust."

Nevertheless, given that the earliest rituals focus on the period from Enoch, the Flood, and the Building of the First Temple, there is reason to suppose that the action was moved to the Second Temple to continue the biblical tradition, and to move away from apocryphal stories. After all, there is no reference in the Old Testament to finding a secret vault containing a pedestal or sacred delta in the books of Ezra, Haggai or Nehemiah.

2.4 A RITUAL TREASURE

In this exquisite hand-written book collected by F.W. Irvin, entitled "Bristol Rituals" and dated 1878, and which is interspersed with cut-out pictures, we find the following rituals: Entered Apprentice, Fellow Craft, Master Mason, Past Master, Royal Arch, 9 Selected Masters, Scotch Knight & Grand Architect, Knight of the East, Sword & Eagle, Knight Templar, Knight Rose Croix; and a Service of Masonic Knights composed for the use of the Encampment of Baldwyn (1813).

After a short Obligation with the penalty left blank, we find this beautiful soliloquy on death, surely one of the great treasures of Masonry:

"In the name of that Great and Omnipotent Being arise (takes him by the hand) and may the remembrance of the spring of acacia which was found on the grave of him who was the Most Excellent of Masons, and who parted with his life because he would not forfeit his honour and [illegible] stimulate his successors to imitate his glorious example, that the essence of virtue may enshrine our Moral Law, and like the Beautiful Rose of Sharon - in conjunction with the Lily of the Valley exalt our intellectual part - when death the grand leveler of all human greatness has drawn his sable curtain around us - and when the last arrows of our mortal enemy hath been dispatched, and the bow of this Mighty Conqueror broken, by the iron arm of time, when the angel of the Lord declares that time shall be no more - and when by this victory God hath subdued all things to Himself, then shall we receive the reward of our virtue, in those heavenly mansions veiled from mortal eyes when every secret of Masonry shall be opened, never never to be closed, then shall the G[rea]t Jeh[ovah], the G[ran]d Master of the Universe, bid us enter into his celestial Lodge, when peace, order, and harmony shall eternally reign."

3. CONCLUSIONS

If we can summarize the situation, so far as we can tell:

1. The fourth degree, later the Holy Royal Arch, existed in some form at least by the 1740s, and therefore predated the Antient-Modern split; it also probably arose around the same time as the 3rd Degree.

2. Following the split, although the Royal Arch was not invented by them, it was seen to be a part of the Antient system of Degrees, and as such officially unrecognized by the Moderns.

3. The ritual itself had many forms, although it taught the same underlying message. This was not standardized even following the Act of Union and the creation of a Grand Chapter, and indeed a unified ritual did not appear until the 1840s.

4. Veils were not peculiar to the Antients - indeed records show that both Antients and Moderns used, or did not use, veils.

5. Despite all this, both Antients and Moderns - even Grand Line Officers - flocked to receive this Degree, as they clearly perceived something in it which was more important than their jurisdictional quarrels.

And yet, despite the contemporaneous development of the 3rd and 4th Degrees, their origins are clearly very different. In no way can the

Royal Arch – even though it is referred to as the "completion of Masonry" – be seen as a natural continuation of the 2nd or 3rd Degree. A.E. Waite states – without citing sources – that: "It follows that in the Royal Arch we are entering a new field of Masonic Symbolism, a new thesis on the preservation and perpetuation of the Secret Tradition, postulating antecedently a traditional history which is not comprised in the Craft. It follows also that, as now known and worked among us, the Arch never formed part of the Third Degree." The discontinuities of time, symbolism, message, language, characters and movement are clear indicators that the inclusion of the Royal Arch Degrees by the United Grand Lodge of England & Wales was more a matter of the preservation of a clearly important and much loved rite, than because it fitted closely with the existing Degree system. It is interesting to speculate why, if the 3rd Degree and the Royal Arch appeared as broadly the same time, why the Premier Grand Lodge embraced the new 3rd Degree with scarcely a murmur, yet refused officially to recognize the Royal Arch.

Similarly, Dr. Oliver regretted that Dunckerley had not improved still further on the ritual of the Royal Arch Degree, from the materials which he had derived from the Antients, observing, with much force, that he could not have failed to see their incongruity.

Earlier we saw a Royal Arch ritual practiced in India around 1800, which mentioned Enoch and the peculiar characters Stolkyn, Jacobert and Giblim. We find these same characters – and the legend of Enoch – in the thirteenth degree of the Rite of Perfection. The Thirteenth, or "Royal Arch Degree" outline almost the exact same story. For example, in the Opening the inspector says: "I dug in the ruins of Enoch. I penetrated through nine arches underground, and in the end I found the Delta which God had promised the Holy Patriarchs should be found in fullness of time." Here the pillars of Enoch are called "Strength and Beauty, and "on the pillar of Beauty, he inscribed the methods of Art, and on the pillar of Strength, he inscribed the rules of moral action." Here we also meet the architects Joabert, Stolkin and Guiblim (or Adoniram according to Albert Pike in Morals and Dogma) in an extremely lengthy lecture which covers history from Enoch, through Noah to their discovery, and which lasts some sixteen pages in my copy.

Further, in *Guide to the Royal Arch Chapter*, pages 17 and 18 we read: "In the year 1755 it was currently reported among the brethren that some of the members of Lodge No. 94 had been on the continent and there witnessed extraordinary manifestations in ancient Masonry, which that Lodge had agreed to practice every third lodge night…The Deputy Grand Master, Dr. Manningham, at once visited the Lodge, and there learned that this pretended Ancient Masonry was nothing more than a mixture of what is now known as Ramsay's Royal Arch with Dermott's Degree, the principal features of which was a transfer of the real Landmark of a Master Mason to a new degree, which was unknown and unrecognized by the Grand Lodge of England." This also suggests France as a possible source of much of the symbolism of the Royal Arch through the Rite of Perfection.

For these reasons I am convinced that the Royal Arch Degree has its origins in France.

As an aside, the veils are preserved in the Scottish ritual of Excellent Master. I had personally wondered if there was any connection between the four veils and the four ancient elements. Many Masonic rituals require the Candidate to be 'tried by the four elements' before being judged worthy to be admitted. In W. Bro. Trevor Stewart's treatise on *Hermetic influence in Masonry*, I found a possible answer: "In some of the early versions of this ceremony (mostly English ones) there were only three veils but in at least one ancient Jewish source (Josephus' Antiquities), the veil of the Temple was composed of four colors: fine white linen)to signify the earth, from which grew the flax that produced it); purple (to signify water because that precious color was derived from the blood of a rare shellfish); blue (which signified air) and scarlet (which signified fire). The ritual of the Excellent Master Degree, however, gives other interpretations to the Candidate at a later stage."

If our ancient Brethren, even knowing the story being told, what persuaded them to exempt this single ritual from the battle for recognition? What did it contain which transcended all material and earthly reason, and why did it attract the greatest thinkers who, like Dermott, Grand Secretary of the Antients, saw in it the "root, heart and marrow of Freemasonry?"

One of the versions of the Royal Arch story found its way into the Rite of Strict Observance founded by Baron von Hund, and thence into the Scottish Rectified Rite penned by Jean-Baptiste Willermoz in the latter part of the eighteenth century. Now, while I have learned from experience that American masons tend to veer away from spiritual or deeply philosophical interpretations of our Degrees, preferring to stick with the safer levels of allegory and metaphor, the equivalent of the Royal Arch Degree in this system – the Master of St. Andrew – specifically states that in this Degree, all symbolism and allegory have been stripped away and that the Candidate now beholds the truth, face to face. This cannot be called yet another interpretation, for this is laid out in the ritual itself, which is considered to be the oldest continually worked ritual in Masonry!

So what is this truth, which is presented in its complete and unveiled form?

While I cannot divulge the exact nature of the ritual itself, of course, I can at least point out some of the philosophy underlying this version of the Royal Arch Degree, written at the time of Dermott, which makes explicit what is only implicit in our modern Degree, and which can safely be ignored by all who do not wish to delve that deeply.

The first temple is Mankind. More specifically it is Adam Kadmon, created by God as the perfect, immortal reflection of Himself, and set to rule the world or universe created by the Grand Architect. The Temple, like our Lodges, rests upon three Pillars, and should one of those be removed the edifice would become unstable. In Kabbalah these three pillars are the two opposing pillars of B and J , or Strength/Severity and Beauty/Mercy, the central of Middle Pillar being the balance of the two poles, or Wisdom. Our ritual tells us that Hiram, the Grand Junior Warden, or the Pillar of Beauty, or Mercy was taken away. This left an excess of Strength with no Mercy to temper it, and as one old ritual states, an excess of Severity (or Strength) is but cruelty. So Adam Kadmon, or Collective Man, attained a state of arrogance and believed himself to be equal to God. However, the First Temple could not endure on two Pillars alone, and the whole edifice collapsed. Thus, for his arrogance, Adam Kadmon was banished to earth and splintered into many pieces, comprising the human race. However, man's sojourn on earth is found in the Royal Arch Degree. For the ruins of the First Temple endured intact, and upon them was build a Second, or very inferior Temple, which caused the old men who remembered the First to weep with frustration and bitterness. Nevertheless, this poor reflection of the first Man in his original state of Glory contained something precious. He still contained a spark of the Divine spirit, or breath, as evinced by the remarkable discovery made by the three workmen: a triangular golden plate upon which was inscribed the sacred name of Deity.

Perhaps it is because they saw a profound message of hope for humanity that those early Royal Arch Masons rose above their temporal quarrels and found a common interest in what is probably the most important lesson in all of Masonry.

APPENDIX 1 - EXCEPTS OF EARLY RITUALS TRANSCRIBED FROM MANUSCRIPTS IN THE U.G.L.E. LIBRARY

Conventions used: personal notes in italics. Incomplete words completed in []; for example, Comps would be written Comp[anion]s. This is only done for the sake of clarity on some places. I do not guarantee that they are all correct. I also cannot guarantee that all abbreviations have been retained: I may have written some abbreviated words in full. Old English 's' retained as 'f'.

A. MS: Sir A. Commins: "Initiation to the Royal Arch according to Sir. A Commins, c.1795"

OPENING

Z. In the b[eginning]...
H. was the W[ord]...
J. and the w[ord was with God].
Z. Om[nopoten]t.
H. Om[mniscien]t.
J. Om[ni]p[resen]t.
All.   Rept - G[od].
Z. Before whom we 3 do meet and agree, in love and unity, the Sac[re]d. W[or]d. to keep, and never to reveal to any in the world, unlefs it be when 3 or more than 3 such as we do meet. They now bow the 3d. time which done they advance to their places, and standing upon the footsteps of their chairs.
Z. I declare this G.R.C. open in the name of G[od]. Then ea[ch]. Laying his right hand upon his h[ear]t, they severally pronounce hkt Eli (this is my Gd.). Bow and sit down.

FORM OF DEGREE
1st Section:

The C[ouncil]. duly opened. All seated. The Scri[be]s with desks, and books open. Z. addrefsing himself to E the P. Seri., says hkt .

Z Is there any thing of which we are not acquainted that requires our present care and attention?

E Looking on his minutes, answrs only our constant duties and the public welfare; except (pointing to the 3 Soj[ourn]ers) those strangers.

Z Addrefsing himself to the strangers. Pray, Sirs, what is your request?

1 SojrWe 1st beg leave to soj[our]n amongst you, and hearing you are about to build a T[emple] to the Lord, we beg your acceptance of our best services to forward that glorious work.

Z Pray what branch of the businefs wo[ul]d you wish to engage in?

Sojrs   We deem the lowest service in the Lord's work an honor, and therefore only beg employ.

Z Your humility bespeaks your merits and we doubt not, but you are qualified for much superior offices; but those being full, and as you are furnished with Tools for the purpose; we at present must appoint you to prepare for the foundation, and must give you this caution, that sho[ul]d you meet with any thing appertaining to the O[l]d T[emple] you will immediately give us information thereof.

The Soj[ourner]s bow and withdraw. Having (namely the Sojrs) waited some short time they give the signal, and N[ehemiah?], going to the door signify their having made a discovery, which they beg leave to communicate to their G[rand] and R[oyal] C[ouncil]. He (namely N.) shuts the door and acquaints the C. who receives orders to admit them. This done.

Z We are told you have made a Discovery which you want to inform us of.

Sojrs   We have. Being at work early this morning in pursuance of your Orders, our Comp. breaking up the ground with his P[ick] ax, we judged from the sound it was hollow. When calling our other Comp[anion] with his Shov[el] to clear away the loose earth and rubbish, we discovered the perfect crown of an A[rch] but not being able to find any way into, I loosened 2 k[ey] stones with my Crow, which having drawn forth and discovered the cavity; it excited our desire to know what it contained. But being apprehensive of danger from damps, or other unknown causes, we cast lots who sho[ul]d go down. The chance fell upon me. Having agreed on proper signals, I was let down by my Comp[anions] by the help of my C[abl]e Tow. Being got to the bottom, and meeting no obstruction, I found somewhat wrought into due and regular form, and also a Roll of a C[harter?]; but the Sun only just now peeping from the portions of the East, and darting his beams parallel to the plane of the Horizon, I co[ul]d not discern what it contained, but giving the signal before agreed on. namely 3 gentle pulls, on my right hand C[able] Tow, I was drawn up by my loving Comp[anions]. On approaching the light we found the [?] contained part of the Holy Law. This gave us much joy and made us resolve on a further search; for which reason, we drew forth a 3rd k[ey] stone, and I was let down a 2 time. The sun was approaching nearer to his meridian, darted his beams on the front of a Ped[esta]l whereon was inscribed the names of the 3 most E[xcellent] G[rand] M[aster]s who presided at the building of 1st glorious T[emple]. On the top was a plate of gold, whereon was inscribed in the form of a O that great mysterious name yhvh, and within that in the figure a [Delta] what we suppose to be the Sac[re]d w[or]d itself. Having made this discovery we again closed [u]p the A[rch], with care as in duty bound, and come to make our report.

etc...

The subsequent sections cover the Qs & As, which later became the Principals' Lectures. Interestingly, the ceremony is performed as though with no Candidates!

B. MS: William Finch, "Ceremonies of Royal Arch & N.R.+", c1800

Book dated up to 1776, written in Bengal or Calcutta, apparently.

The Mode of Opening the Grand Royal Arch Chapter of Jerusalem. Usual opening In the beginning...Om...Om... Om... (kneel) before whom we three do agree in love and unity the Sacred Word of Royal Arch Mason to keep and never to reveal it to any in the world unless it be when the sign, word demand me. Shortly after, each with right hand on left breast: "We three do agree the Royal Arch to raise. We three do agree the Royal Arch Word to seek. We three do agree the Royal Arch Word to keep."

Here we find the mysterious reference to the names of the 3 Sojourners. this time set in the time of King Solomon. The story opens with Enoch taken to heaven to be shown the triangular plate bearing the name of God, then to a vision of an underground vault of 9 perpendicular arches in which was a white marble pedestal. God commands him to build this and he does. Then the wickedness of the world brings about the flood. After having the two pillars of brass and brick created upon which are engravers all the arts and sciences. Solomon dreamed that on completing the Temple the true name of God revealed to Moses would be restored Also, he is commanded to build a corridor. So Solomon builds the vaulted walk from his apartment to beneath the Sanctum Sanctorum, there placing a pedestal of white porphyry called 'Abeshasco' or 'Abenshasco'. This was the second Vault of Wisdom, where the 3 GMs met. Next to Mount Moriah was Mount Calvary(?), and on building foundations they had come across the ruins of a more ancient building. So Solomon sent for his 3 Chief Grand Architects Stolkyn, Jacobert and G-l-m to explore. The first one let down by rope is Stolkyn, who explores the first 3 arches before his courage fails him. In fact, the arches are one atop of another, similar to the vault of Enoch. Each keystone comes with a ring which Stolkyn uses to prise open with his crowbar. Jacobert then goes down and opens up the next 3 arches. Then G-l-m goes down with a lighted flambeau, and in the 9th arch, which is illuminated by the brilliant light coming from the 12 jewels in the High Priest's breastplate, he finds the pedestal and instinctively gives the Sign of Admiration.

Also mentions the "different mystical ages of Masonry 3-5-7-9, and the mystical numbers, of the 12 Grand Names (tribes??) 3 with 3 letters, 3 with 5 letters, 3 with 7 letters, 3 with 9 letters. These are the mystical numbers of the degree of perfection. These add up to 72."

C. MS: John Knight, "Sub. Deg. Of R.A. Mas." (manu) 1791?

This is clearly the Antient Ritual (as opposed to the Domatic version elsewhere). Written in Redruth, Cornwall, where he was a member of the Druids Chapter of Royal Arch Masons No. 79 in 1791 . However, John Knight lists himself as "MEGP Z" and the other Principals EGP H and EGP J, so Zerubbabel was still the senior officer. The Candidate is examined in a MM Lodge to ensure he has gone through the Past Master Degree (evinced by giving the sign of a Master of Arts & Sciences), after the Chapter is Opened with "In the beginning.... Om/Om/Om").

The cipher is confusing, substituting letters for others. However, after the opening prayer the Opening continues (probably)!:

Z From whence came Joshua (Jeshua)?
J From Babylon.
Z Where going?
J To Jerusalem.
Z What sho[ul]d induce him to leave Babylon and go to Jerusalem?
J To afsist in clearing away the Rubish from the Building of the First Temple in hopes of finding the S. W. of Mcspnry [Masonry].
Z Was the S.W. lpst [lost]?
J It was.
Z How came it to be lost?
J By the D[eath] of our G[ran]d M[aste]r HAB.
Z Let us then Search and use our best endeavours to find the S[acred] W[ord]....

Candidate enters, prayer said then led round with Scriptural reading: "I will bring him by a way that he knows not", etc. He kneels a first arch but finds nothing. Kneels at second arch and finds Law which he takes to Jeshua. Kneels at third arch and finds S.W. of God. Two prayers and Obligation including the words: "so that I will not in any wise aiding or afsisting at the Exaltn of a MERAM except it be in a regularly constituted Chapter under Warrant or Sanction of His Royal Highness the Duke of Cumberland Deceased of his Succefsor." Then welcomed into Order and Catechism given. Followed by Lectures.

As an interesting variation the triple tau is seen as a 'T' above an'H' to stand for Templum Hierosalymum - Temple of Jerusalem. Also, the triangle stands on a pedestal so the "Sacred name of God shod never fall to the ground." Called "Royal" because it is presided over by a descendant of King Solomon.

Note no mention of veils!

D. MS: Anon., "Arundel Chapter index", c. 1808

Penalty "as the High Priest" shorthand indicates: "may my right arm be withered and changed to a state of Leprosy and left arm struck by a Serpent and the contaminated matter (?) circulate through every vein of my body that this corrupt frame of mine is totally ... [illegible]."

E. Com. G. Claret, "The Ceremonies, Etc. of The Holy Royal Arch also Passing the Vails", pub. London 1845 (first published H.R.A. Ritual)

This is broadly in line with modern working. However, the explanation of the signs is most interesting:

"On the front of the Pedestal are graven the names of the three Grand Masters, who presided at the building of the former Temple, viz. Solomon King of Israel, Hiram King of Tyre, and Hiram Abbiff, and are meant to perpetuate their names, as well as to commemorate the proceedings during the erection of the former temple; there is likewise a Triple Tau, or letter T, a mark or character affixed to the summonses of R.A. Masons, when summoned on other than usual occasions. The triple Tau or letter T is translated from the Hebrew, a mark or sign, spoken of by Ezekiel, when he said to the man with the inkhorn: "go thy way thro' the midst of the city of Jerusalem, and set a mark on all those who sigh and lament for the abomination thereof", by which mark they were saved from among those who were, slain for their idolatry, by the wrathful displeasure of the Most High. In ancient times this mark was placed on the forehead of all those who were acquitted by their judges, as proof of their innocence; and military commanders caused a T to be placed on all those who had escaped unhurt from the field of battle, denoting that they were in perfect life, it has ever been considered the mark of life. The union of the three Ts, allude to the grand tri-union of the Deity by whom the horrific, gloomy and unshapen chaos was changed into form and existence. The Word you observe on the triangle is the sacred word, which you have promised and sworn never to divulge unless with the assistance of two or more R.A. Masons, lawfully congregated, constituted and dedicated, which as Principal of this Chapter, I am authorized to pronounce. It is in itself a compound word, and its combination forms the word J.B.O. J. the Chaldean name of God, signifying His essence of majesty incomprehensible, it is also a Hebrew word, signifying I AM, and shall eternal existence of the Most High. B. is an Assyrian word, signifying Lord or powerful. It is also a compound word; from the preposition Beth; which signifies in, or in heaven, or on high, therefore this word means Lord in heaven, or on high. O. is an Egyptian word, signifying father of all, it is also an Hebrew word implying strength, power, and expressive of the omnipotence of the father of all. Taking each together will read thus: I AM and shall be, Lord in heaven, father of all in every age, in every clime adored by saint, by savage and by sage, Jehovah Jove or Lord. The word on the circle is the grand, awful, tremendous and incomprehensible name of the Most High, signifying I AM the beginning and the ending, which was and is to come, the actual future, and all sufficient God, who alone has His being in, and of himself, and gives to all others their being, so that He was, what he is, is what he was, and shall be both what he was, and what he is, from everlasting to everlasting, all the creation being dependent on His mighty will. The Circle also typifies the Omnipotent and Almighty author of the universe, having neither beginning nor ending; it also calls to our remembrance the grand and awful hereafter, or futurity, where we hope to enjoy endless bliss, and everlasting life. The characters which are placed on each angle of the triangle are Hebrew, and particularly worthy of your attention, the Aleph answering to our A. the Beth to our B. and the Lamed to our L. Take the Aleph and the Beth,

246

they form the word Ab, meaning father. The Aleph and Lamed the word Al, which means word. Take the Lamed the Aleph and the Beth, they form the word Lab, meaning Spirit. Take the Beth, Aleph and Lamed, the word Bul, meaning Lord. Take each angle of the triangle, they will form the following sentence, Father Lord, Word Lord, Spirit Lord.

"The triangle; was in the days of Phygoras (sic!) esteemed as the most sacred of all emblems, and when any oath of more than usual import was to be administered it as given on the triangle, and when so administered, none were even known to have violated it, the ancient Egyptians called it the sacred number three, or number of perfection, and was an object of worship amongst the ancients as the grand principle of animated existence, and they gave it the name of God, representing the animal vegetable and mineral creation, it was also called Avolet, that is to say the soul of nature. The sacred Delta is usually placed in the midst of squares and circles, indicating the vivifying principle, extending its ramifications, throughout all created matter, it is therefore denominated the great all, or summum bonum.

F. Province of Bristol Ritual of the Degree of the Holy Royal Arch copied from the Standard Ritual 1949

Z. Companions, assist me to open this Chapter. Ex. Comp. J., what is your duty?
J. To aid and assist in promoting the Lord's work.
Z. Ex. Comp H., what is your duty?
H. To aid and assist in protecting the Lord's work
Z. Let us pray. Almighty, Supreme and Incomprehensible Jehovah, assist us mercifully in this our undertaking. Grant that our endeavours to spread the knowledge of Thy Holy Word may be crowned with success, through Thy All-powerful protection.
All   S.M.I.B.

All 3 rise and take the VSL each in his right hand.

Z. In the beginning was the Word.

H. And the Word was with God.

J. And the Word was God.

Z. What are the attributes of this omnific Word?

J. Omniscience.

H. Omnipotence.

Z. Omnipresence. To the All-wise, All-powerful and Ever-present Being around whose throne may we hereafter assemble.

Each kisses the VSL in turn They proceed to the East.

Candidate is asked to give proofs of EA, FC and MM by signs and words. Then quizzed more completely on the 3rd Degree: how prepared, how received, differences in the Lodge room, death as the peculiar subject of the Degree, who killed, the instruments used, explain the meaning of FPOF. Pledge of fidelity.

Principle Sojourner now reads Exodus III, v1 -5 (Can removes shoes); v6 (Can. covers face with left hand); v 13-14; Exodus IV,v 1 -3 (Can throws down rod); v4 (Can picks up rod); v5. Then PS says : The Sign of the First Veil is ___. The Password is ___.. Can, led by DC now passes first veil. Ditto Veils 2 – 4. 2nd AS at first veil; 1st AS at second veil, PS at third veil.

Candidate readmitted.

Z. Then Bro, I exhort you to persevere with fidelity and firmness, and not to fall away as our forefathers did the time of need, when the wrath of God fell upon them for their disobedience as foretold by Jeremiah, and other prophets by whom he declared that for having forsaken His laws, and disobeyed His commandments, their city should become a desolation, their Temple reduced to ruins, and that they should feel the weight of His displeasure for seventy years. This prophecy began to be fulfilled in the fourth year of the reign of Jehoiakin, Anno Lucis 3398. An account of the destruction of the Temple will now be read by Ex. H. (reads II Chronicles XXXVI, v14-21). Long perambulations and scriptural readings of an eclectic nature, including Proverbs II vl-5 and III v13-26 (then Obligation taken -

penalty: "than that of having my hand struck off with the sword of human justice, and publicly exposed in token of my infamy, or the Royal Arch fall in upon me and crush me beneath its ruins" - sealed four times on VSL); Exodus XXVIII (1st time), 36; Ezra III v8-10(2nd time); Nehemiah IV vl-6 & 16-18 (3rd time); Psalms LXVIII v4 (4th time); Haggai I v1-5 (5th time); Ezech VIII vl-3 (6th time); St. John I v1 (7th time).

Z. Who are you? Are you of the lineage of that set of traitors who fell away during the siege and went over to the enemy when liberty and kindred had most need of their assistance, or are you of the poor of the people, left in the land of Judah by Nebuzaradan, the chief of Nebuchadnezzar's officers to cultivate the fields and vineyards, or are you (as we are more inclined to suspect) descendants of those princes carried away captive into Babylon with King Zedekiah? Speak, who are you?

PS We are not, Most Excellent, of that timorous race of parasites, who, when their city was besieged and the Temple destroyed, basely fell away and deserted their trust; neither are we of the lower class, left behind by Nebuzaradan to cultivate the vineyards, till the land, and perform other servile offices; but as you rightly suspect, we are descendents of those brave but unfortunate princes carried away into Babylon with King Zedekiah. We now come to offer our best services in repairing the walls of our city, and rebuilding the Temple of our Lord.

Z. How have you been engaged during your captivity in Babylon?

PS In Masonry, Most Excellent.

Z What do you mean by Masonry?

PS That grand and comprehensive science which more especially teaches us the knowledge of ourselves and the duties encumbent upon us as men and Masons.

Z That is worthy of your noble ancestors. In what labor do you wish to be engaged?

PS We deem the lower situation in the Lord's house an honour, and therefore only seek employment.

BIBLIOGRAPHY

For Early Ritual of the Holy Royal Arch

BOOKS

· A Basic Historico-Chronological Model of the Western Hermetic Tradition, by Wor. Trevor Stewart, Past Master of the QCCC, pub. Privately 1999.

· The Ceremonies, Etc. of The Holy Royal Arch also Passing the Vails, Corn. G. Claret, pub. London 1845 (first published Holy Royal Arch Ritual)

· Glimpses of Masonic History, Charles W. Leadbeater, orig. pub. 1926, edition used Kessinger Publishing Company, ISBN 1-56459-613-3

· Guide to the Royal Arch Chapter, John Sheville and James L. Gould, orig. pub. 1867, edition used Macoy Publishing, ISBN 0-88053-021-9

· Institution of Freemasons Catechism, 1725, - brad_quinn.tripod.com/catechisms/ catechism01 .html

· …Neither Arch, Royal Arch or Antient..., A Healthy Re-examination of Some Old Material concerning the Delayed Recognition of the Royal Arch by the Premier Grand Lodge, by Wor. Trevor Stewart, Past Master of the QCCC, pub. privately 2003

· A New Encyclopædia of Freemasonry, Arthur E. Waite, orig pub. 1921, edition used Wings Books, ISBN 0-517-19148-2

· The Pocket History of Freemasonry, Fred L. Pick & G. Norman Knight, pub. Frederick Muller Ltd, London 1953, ISBN 0-584-10256-9

· The Royal Masonic Cyclopædia, Kenneth Mackenzie, orig. pub. 1877, edition used: The Aquarian Press, ISBN 0-85030-521-7

· Royal Arch Scarf & Apron (pictures) - www.phoenixmasonry.org/rnasonicmuseum/ RAM 1800s Apron.htm

MANUSCRIPTS IN THE LIBRARY OF THE UNITED GRAND LODGE OF ENGLAND

· Sir A. Commins: "Initiation to the Royal Arch according to Sir. A Commins", c.1795

- W.H. Dee (Z of the Chapter of Goodwill, Braintree - exalted in 1796) "Royal Arch Ritual & Discourses, 21S` May, 1812"
- William Finch, "Ceremonies of Royal Arch & N.R.+", c1800
- John Knight, "Sub, Deg. Of R.A. Mas. (manu)", 1791?
- 11.H. Sadler, "Royal Arch", c.1805
- Anon., "Arundel Chapter Index", c.1808
- "Province of Bristol Ritual of the Degree of the Holy Royal Arch". copied from the Standard Ritual 1949
- F.W. Irvin (collector), "Bristol Rituals" (manu), 1878.

A BRIEF LOOK AT THE TRIVIUM & QUADRIVIUM

A key focus in the Fellowcraft Degree is the Seven Liberal Arts and Sciences. Why are these important, and what does that have to do with the Royal Arch Degree?

While Plato initially came up with the idea of a formal syllabus for study, building upon an idea formulated by Pythagoras of a school where both men and women could study, the idea was expanded in a book by a moderately obscure author of the 5th Century, a pagan living in North Africa called Martianus Capella. In his book De nuptiis Philologiae et Mercurii (On the Marriage of Philology and Mercury), he outlined the seven liberal arts and sciences in a wordy book full of allegory and poetry, in which each Art or Science is explained in great – sometimes bizarre – detail by seven maidens who will serve Philology on her marriage to Mercury. The reason attention was drawn to the fact that Martianus was a pagan is because it was this book which ultimately led to the establishment of the formal educational system throughout Western Europe. Of course all early schools and universities were run by or controlled by the Church, and so it is interesting to note that the very skills taught as a means towards greater understanding of the world and man in the context of theology should be formulated by a non-Christian!

The Seven Liberal Arts and Sciences were divided into two courses, reflected even today in most European University Degrees by a division into two streams of basic and advanced studies. For example, in Oxford the first two or three terms lead to examinations called Preliminaries, or 'Prelims'; while the next two years of study lead to the Finals, or 'Schools'. So in the classical educational system, we find the Arts and Sciences presented in two groups, called the trivium (or three roads) and quadrivium (or four roads). The trivium was comprised of Grammar, Logic and Rhetoric; while the quadrivium was made up of Arithmetic, Geometry, Music and Astronomy/Astrology. This approach to university education lasted from the early Middle Ages right up to the 18th Century. Its function is well described in an article in The New Atlantis: "At the center of the liberal arts were the humanities, the education of how to be a human being. Each new generation was encouraged to consult the great works of our tradition, the vast epics, the classic tragedies and comedies, the reflections of philosophers and theologians, the revealed Word of God, those countless books that sought to teach us what it was to be human — above all, how to use our liberty well."

As Freemasonry in its present form began in the early 18th Century, it was expected that all educated men would have been taught the liberal arts and sciences at university, and no doubt those members of the Royal Society and many founders of Freemasonry would have had that background. Therefore, an education in these subjects was seen as an essential part of becoming a refined gentleman, capable of holding elegant discourse in parlors and possessing the skills to discuss the important topics of the day; and to participate in the great social and scientific experiments of the Age. It was not until later that, despite ferocious opposition from the Establishment and the Church, the subjects taught in universities began to move away from the subjects which had been taught since their creation, and a more objective and scientific approach began to replace them. However, this new form of thought had little time for the introspection and philosophy of old educational values, and subjective contemplation was replaced by objective observation. It is interesting to see that the Fellowcraft Degree still retains the lesson that it is valuable for us to study the original topics which leads to philosophical inquiry, and ultimately a better understanding of ourselves and our relationship with God and man.

Now, it is no coincidence that there was seven liberal arts and sciences, not six or eight! Seven had always been seen as a powerful and mystical number, which signifies completion or perfection. From the earliest chapters in Genesis, we are shown that 'seven' is a very special number. We do not need to go into the many examples in nature, in books and in Masonry where the number seven appears in a significant role. Of course in the case of Martianus, who was a pagan, his focus on the number seven was more likely due to the number of planetary intelligences, or the major Gods of Egypt!

Just as the trivium and quadrivium were made up of three and four grades, degrees or steps, so we see that our own rituals reflect this perfect journey of seven steps in the three Blue Degree and four Capitular Degrees.

The first three subjects of the trivium are Grammar, Logic and Rhetoric. We are given a framework in which to work. Then we are given the tools to analyze a situation; and finally the ability to communicate this effectively. Indeed, these three subjects have been referred to as: Knowledge, Understanding and Wisdom, words familiar to a Mason. The Blue Lodge is the realm in which the basic tools are provided to allow a man to work upon himself and to knock of the 'superfluous knobs and excrescences' thereby allowing him to become a perfect living stone, fit for the celestial temple.

Another way of looking at the trivium is that it gives us the skills to formulate, to build hypotheses about what we experience, and finally to communicate these ideas to others. This realm is dedicated to man: to the individual and to mankind. Louis-Claude de Saint-Martin, an 18th Century French philosopher and mystic, described two Great Books of learning, the Book of Man and the Book of Nature. The trivium refers to the Book of Man.

The quadrivium refers to the Book of Nature. It considers the cyclical nature of all things, how they come into existence or are born, live, and die or are destroyed. We see this in all of Nature, in seeds and flowers, in the harvest, in animals and in mankind. In a slower cycle we learn in our history books about the rise and fall of clans or royal families – even of civilizations and nations. We identify patterns and learn to apply these in order to learn. If the trivium focuses on language, the quadrivium focuses on number.

Arithmetic considers Number. Geometry considers number in Space as dimension. Music considers number in Time. Finally, Astronomy consider number in Space and Time. In studying these, we come to appreciate the oneness of everything, and how everything is interrelated. We also learn to use those skills of communication we received in the trivium to analyze what we perceive with our five senses, and learn the art and science or mind as well as the art and science of matter.

Freemasonry does not require us to make a personal study of the seven liberal arts and sciences (though there is nothing to prevent the interested Mason from doing exactly that!). When it talks about the Arts and Sciences it is employing allegory and analogy as it does so often in its lessons. It is telling us to look beyond the obvious, deeper than the superficial, to examine and contemplate the symbols it places before us to see the truth within.

If the seventh Liberal Art is astronomy, the study of Time and Space, an Art which requires you to look up at the sky and consider in humility our unimportance in the great scheme of things – yet also our centrality in the Divine Plan – then we should expect this Degree, the Royal Arch, to contain messages and lessons which will lift us out of the mundane world and furnish us with an appreciation of an altogether higher plane of existence, where we will learn important truths about ourselves.

The previous six Degrees will then have been but a preparation for this final, seventh step. Here we arrive on the threshold of Time and Space where learning ends, and, having examined ourselves, and then the universe around us, it is now for us to put the pieces together and understand the profound lesson we are being led to learn.

THE GEORGE WASHINGTON INAUGURAL BIBLE – A NEW THEORY

NOTE: It seems appropriate to end this series of Masonic talks with a new theory on how and why the Bible of St. John's Lodge No. 1, A.Y.M. of New York City came to be used as the Bible on which George Washington took his oath of office as first President of the United States (and on which several subsequent Presidents have taken the same oath). I joined St. John's Lodge upon moving to New York, having been a Mason in England for twelve years. Over the past twenty-five years I have traveled around the United States with the Lodge Bible, giving talks and exhibiting it along with two other Brothers of our Lodge (our Bylaws require three Brothers to travel with it). For many years I have delivered the 'traditional' story of its use, but over time, and in light of later findings, I believe the version I now tell to be far closer to the truth. We will never know the whole story, so all I can do is offer this interpretation for your consideration.

Fig. 1 – George Washington Inaugural Bible
Photograph reproduced by kind permission of © Jason P. Sheridan

With the fever of the Presidential Inauguration only just past (this was originally written in a shortened form as an article in the MSA series of Short Talks, in time for the Presidential Inauguration in 2013), it is an appropriate time to share some thoughts I have been developing about the original use of the St. John's Lodge Bible in the Inauguration of President and Brother George Washington.

Like all apprentices I learned the history of the Bible from my predecessors, and initially never thought to question their stories. In brief, although the planning of the first Presidential Inauguration – to be held at Federal Hall in Wall Street, New York, since New York was the first Capital of the Nation for a few months – had been extensive, they had forgotten to provide a Bible for the Inauguration Ceremony. General Jacob Morton, Master of our Lodge and Equerry to Washington ran down the road to get the Lodge Bible, since St. John's Lodge then met nearby. It was opened at random, and Washington laid his hand upon it to take his Oath, whereupon Chancellor Robert R. Livingston (who was also Grand Master of Masons in New York) turned down the corner of the page to preserve it for posterity.

Yet the story of the Inauguration simply didn't make sense to me. Why would they forget the Bible at the event if they had laid out every detail, even down to the number of bales of hay that were needed for the horses?

Firstly, we need to go back to December 1757, and the founding of St. John's Lodge No. 1 by means of a Charter issued from the Premier Grand Lodge of England (it was still 56 years before the Antients and Moderns would join to form the United Grand Lodge of England & Wales). Although most military Lodges were warranted by the Antients, St. John's, unusually, was a Modern Lodge.

They met for a few years in Lower Manhattan, but a great fire in March 1770 wiped out many of the wooden buildings, including the venue at which the Lodge met. As a result, all the furniture and regalia had to be replaced. The incoming Master, Jonathan Hampton, ordered a King James Bible from England to replace the one which had burned.

In those days, since the monarch owned the copyright to the King James version of the Bible, he appointed a printer (in England, of course) who typeset and printed all the bibles to be sold. It was illegal to print bibles in the colonies. When the bible arrived it was presented to the Lodge in 1770. Richly bound in red calfskin, it bore the following inscription in gold letters: "God shall establish; St. John's Lodge constituted 5757; Burnt down 8th March, 5770; Rebuilt and opened November 28th, 5770. Officers then presiding: Jonathan Hampton, Master: William Butler, Senior Warden: Isaac Heron, Junior Warden." In those days the Masonic custom was to add 4000 to the actual year, to reflect Bishop Ussher's calculation using timelines in the bible to claim the world was created in 4004 B.C.E. (Sir Isaac Newton actually claimed it was 4000 B.C.E.). To bolster the claim that Freemasonry was as old as mankind – indeed, even Adam wore an apron made of skin according to some translations from the Hebrew! – they counted their years from the year 4000 B.C.E. And so St. John's continued to meet in Lower Manhattan: indeed, it was one of the only Lodges which continued to meet in the city during the Revolutionary War (most of the others either moved upstate or closed their doors).

But what of the romantic story of how this very bible became intimately connected with the founding of the United States?

One of our Brothers located a pamphlet from the time of the first Inauguration. This revealed that, far from the romantic notion that Washington had sailed across the Hudson and gone straight to Federal Hall, he had actually crossed the Hudson from Elizabethtown (now Elizabeth) in New Jersey weeks before the Inauguration. A house had been prepared for him, in which he would clearly have spent much time with his Officers and key civilians, planning every detail of his Inauguration. He was also a religious man – not in the mold of Thomas Jefferson (who took a pair of scissors to the New Testament in order to expunge the miracles), but a 'traditional' Anglican Protestant, whose household contained a Bible which was read every day; and we know he traveled throughout his campaigns with the Good Book beside him. With all this time to plan there is no doubt in my mind that the Bible was always an integral part of the ceremony.

So my interpretation is quite different to the traditional view.

At the time of the Inauguration New York was then, as now, a melting pot of nationalities and religious backgrounds. Both residents of New York and the many spectators were inheritors of diverse

Christian beliefs, for which they had been persecuted in their home-lands. How, then, could they select a Bible to use at the Inauguration, without the Church from which it had come claiming that their form of Christianity had therefore been adopted as the 'official' religion of the United States?

Freemasonry was very highly regarded in the colonies at the time (this was decades prior to the Morgan Affair and the rise of the Anti-Masonic Party). By using a Masonic Bible, a noble Order was being represented but, more importantly, it could be claimed that this Bible had never seen service in a church, and was therefore clear of any de-nominational issues.

That the event planning was under the control of Freemasons is very eloquently demonstrated by the fact that Washington and his Aide-de-Camp Morton, who was responsible for the logistics of the Inauguration, were both Masons. Chancellor Livingston, who would administer the Oath was Grand Master of Masons in the State of New York. Even the chef, Samuel Fraunces, who would be responsible for the banquets, and would later become George and Martha Washington's personal chef when they set up residence in New York, catering the weekly banquets, was initiated into Holland Lodge No. 8 barely two weeks prior to Washington's arrival in Manhattan.

General Jacob Morton was a friend of Washington and his Lodge was nearby. I have no doubt the Bible was collected days before the Ceremony, and that Chancellor Livingston did not turn down the page corner after, but actually *before* the event, so he would know where to open it. But this would mean that the passage used was not randomly selected, but very carefully chosen. This is borne out by the fact that the passage used, Genesis Chapter 49, is towards the very front of the Bible: most people would open a book 'at random' in the middle. In-deed, when I was interviewed by Mo Rocca for CBS at the time, we tried the experiment on camera, and the bible opened at the Book of Job: hardly an auspicious reading for the birth of a country, Mo Rocca wryly commented!

On a more practical note, ambassadors from all the known coun-tries were present to witness this unprecedented event in the history of mankind. Some, like France, were there as friends and allies; some, such as England, less so. It would have been of paramount importance that absolutely nothing could be left to chance, so that a hesitation, a mistake or a trip could be gleefully reported to the Heads of State. Everything had to proceed like clockwork: and that meant everything had to be planned beforehand.

Why, then would George Washington and his Masonic colleagues have chosen Genesis Chapter 49 as the perfect passage on which to take his oath as First President of the fledgling Nation?

In Genesis Chapter 49. Jacob calls his twelve sons to bless them. That makes 1 + 12, or 13 people. At the time there were thirteen colonies, and New York was the Empire State, New York then being the capital of the new country. Jacob blesses his sons, and Washington blesses the colonies. If we accept that Washington was a devout man who knew his Bible, and that the passage was selected most carefully indeed prior to the Inauguration, what could be a more appropriate and uplifting passage to be used at the founding of this Brave New World, as a new country launched itself upon the world stage beneath the stern gaze of Europe?

Made in United States
Orlando, FL
13 July 2023

35102122R00167